The South African
MICROWAVE
Cookbook

This book is dedicated
to all microwave owners who would
like to make the best
use of their appliance

The South African MICROWAVE Cookbook

Shirley Guy and Marty Klinzman

Photography by Peter Brooks

C. STRUIK PUBLISHERS

C. Struik (Pty) Ltd
Struik House
Oswald Pirow Street
Foreshore
Cape Town 8001

First edition published in hardcover 1984
Second Impression 1985
First published in softcover 1987
Second Impression 1988

Designed by Martin Field, Cape Town
Sketches by Andrea M. Bagnall, Cape Town
Typeset by McManus Bros (Pty) Ltd,
Cape Town (10,5/10 set Times Roman)
Lithographic reproduction by Unifoto,
Cape Town
Printed and bound by
Tien Wah Press (Pte) Ltd, Singapore

ISBN 0 86977 583 9

Acknowledgements

Once again special thanks to Heather
Carstensen and Fiona Sadman for
their many hours of work on the
manuscript, and to Peter Brooks for
his calming influence during the
photographic sessions.

Thanks also to THORN EMI
Kenwood for the loan of microwave
ovens for recipe testing and
development, to *Style* magazine
for permission to use several
photographs, and to D.H. Kahn
for china and glassware used
in the photography.

Contents

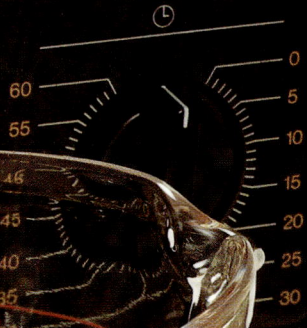

Microwave energy— a new dimension

Microwave cooking is fast becoming part of the South African way of life, but many microwave owners do not realize the full potential of this electronic cooking wonder. And, even though it has been available in this country for well over a decade, the microwave is often still thought of only in terms of thawing frozen food, or warming yesterday's casserole. It is our hope that you will discover that microwave cooking is a very versatile and efficient way to prepare a wide spectrum of tasty foods, without mess or fuss. There is nothing difficult about cooking food in the microwave once you have mastered the basic techniques, all of which have been thoroughly dealt with in this book. However, like any other appliance it has certain limitations, as not all foods are suitable for microwaving. Accept these limitations, and use the microwave in conjunction with your conventional stove. This way you will enjoy the benefits of both methods. Before attempting any recipes read 'How to use this book' on page 24.

Microwave energy

Microwave ovens have been in commercial use for several decades while models for home use have been manufactured for a number of years and are becoming increasingly popular. They are now accepted by many as indispensable items of kitchen equipment. Microwave cooking is, however, a completely new concept and before you begin to use your oven, it is important to have a good understanding of what microwave energy is, how it works, and how it can save time and effort in your kitchen.

What is microwave energy?

Microwaves work on the same principle as radio, television or light waves. They are simply a form of high-frequency electromagnetic energy that produces heat, depending on the substances it comes into contact with. Microwaves are not attracted to all substances; for example they cannot penetrate metal and so they are reflected by it. For this reason metal makes an ideal lining to microwave ovens as the waves bounce off the oven walls. Many other substances allow microwaves to pass straight through them without producing heat; for example, glass, pottery, china, paper, wood and some plastics. These make ideal containers as microwave energy passes through them directly into the food.

Microwaves are attracted by the moisture, sugar or fat content of foods and, depending on the size and density of the food, penetrate to a depth of 2 to 4 cm. The microwave energy causes molecules to vibrate at very high speeds – over two thousand million times a second – producing heat through friction. This heat spreads rapidly throughout the food from the point of penetration, thus cooking the food by conduction. However, smaller pieces of food are penetrated completely by the microwaves and therefore cook more quickly than larger, more solid foods. It should also be remembered that larger quantities will take longer to microwave than smaller quantities because the microwave energy within the oven remains constant. Microwave ovens do not need preheating like conventional ovens, as microwave energy reacts with the food instantly.

What happens in the microwave oven?

When the microwave oven is plugged in, power flows to the magnetron which converts electrical energy to microwave energy. This energy passes through a wave-guide that directs it into the oven cavity. A wave-stirrer or fan distributes the microwaves in an even pattern around the oven. The metal lining reflects the microwaves which are then attracted by the food.

Are microwave ovens safe?

The microwave oven has no sharp edges or moving parts, and its form of heat generation helps prevent burns and scalding. As microwaves heat only the food, no energy is wasted heating the air inside, which remains cool, or the container. However, as the food is heated the container may become hot by conduction, so care should always be exercised when taking food out of the oven. Manufacturers have designed microwave ovens so that no microwaves escape. Special safety features are built into microwave ovens, making them one of the safest kitchen appliances. The see-through oven door incorporates a reflecting metal screen and the door frame is designed with special seals to keep microwaves safely within the oven. Cut-out devices ensure microwave energy is automatically switched off when the door is opened.

More about microwave energy

Although microwaves are similar to radio and television waves, they are of a much higher frequency. The number of cycles the wave completes in a second (the frequency) is measured in hertz (Hz) and megahertz (MHz).

1 Hz = 1 cycle per second

1 MHz = 1 million cycles per second

Radio waves have a frequency of	0,56 – 8 MHz
Television waves have a frequency of	30 – 300 MHz
Microwaves have a frequency of	2 450 MHz

It is this high frequency which causes molecules in the food to vibrate at such high speeds that they produce heat. Microwaves should not be confused with X-rays, ultra-violet or gamma rays, all of which are ionizing and cause irreversible, chemical and cellular changes with little or no temperature change. Microwave energy is a non-ionizing form of electromagnetic energy transmitted through space by microwaves, which are very short and travel in straight lines. Being non-ionizing, microwaves are not harmful, as they do not damage cells, nor do they accumulate in foodstuffs cooked in a microwave oven.

Microwaves have three important characteristics: they can be reflected by metals, attracted by foodstuffs and they can pass straight through certain materials, such as glass, plastics and paper, without affecting them.

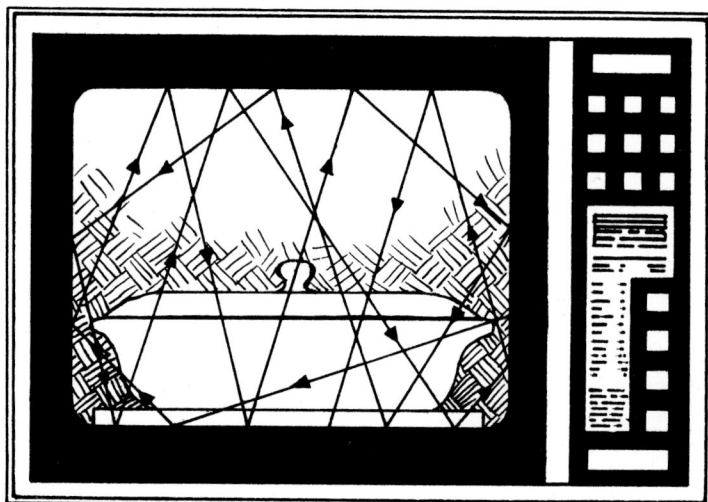

Microwaves are reflected by the metal lining of the oven and attracted by the moisture in the food

Advantages of microwave cooking

There are many advantages to cooking in a microwave, as you will discover as you continue to use yours. The microwave oven is useful in busy households where family members can't always be together at meal times or when quick meals are needed, while anyone living alone will find it ideal for cooking small quantities. Here are some of the more obvious advantages:

Speed: This is one of the greatest advantages, as microwaving takes about one third to one quarter of conventional cooking time.

Economy: Not only do microwave ovens use less power than conventional ovens (650 watts as opposed to the 2 200 watts of one element in a conventional oven), but they are on for a shorter time. Moreover, there is no need to preheat the microwave, as heat is generated instantly in the food when the oven is switched on. It also switches off at the end of the set cooking time, so no power is wasted.

Mobility: Microwave ovens use a standard 15 amp plug and household current, so they can be used almost anywhere where there is a stable surface. Although they can be placed in any area of the kitchen, counter height is usually the most convenient. Some people find it handy to place the microwave on a sturdy trolley, so that it can be wheeled from kitchen to dining room or patio.

Safe and easy to use: Microwave ovens are simple to operate and most dishes remain cool enough to handle easily. This means they can be used safely by the young, the elderly and the disabled, with little danger of burning.

Defrosting: There is no need to panic if you have forgotten to take a roast or casserole from the freezer. The microwave will defrost foods quickly and effectively without affecting the flavour or texture of the food.

Flavour and nutrition: Many foods cook in their own juices, or with the addition of very little liquid, thus retaining their natural flavour and most vitamins and nutrients. Many foods can be cooked in the microwave without the addition of oil or butter, making it useful for people on slimming diets or for those who are avoiding cholestrol.

Reheating: The microwave oven will reheat foods, such as casseroles, soups or individual plates of food, with no added moisture and no change in texture or flavour. Leftovers are just as appetizing as the first time they were served, and a plate of food saved for a latecomer will look and taste as fresh as newly cooked.

Cooler cooking: The microwave oven itself does not get hot, so even during long cooking periods, or when the temperature inside the oven is extremely high, the kitchen will stay cool. This is a great help with processes like preserving fruits and vegetables in the middle of summer.

Easy cleaning: The microwave oven is easier to clean than a conventional oven as foods do not often boil over and do not burn onto the oven surfaces. If spills occur, the metal or acrylic surfaces inside are easy to wipe clean.

Saves washing up: Food can often be cooked and served in the same container, so there is less washing up to do after cooking in the microwave oven. Food does not burn easily in the microwave, and containers heat only from contact with hot food, so there will be fewer sticky or crusty pans to wash.

Microwave features

You don't need great mechanical ability to use your microwave oven, but it is necessary to read and follow the manufacturer's operating directions carefully. Be sure you understand all the features of the oven and how they work. Some or all of the following features will be used in your oven.

On/off control: This operates the fan and interior light, but usually does not control the microwave supply.

Cook or start control: This switch or button starts the microwave process but cannot be operated until the oven door is securely closed. When the door is opened, the microwave energy is automatically cut off.

Oven door: Most models have doors that open to the side. The door consists of a metal mesh panel and a glass panel fitted in a metal frame. You can watch food as it cooks, but the metal mesh stops microwaves from

penetrating the glass door. Microwave ovens cannot be operated until the door is firmly shut.

Timer: Timing controls may be in the form of a dial, a sliding device or touch controls with a digital display. Timers that can be set for seconds as well as minutes give the most accurate cooking control. Some ovens can be timed for lengths of 25 to 30 minutes, while others have timing controls that can be set for longer periods. A bell or buzzer sounds when the cooking time is up.

Oven cavity: The metal lining is coated with acrylic and keeps the microwaves inside the oven. Food is cooked on the base of the oven or on specially designed glass or ceramic trays, shelves or turntables. The interior of each make of oven has been designed to allow microwaves to penetrate the food from all angles. Most ovens have an interior light that comes on when the oven door is opened and also operates during cooking.

Oven vent: All microwave ovens have a vent to allow moisture and air to escape during cooking. It is important that the vent be kept free whenever the oven is in operation. Built-in microwave ovens need space at the back or top for ventilation purposes.

Power control: This allows you to select the power level you want to use to cook food. Variable power offers flexibility in cooking so you can control the speed at which the food cooks. The number of power settings varies according to the model, so follow the manufacturer's instructions carefully. See page 24 for power levels used for recipes in the book.

Turntable: Most microwave ovens are likely to have hot and cold spots, so it is important that food be turned occasionally during defrosting, heating or cooking. Some microwave ovens have a turntable or rotating platform that automatically rotates the food during the cooking time, eliminating the need to turn or rotate containers and promoting even cooking. Follow the manufacturer's directions for using the turntable. In some models, the microwave oven should not be used without the turntable in position.

Temperature probe: This takes the guesswork out of timing, and allows you to control the internal temperature of the food. The probe is especially useful for cooking roasts or whole poultry, for reheating foods

A temperature probe takes the guesswork out of timing

and, in some cases, for simmering and slow cooking. Follow directions for its use. The probe's flexible connection fits into a socket inside the oven and the point is inserted into the food being cooked. The placing of the probe is important, usually in the thickest part of the poultry or meat, or in the centre of a casserole or stew. Foods cook to a pre-set temperature, then the oven automatically turns off. However, food continues to cook even after the oven switches off, so you may wish to select a lower temperature. It is always easy to microwave the food for a few minutes more, but it is impossible to remedy overcooking.

Warning: Never use a conventional meat thermometer made of metal in your microwave.

Additional features

Defrost control: The defrost setting on the power control enables you to defrost large or small amounts of food easily and quickly. When the defrost setting is in use, the microwave energy inside the oven is turned on and off automatically, allowing rest periods between bursts of energy, so that foods are defrosted but not cooked.

Browning element: Manufacturers incorporate a browning element, similar to a grill unit, in some microwave ovens. It is used to brown food before or after it is cooked.

Touch controls: A few microwave models are operated by touching a control panel on the outside of the oven. Many of these have a digital display to show power level, cooking time and any special instructions. They also incorporate a clock on the front panel.

Memory control: The use of the 'memory' on a microwave oven allows it to be programmed for two power settings and sometimes for special instructions such as 'hold'. The cooking will automatically be changed from one power level to another. With this feature, you do not have to wait for cooking time to finish at one level before physically resetting the oven.

Automatic start: Some ovens can be programmed to start at a pre-set time and continue cooking for a predetermined period.

Slow cook or simmer control: This is a setting or power level that reduces the energy used, therefore slowing down the cooking time. It is useful for recipes that require long slow cooking to develop flavour or tenderize ingredients.

Care and cleaning

As with any other appliance, it is important to read the manufacturer's instruction book on the cleaning and care of your oven. However, certain general guidelines can be followed:
* Wipe the inside surface of the oven with a damp cloth after each use. Also wipe moisture from the inside of the oven and door.
* For thorough cleaning, remove the base, glass shelf or turntable and wash with warm, soapy water if necessary.
* Harsh abrasives or oven cleaners may damage the inside surfaces of the oven and scratches may distort the microwave pattern within the oven.
* Since the interior walls of the oven remain relatively cool, splashing and spills should not burn on. Be sure to clean the oven interior if any spillage occurs, as the food particles left adhering to the oven surfaces will attract microwave energy and slow down cooking the next time you use the oven.
* Be sure to clean any grease or food particles from around the door seal. It is important that a good seal be maintained.
* To remove stubborn food particles from the inside surface, place a cup of water in the oven and let it boil for a few minutes. The moisture should loosen the pieces of food and they can then be wiped away.
* The outside of the oven can be wiped over with a damp cloth. Wipe exterior vents occasionally to remove any condensation, but do not splash water over them.

SAFETY
* Do not attempt to operate the oven with the door open. Do not tamper with the safety locking systems.
* Do not place any object between the oven door and the front of the oven. Make sure that sealing surfaces are clean.
* Do not operate the oven if it is damaged in any way. It is important that the oven door closes properly.
* Do not allow the oven to be adjusted or repaired by anyone other than qualified microwave service personnel.
* Do not remove the outer casing or oven door at any time.
* Never line the oven with foil, paper or any other material.
* Do not lean heavily on the oven door.
* Do not use the oven for storing utensils.
* Do not operate the oven when it is empty, as this may damage the magnetron. A cup of water left in the oven when it is not in use will attract the microwave energy if the oven is accidentally turned on.

Microwave techniques

Many of the techniques used in microwave cooking are similar to ones used in conventional cooking. Methods such as turning, rearranging or stirring foods are used to promote fast and even cooking. The application of these techniques is slightly different when microwaving, so for best results, be sure to follow recipe instructions when any of the following techniques are called for:

Standing time

Food continues to cook after it has been removed from the microwave, so it is important to let it 'stand' before serving. The length of standing time varies, but in general depends on the volume and density of the food. Meat dishes such as roasts or poultry will continue to cook for 10 to 20 minutes after the microwave energy has been turned off. Other foods, such as cakes or puddings, depend on standing time to finish cooking. Because of this it is important to take standing time into consideration when experimenting with foods or trying new recipes, so that foods will not be overcooked. It is always better to slightly undercook foods, as they can easily be heated again if they are not done. Follow recipe directions for standing time.

Stirring

In conventional stove-top cooking, food is stirred from the bottom up to ensure even heating. Since the outer edges of food normally cook first in microwave cooking, foods should be stirred from the outer edges inward to promote even cooking. Foods that normally need constant stirring, such as sauces or custards, need only occasional stirring in the microwave oven. However, these foods may need to be stirred a little more frequently in a microwave oven without a turntable.

Turning

Foods that cannot be stirred during cooking need to be repositioned to heat evenly or to brown each side.
- Large roasts, poultry, pieces of vegetables or meat, should be turned during the cooking time to ensure even heating.

Stir from the outside inwards

Turning ensures even cooking

Arrange equal-sized portions in a circle

- Foods microwaved in a browning pan, such as hamburgers, steaks or chops, will need turning to ensure even browning.
- In microwave ovens without a turntable it is advisable to rotate the container a quarter or half a turn during the cooking time if the food appears to be cooking unevenly.
- Foods defrost more evenly if turned during the defrosting time.

Arrangement

The arrangement of food in the microwave oven is another important factor for even cooking:
- Always place the thicker or larger portions of food towards the outside of the container because microwaves penetrate the outer edges of food first. For example, chicken legs or fish steaks should have the thinner part towards the centre of the dish.
- Arrange foods of equal size in a circular pattern. For example, potatoes to be baked or individual portions of custard or eggs can be placed in a ring pattern or circle in the microwave oven. If possible, do not place an entire portion in the centre. Foods such as meatballs will cook more evenly if arranged in a circular pattern in a round dish with the centre empty.
- For even cooking, food should be arranged to a uniform depth.
- Vegetables should be spread out rather than heaped in the middle.
- When reheating a meal on a plate, keep foods at an even depth, and arrange denser or thicker foods towards the outside of the plate.
- By rearranging food during cooking you help it cook more evenly. Moving foods from the centre to the outside, or from the outside towards the centre, gives more evenly cooked results, and can help shorten the cooking time.

11

1

2

3

6

7

Covering and wrapping

In conventional cooking, many foods are covered to retain moisture and decrease cooking time. The same techniques are used in microwave cooking, but the application may be different. Follow the recipe directions for covering food; if no mention is made microwave food uncovered.

Plastic wrap: A tight cover of plastic wrap (1) holds in steam as well as heat. Turn back one corner, or make two slashes in the wrap to prevent it from 'ballooning' during the cooking time. The lid of the dish (2) can be used instead of plastic wrap when microwaving vegetables, casseroles and meats that require moisture.

Waxed or greaseproof paper: A loose cover of waxed or greaseproof paper (3) holds in heat without steaming the food. It is used to cover foods such as fruits, hamburgers, chicken, bacon or roasts where steam is not needed to tenderize the food.

Cooking bags: Cooking bags (4) hold in steam and help to tenderize meat or poultry. Do not use a metal or foil strip to seal the bag. Fasten with string or an elastic band and make one or two slashes to prevent the bag from 'ballooning' during cooking.

Paper towel: A paper towel (5) allows steam to escape, promotes even heating and prevents spattering during cooking. It also absorbs excess moisture from foods. Use a paper towel to cover bacon during microwaving or to absorb moisture when drying herbs or freshening chips, pretzels or savoury biscuits. Porous paper towels can be used to wrap such foods as hamburgers or hot dogs in rolls, bread rolls or pastries for heating. Use damp paper towels to steam fish fillets and scallops, or to soften crêpes in a few seconds.

Shielding

Sensitive areas of food should be shielded so that they do not overcook. Use small strips of aluminium foil (6) to shield thin parts of poultry, such as the tips of wings and legs or the breastbone, and bones on thin parts of joints of meat. Shielding can be useful in baking too. Use small pieces of foil (7) to shield the corners of square and rectangular dishes as these would overcook before the centre is done.

Browning

The attractive browning of foods during cooking is due to a chemical reaction between food sugars and amino acids which takes place slowly at low temperatures and more quickly at higher temperatures. During quick microwave cooking, the surface temperature of foods does not change enough to bring about natural browning, so foods do not have the same appearance as when cooked conventionally unless first brushed with a browning agent. Refer to chart on page 22. Foods such as large roasts and poultry will brown slightly if they are cooked longer than about

4

5

8

9

25 minutes because the fats reach a high temperature, causing some change in colour.

Some microwave ovens have a special element to brown food either before or after microwave cooking. Browning dishes (see page 16) designed especially for microwave ovens sear and brown foods (8) the way a frying pan does, giving chops, steaks, sausages and hamburgers an appetizing appearance. Many recipes in this book make use of special toppings to improve the look of the food, and on page 22 there is a special section giving tips and hints on how to make microwaved foods look good.

Heating

Heating home-prepared meals, leftovers and 'fast foods' is one of the best features of microwave cooking. Many foods can be prepared ahead of time and reheated with no loss of flavour or texture. While heating, most foods should be covered with greaseproof paper (9) to hold in the heat and at the same time allow steam to escape. The plate or dish may need to be rotated if no turntable is used.

- Baked foods such as rolls and mince pies must be heated with care as they are easily overdone.
- Stews and casseroles may need to be stirred during heating.
- A plate of food that needs heating should have all the foods at the same temperature and arranged so that the one which takes longest to heat is on the outside.
- Canned foods need only be heated before serving.

Defrosting

Defrosting food in the microwave oven is not only quick and convenient, but most of the flavour or moisture is retained, and there is little risk of bacterial growth. When the defrost setting is used, the power is cycled on and off to produce a slow heating process. Defrosting charts for fish, poultry, meat, vegetables and baking are given in the relevant chapters.

- Defrost food slowly so that it does not begin to cook on the outside before it is completely thawed.
- Large roasts and poultry may need to stand after defrosting so that heat from the thawed outer layers will penetrate to the centre. The latest models incorporate this standing time automatically. For best results, be sure meat and poultry are completely defrosted before microwaving.
- It is often necessary to reposition or turn foods so they defrost evenly.
- Place frozen food in a container suitable for microwaving. Be sure the container is large enough to hold the food after thawing, and to allow for stirring if necessary.
- Foods frozen in foil trays or wrapped in foil should be removed from the container or wrapper and placed in a suitable dish.

Microwave equipment

Substances such as glass, pottery, porcelain and paper allow microwave energy to pass through them, so containers made of these materials are ideal for use in the microwave. Because metal reflects microwaves, containers of aluminium, copper, stainless steel or aluminium foil are not suitable and may cause arcing which will damage your appliance.

Equipment made of materials that meet the special requirements of microwave cooking is now available. However, there is no need to rush out and buy a complete new range of cookware. Although you will not be using metal pots or baking pans, many utensils you already have are suitable for use in the microwave. These include such items as paper plates, paper towel, ovenproof casserole dishes and glass measuring jugs. It is often possible to cook and serve in the same container, saving not only time, but washing up too.

Testing containers for microwave safety

Measure 250 mℓ water in a glass measuring jug. Place the container you wish to test in the microwave oven and stand the jug on it. Microwave on full power for about one minute. At the end of that time, the water should be warm and the container cool. If so, the container is ideal for microwave use. If both the water and container are warm, the container can be used, but the cooking time must be increased, as it has attracted some of the microwave energy. If the container is warm but the water is cool, the container has attracted much of the microwave energy and should not be used for microwave cooking.

Ideal containers for microwave cooking

Heat retention

Because microwaves pass through the container directly into the food, the dish stays relatively cool during the cooking process. However, as the food becomes hot some of the heat is absorbed by the container, so care should be taken when removing it from the microwave oven. Foods that are high in fat or sugar content or ones that have a long cooking time transfer heat more readily. ·

Materials suitable for microwaving

Paper: This is a good material for microwave use especially with foods that require low heat and short cooking times. Thawing, reheating and some cooking methods can make use of paper napkins, towels, cups and plates.
- Paper towel is useful for covering fatty foods such as bacon while cooking, as it absorbs excess fat and prevents spattering. Paper towel can also be used to line cake pans. Just cut to fit, then spread the cake mixture over. The paper towel absorbs excess moisture and makes turning the cake out easy.
- Waxed paper and greaseproof paper can be used as light covering while foods cook because they hold in heat but allow steam to escape.
- Wax-coated paper plates and cups should be used only for heating foods for short periods, as high temperatures cause the wax to melt.
- Paper baking cups not only reduce washing up, but they absorb excess moisture when microwaving small cakes or muffins.
- White paper products are the best to use, as coloured ones may transfer their colours to the food.

Plastic wrap, cooking bags and plastic bags: Plastic wrap makes an excellent cover for microwaved foods as it keeps in both heat and moisture. To prevent the wrap from 'ballooning' during cooking, make two slits in the surface or turn back one corner of the wrap.

Cooking bags are convenient for a variety of foods as they promote the browning of roasts and poultry while retaining moisture and heat. They also help cook vegetables or fruit with very little added moisture. As with plastic wrap, it is important to make two slits near the top of the bag. Do not use the metal ties that come with the bags, but fasten them with string or an elastic band.

Do not use ordinary plastic bags in the microwave oven, as they will melt at high temperatures.

Plastic containers: 'Dishwasher safe' is a useful guideline when determining if a plastic container is safe for use in the microwave oven. Rigid plastic dishes made of thermoplastic material and usually marked 'dishwasher safe' or 'boilable' can be used for heating foods or microwaving for a short time. Special plastics have been developed for use in both microwave and conventional ovens, and may be safely used to cook any food item in the microwave.

Do not use:

- Freezer containers, as they absorb heat from the food during cooking and distort or melt.
- Plastic cream cartons or yoghurt cartons or any other lightweight plastic containers.
- Stryrofoam trays for reheating or cooking, but they can be used for defrosting.
- Melamine as it absorbs microwave energy.

Glass: Ovenproof glass such as Pyrex and glass ceramic containers such as Corningware are ideal for both heating and cooking in the microwave. Such items are fairly inexpensive and readily available in hardware stores and supermarkets. Clear glass containers allow you to see what is happening to the food. For anyone using a microwave oven for the first time, this is important, especially when checking bases of cakes or puddings to determine whether they are cooked. Ordinary glass without any lead content may be used for heating foods for a short time, but do not use ordinary glass for foods with high sugar or fat content, as the high temperatures reached by those ingredients may crack the glass.

When purchasing glassware for microwave use, remember that round shapes will give more even results than rectangular ones. A deep glass bowl

For more even cooking, choose ring pans and shallow round dishes rather than rectangular and deep ones

and two sizes of measuring jugs will be useful additions to your microwave cookware.

Pottery and china: Sturdy china and stoneware pottery containers without metal trim or content are usually suitable for microwave cooking and can be used in the same way as glassware. Foods can be cooked and served in the same dish, making cleaning up easy. Dark pottery or china slows the microwave cooking process slightly and may become fairly hot to the touch. Avoid containers with a shiny or metallic sheen. If you are unsure whether to use a stoneware or pottery container, test the container as described on opposite page.

Clay pots: Use a clay cooking pot or Römertopf for meat casseroles, poultry or joints of meat. Presoak the lid and base according to the manufacturer's directions. The cooking time is somewhat longer than in an ordinary casserole dish because the moisture in the pot attracts some of the microwave energy. These pots become hot during cooking, so use oven gloves when handling them. Do not add cold liquid during the cooking period, as the sudden change in temperature may crack the pot.

Other materials

Natural shell: Scallop shells make attractive containers for individual servings of seafood and are safe to use in the microwave. Remember that the cooking time should be reduced for individual servings.

Wood: Items made of wood contain some moisture that evaporates during microwave cooking and eventually they may become so dry that they crack. Use wooden boards or platters for short-term heating rather than actual cooking. Small wooden utensils, such as wooden spoons, are ideal for use in the microwave.

Wicker and straw: Baskets made from wicker or straw can be used in the microwave oven for short periods, such as when bread rolls need to be thawed or heated for a few seconds. Long periods of heating may cause the wicker or straw to dry out and crack.

Aluminium foil: Many microwave oven manufacturers agree that small pieces of aluminium foil can be used to shield corners of a baking dish, or to prevent chicken legs or wings, or bone-ends of meat from overcooking.

Warning: Aluminium foil should not be used as a covering or wrapping as it may cause arcing and flashing which will damage your appliance.

Microwave cookware

Many new items on the market are marked 'safe for microwave use' by the manufacturer. Lugs and handles make containers easier to use as they generally stay cool even though the dish itself may become warm. A round container is more suitable for microwave use than an oval or rectangular one, and a dish with slightly rounded corners rather than square corners helps prevent food from overcooking at the edges. Small deep bowls are not as suitable as larger shallow ones, because food with a greater surface area cooks more evenly. It is important to have a few deep containers for making sauces, puddings, preserves and cream mixtures, as these may rise to almost double the volume during cooking. Avoid any ovenproof containers or plates that have metal trim, as the trim will reflect microwaves.

Due to the increasing popularity of microwave cooking, special microwave cookware has been developed. Designed of specially made plastics, many microwave containers can be used, within certain temperature ranges, in a conventional oven, and are safe to use in the dishwasher. It is now possible to purchase microwave containers such as ring moulds, roasting pans, cake dishes, muffin pans, bacon racks and loaf pans. Be sure to follow instructions for use and care.

Browning dishes

Because they cook quickly, many microwaved foods do not have the browned appearance associated with conventional cooking. With a special browning dish it is possible to brown such foods as hamburgers, steaks, chops and toasted sandwiches, and to fry eggs so that they have an appetizing appearance. Browning dishes are made of glass ceramic and have a special coating under the base. This coating absorbs microwave energy when the empty dish is preheated in the microwave oven, and the bottom of the dish becomes hot. Thus, the surface of food is seared and browned when placed in a preheated browning dish, while the rest of the food is cooked by microwave energy.

Foods such as steaks, toasted sandwiches or chops are normally turned during the cooking time to brown both sides. Preheating times will vary according to the size and shape of the dish, and the type of food to be cooked, so always follow the manufacturer's and recipe directions.

Special plastic cookware and ordinary paper products are a boon to microwave users

BROWNING DISH CHART

Always use full power when using the browning dish. Add butter or oil once the dish has been preheated. Do not use non-stick sprays or coatings as they scorch.

FOOD	PREHEAT TIME	BUTTER OR OIL	FIRST SIDE	SECOND SIDE
125 g/4 oz almonds	–	–	4-5 minutes, stir every 1 minute	
4 chicken pieces	5-6 minutes	1 tbsp	6 minutes	4-5 minutes
4 chops, lamb	5-6 minutes	1 tbsp	3 minutes	1-3 minutes
4 chops, pork	5-6 minutes	1 tbsp	4 minutes	5-7 minutes
2 eggs (yolks pricked)	2-3 minutes	1 tbsp butter	1½-1¾ minutes	
4 fish portions	4-5 minutes	1 tbsp	2-3 minutes	4-5 minutes
6 fish fingers (frozen)	5-6 minutes	brush food with melted butter or oil	2 minutes	1-2 minutes
2 toasted sandwiches or pieces of French toast	4-5 minutes	1 tbsp butter	30-40 seconds	15-25 seconds
4 hamburgers	4-5 minutes	–	2 minutes	1-2 minutes
250 g oven chips	4-5 minutes	–	2-3 minutes	2-3 minutes
4 sausages	5-6 minutes	1 tbsp	1½-2 minutes	1½-2 minutes
2 steaks	6-8 minutes	–	3 minutes	2-2½ minutes
2 veal escalopes (crumbed)	5-6 minutes	2 tbsp butter and 2 tbsp oil	45 seconds	1-1½ minutes

The browning dish does get hot, so wear oven gloves when handling it, and do not place the hot dish directly on the counter or work surface. The bottom of the dish cools as the food browns, so before browning a second batch of food, wipe the dish clean and reheat for about half the original time. Covering the dish with a lid or with greaseproof paper will reduce any spattering and splashing that may occur with fatty foods during cooking. Refer to the chart for specific cooking times.

EQUIPMENT THAT CANNOT BE USED IN THE MICROWAVE

The following equipment is unsuitable for microwave cooking:

- Metal or part-metal pans or baking tins.
- Metal thermometers, skewers or baking sheets.
- Foil baking dishes, trays, or foil-lined paper containers or boxes.
- Porcelain or ceramic dishes with metal trim.
- Melamine dinnerware and some oven-to-table ware. Check with the section on testing containers for microwave safety on page 14.
- Soft plastic containers or plastic yoghurt, margarine or cottage cheese containers.
- Metal or wire ties for cooking bags.

Equipment unsuitable for use in the microwave

Helpful microwave hints

- Read the manufacturer's instruction book carefully before using your microwave oven. Microwave ovens vary from model to model and it is important to know all the features of your oven.
- Do not switch on the oven when it is empty, as this could damage it. A cup of water left in the oven when not in use will attract microwaves if the oven is accidentally switched on.
- Be sure to remove any metal ties or twists before defrosting frozen foods in the microwave.
- Standing time is required for even distribution of heat throughout many foods in the microwave.
- Remember that containers absorb heat from the cooked food and may become warm to touch. Take care when removing them from the microwave.
- Best results are obtained if the food to be cooked is at an even temperature throughout. Make sure foods are completely defrosted

before cooking, unless otherwise indicated in the recipe.
- The microwave cannot improve the quality of food. Always start with good quality ingredients to ensure the best results.
- Cover food to keep it moist. Use pierced cling film or a non-metallic lid.
- Arrange food carefully for even cooking. As a general rule, place the thinnest part towards the centre, and place items such as potatoes or mushrooms in a circle rather than in rows.
- Cut food into even-sized pieces. Irregular sizes will cook unevenly, so some of the food may be overcooked while other pieces will be underdone.
- If your oven does not have a turn-table, you may need to stir, rotate or rearrange food more frequently.
- When using boiling or roasting bags, always prick them to prevent them from bursting. Use string or elastic bands instead of metal ties or twists to close cooking bags.

When cooking whole vegetables or fruits, prick the skins to prevent them from bursting. Similarly, prick yolks before frying or poaching eggs in the microwave

- If a recipe has been doubled, allow one third to one half extra cooking time. When halving a recipe, use two thirds of the cooking time.
- Always check foods at the minimum suggested time. It is safer to undercook, as food can always be cooked for a few seconds more, but overcooking can spoil some dishes.
- Never attempt to deep-fry in a microwave oven.

How to check whether food is ready

The major difference between conventional recipes and microwave recipes is the cooking time. The appearance of some foods cooked in the microwave differs from that of foods cooked conventionally, but many of the methods used for checking whether the food is done remain the same. Personal preference will decide the readiness of some foods, so cooking times will have to be adjusted accordingly. It is important to learn when to remove the food from the oven. Some foods must be removed while they look only partly cooked, as they will finish cooking during the standing time. Always undercook until you learn to judge accurately cooking times in your microwave, and become familiar with how the food should look.

Cakes and sponge puddings are done when a toothpick or skewer inserted in the centre comes out clean. Moist spots on the surface of the cake or pudding will dry during the standing time. Timing is very important with cakes and puddings, as overcooking will cause the outer edges to become hard and dry. Check whether cakes or puddings are done at the minimum suggested time.

Shortcrust pastries should be flaky, and the base should be dry and opaque. The pastry will not turn golden brown although a few brown spots may appear.

Custards and quiches should appear soft in the centre. A knife inserted halfway between the centre and the outer edge should come out clean. The centre will set during the standing time.

Reheated meals on plates are hot enough to serve when the base of the plate feels warm all over.

Vegetables should be fork-tender but not mushy because they continue to cook during the standing time.

A baked potato is heated through in 4 to 5 minutes, but if cut in half reveals an uncooked centre. The potato will finish cooking during standing time, and stay hot enough to serve for up to half an hour if wrapped in aluminium foil after cooking. This factor is a great help when planning menus.

Meat should be fork-tender when done. Less tender cuts should split at the fibres when tested with a fork. A temperature probe is one way of insuring meat is done as desired, but remember meat continues to cook during standing time. Only special microwave meat thermometers can be used in the microwave oven during cooking, but a conventional meat thermometer can be inserted to check the temperature after the joint has been removed from the oven.

Whole chicken feels soft when pinched and the leg moves easily at the joint. The juices should run clear with no trace of pink. During standing time, cover the chicken with a tent of aluminium foil, shiny side in, to keep in the heat.

Fish flakes easily with a fork when it is cooked. The centre of a piece of fish may be slightly translucent, but will finish cooking during standing time. Fish becomes tough and dry if overcooked.

Shellfish turn pink and opaque when cooked. To avoid toughening, undercook slightly and let stand.

Using a combination of microwave and conventional cooking

Many foods can be quickly and easily prepared by using a combination of microwave and conventional cooking. Use the microwave for its speed and conventional cooking for browning or baking. Remember to use a dish suitable for microwaving if you are cooking in both the conventional and the microwave oven.

- For toasted sandwiches, toast bread conventionally, then place the sandwiches in the microwave to heat fillings and melt cheese.
- Brown meats on a conventional stove top, then finish cooking in the microwave but reduce the cooking time by a quarter to a half.
- Make pancakes or crêpes conventionally, but heat fillings and toppings in the microwave.
- Partially cook chicken pieces or ribs in the microwave, and then finish cooking them on a barbecue.
- Bake double-crust pies conventionally, and reheat or defrost in the microwave oven.
- Prove yeast doughs in the microwave oven and bake conventionally for a crusty loaf.
- Bake a flan or quiche case conventionally, then add the filling and use the microwave to cook it quickly.

Combination ovens: In some microwave models it is possible to cook by microwave energy or by conventional power in the same oven although not, of course, at the same time. Conventional cooking for part of the period and microwave cooking for part of the time will give results that are similar to conventionally cooked dishes, but in a shorter time. The conventional oven in these models usually has a fan to distribute the heat and aid cooking.

Cauliflower cheese (p. 101) cooks to perfection in the microwave oven

Converting conventional recipes to microwave

Many of your favourite recipes can be adapted to microwave cooking with few changes other than shortening the cooking time. However, it is wise to understand microwave cooking thoroughly before attempting to convert conventional recipes. Study each recipe to determine whether it is suitable for microwave cooking. It is best to start with a familiar recipe because if you already know what the food should look and taste like, the conversion to microwave cooking will be easier. Look for cooking methods that are similar to both conventional cooking and microwaving, such as steaming and poaching. Also check the list of foods that microwave well (page 18) and those that should not be microwaved (page 19) before deciding to prepare a conventional recipe in the microwave oven. For example, if foods should have a crisp, fried crust, or a very dry surface, they are better prepared by conventional cooking.

You will want to experiment as you learn to use your microwave oven, adjusting cooking times, seasoning and methods to suit your tastes. It is important to select foods that microwave well and look for cooking methods that are successful in the microwave, such as:

Roasting meat or poultry is so easy in the microwave. Place the meat on a rack in the microwave, cover if moist heat is desired, and microwave on medium or full power until done.

Braising and stewing can be done in the microwave. Meat pieces are not browned first, and cooking liquid is reduced. The microwave dish should be covered and the power level set for the type of food to be cooked.

Poaching is a pleasure in the microwave, as foods cook with less liquid than in conventional cooking and retain good texture and flavour. Reduce the poaching liquid and cover the dish. The power level will depend on the type of food cooked.

Steaming may be done by placing foods in a tightly covered dish with very little water. If plastic wrap is used as a cover, make two slashes in it with a sharp knife to prevent 'ballooning'.

Stir-frying can be done in a browning dish. Preheat the dish, add a little oil or fat, then the food and stir it every two minutes during cooking time.

Frying can be simulated by the use of a browning dish. Preheating the dish, then adding a small amount of fat or

SAMPLE RECIPE CONVERSION

Banana and granadilla slice

Crust

100 g blanched almonds, chopped	1. *Toast in microwave (see page 23).*	2. *Combine, rub in margarine, pack half into loaf pan. Microwave on full power for 2 minutes. Cool.*
75 g coconut		
45 mℓ sugar		
80 g margarine		

Filling

30 mℓ water	3. *Combine, stand for a few minutes, microwave on medium for 1 minute.*	4. *Combine and continue according to recipe instructions.*
15 mℓ gelatine		
400 mℓ natural yoghurt		
45 mℓ honey		
2 granadillas		
2 egg whites		
2 bananas, sliced		

To make the crust, combine almonds, coconut and sugar, and rub in margarine. Press half the crust into a lined and greased 26 x 12 cm loaf pan. Bake at 160 °C for 15 minutes. Allow to cool. Place remaining crumb mixture onto a baking sheet, place in the oven for 8 – 10 minutes, until golden brown. Cool and reserve.

To make the filling, place water and gelatine in a heatproof jug, and allow to stand for a couple of minutes. Stand gelatine mixture in a pan with 3 cm of boiling water, stir until dissolved. Combine yoghurt and honey, add granadilla pulp. Beat egg whites until stiff. Stir dissolved gelatine into yoghurt, then fold in egg whites. Arrange bananas on the crust and pour yoghurt mixture over. Sprinkle with remaining crumb mixture. Chill for 4 hours. Turn out and cut into squares or slices. This pudding may also be made in two 21 x 11 cm loaf pans.

Serves 8

oil, will give a nicely browned surface to many foods.

Sautéing can be done by heating a small amount of fat or oil, then adding food and cooking it for the required time. The food will not brown as in stove-top cooking.

Baking many foods is successful in the microwave. See the chapter on baking for specific information. Some baked foods, such as angel or chiffon cakes and sheet cakes, puff or choux pastries, double-crust pies and some yeast breads are not suitable for microwave cooking.

The following guidelines will give you a good start on converting your own recipes to microwave cooking:
- In general, foods cook in about a quarter to a third of the time required for conventional cooking. Microwave ovens vary in speed and evenness of cooking, so always underestimate the cooking time and test whether foods are ready at the minimum time. Remember that foods continue to cook after removal from the microwave, so allow for standing time.
- Watch the cooking process closely and check the food often. If the

food seems to be cooking unevenly, stir, rearrange or rotate it.
- Reduce the amount of herbs and spices used, especially strongly flavoured ones, as they keep their flavouring power in the microwave. For many casseroles and meat dishes the seasoning can be added near the end of the cooking time.
- Select containers that are larger than those used in conventional recipes and fill one third to one half full, as foods tend to rise higher and increase in volume in the microwave.
- As a general rule, use less liquid when cooking vegetables, stews and casseroles. Watch the dish and add a little more liquid if necessary during the cooking time.
- Converting recipes containing raw pasta or rice can be difficult. These ingredients need time to absorb moisture and become tender, so other ingredients may cook much more rapidly in the microwave, and you may find that when the meat or vegetables are cooked, the pasta or rice is still too raw to serve.
- Some changes may be needed in piece size of ingredients. Pieces of a uniform size cook evenly, and small pieces cook more rapidly than large ones.

Improving the appearance of microwaved foods

Food cooked in a microwave oven does not brown to the same degree as food cooked conventionally. Glazes, coatings, icings and garnishes help to improve the appearance of the food.

Cakes do not brown as they do in a conventional oven. Cakes and bars are usually iced before serving, so the difference in appearance is not noticeable. If no icing is used, there are several toppings that improve the appearance. A mixture of cinnamon and sugar, toasted coconut or chopped nuts, or a blend of soft brown sugar and nuts can be sprinkled on top of the cake or loaf before microwaving or after part of the cooking time. Sifted icing sugar on top of a baked cake also looks good.

Breads can be brushed with beaten egg or milk and sprinkled with seeds, bran or wheat germ before microwaving to give good colour to the finished product. Breads can also be browned under the grill for a few minutes, but be sure the container will withstand the heat. Many of the recipes in the chapter on baking include toppings which add both colour and flavour.

Meat cooked in small portions does not brown in the microwave oven because of the rapid cooking time, although larger roasts and whole poultry develop some natural colour when microwaved for longer than about 25 minutes. Soy sauce or Worcestershire sauce, dry onion soup, herbs, or beef stock powder brushed on before microwaving improve the appearance of beef, lamb and pork. Microwaved meats basted with a marinade during cooking or served with a sauce also have a better appearance and flavour.

Chicken can be brushed with melted butter and sprinkled with herbs, paprika, dry onion soup or chicken stock powder before microwaving, or small portions can be coated with egg and crumbs to develop a 'crust' during cooking. Soy sauce, Worcestershire sauce or braai sauce are useful coatings for poultry that needs extra colour.

Ham and poultry can be successfully glazed with fruit preserves or marmalade to add colour and flavour to the dish.

Casseroles can be topped with crushed potato crisps, buttered breadcrumbs, grated cheese or crumbled cooked bacon to give an attractive finish.

Clockwise from the bottom: plain microwaved cake, topped with toasted almonds (p. 23), streusel mixture (p. 122), cherry pie filling, icing sugar and chocolate icing

The following chart gives useful ideas for improving the appearance of many microwaved foods:

BROWNING AGENT CHART

AGENT	FOODS	METHOD
Soy sauce	Hamburgers, beef, lamb, pork, poultry and sausages	Brush onto meat or poultry, or add to marinades
Melted butter and paprika	Poultry and fish	Brush food with butter, sprinkle with paprika
Worcestershire sauce	Hamburgers, beef, lamb and pork	Brush on or add to marinade
Brown onion soup powder	Hamburgers, beef and lamb	Sprinkle on before microwaving
Braai sauce and steak sauce	Hamburgers, beef, lamb, poultry and sausages	Brush on or add to marinade
Bacon strips	Hamburgers, beef, lamb and poultry	Lay on food, which browns under bacon as it cooks
Streusel topping	Cakes and puddings	Sprinkle on before microwaving
Biscuit crumbs, cinnamon sugar or nuts	Cakes and puddings	Sprinkle on before microwaving
Wheat germ, oatmeal, crushed cereal, sesame or poppy seeds	Bread and rolls	Brush food with milk, then roll in topping
Breadcrumbs	Scones and casseroles	Brush scones with melted butter, sprinkle with crumbs. Combine crumbs with a little butter, sprinkle onto casseroles

Special uses for the microwave

- Individual meals can be heated on the serving plate. Family members who arrive late for a meal can still have appetizing food.
- Blanching vegetables for the freezer takes seconds in the microwave, and colour, texture and flavour are retained (see page 54).
- To eliminate a soggy top on an individual meat pie, cut a small piece of foil the same size as the pie and place it, shiny side up, on the bottom of the microwave oven. Cover with paper towel. Place pie upside down on the paper towel and microwave on full power for 3 to 4 minutes if frozen, or 1 to 2 minutes if thawed.
- To blanch almonds, microwave 250 mℓ water for about 2½ minutes on full power, until it is boiling. Add the almonds and microwave for 30 seconds. Drain, then slip the skins off.
- To toast almonds, place the flaked or blanched nuts in a browning dish and microwave on full power for 4 to 5 minutes, stirring every minute.
- To soften jams and jellies to a spreading consistency, microwave on full power for 3 seconds per 250 mℓ.
- Heat brandy for flambéing desserts or meats by microwaving on full power for about 15 seconds. Pour over the food and ignite.
- Place chocolate to be melted in an ovenproof glass bowl. To obtain a dipping consistency, microwave on defrost for about 2½ minutes per 30 g. For general purposes, microwave on full power for 30 to 45 seconds per 30 g.
- To shell pecans or walnuts, place the nuts in a glass bowl, add about 60 mℓ water, cover and microwave on full power for 1 to 2 minutes. Dry before shelling.
- Toast coconut by evenly spreading 100 mℓ desiccated coconut on a paper plate. Microwave on full power for 5 to 6 minutes, stirring every minute.
- For warm finger-towels, wet face cloths with water and lemon juice, wring out and roll up. Place in a wicker basket and microwave on full power for about 2 minutes.
- To plump raisins and dried fruit, heat 250 mℓ water on full power for 2 to 3 minutes, then add the dried fruit and stand for a few minutes.

To improve their appearance, meats can be brushed with soy sauce or sprinkled with brown onion soup mix. Casseroles can be topped with crushed potato crisps and grated cheese

- To peel tomatoes, place them in a circle on paper towel in the microwave oven and microwave on full power for 10 to 15 seconds. Stand for about 5 minutes, then peel.
- To marinate meats quickly, microwave the marinade on high for 1 or 2 minutes, then pour it over the meat.
- To soften hard brown sugar, place 200 g sugar in a glass dish. Add a slice of white bread or a wedge of apple, cover and microwave on full power for about 25 seconds. Stand for several minutes.
- To obtain all the juice from fresh citrus fruits, prick the skin lightly and warm in the microwave for a few seconds.

- For chicken on the braai, cook the chicken pieces in the microwave until partially done, then finish on the grill. Brush them with sauce or marinade during cooking.
- To reheat cold fruit pie, place a slice on a serving plate and cover with paper towel. Microwave on full power for a few seconds.
- To dry lemon or orange rind, place on a glass pie plate and microwave on full power until all moisture is gone. Crumble and store in an airtight container.
- Heat ice-cream toppings or sauces in a wide-mouthed glass jar without a lid on full power for 30 to 45 seconds.
- To separate bacon slices easily, microwave on full power for a few seconds. Do not microwave foil packets.
- To peel peaches, place a small amount of water in the bottom of a glass dish. Prick the peach skins, place the peaches in the bowl, cover and steam for 1 to 1½ minutes on high. Stand for 5 minutes, then peel.
- To make a quick glaze for ham or carrots, combine 150 g brown sugar with 10 mℓ dry mustard and 45 mℓ red wine in a glass measuring jug. Microwave on full power for 1½ to 2 minutes, then stir well.
- Dry a damp newspaper by microwaving on full power for about 15 to 20 seconds.
- To dry herbs, place 250 mℓ fresh herbs between layers of paper towel on a paper plate. Microwave on full power for 4 to 6 minutes until dry and brittle, rearranging the herbs halfway through the cooking time. Cool between the layers of paper towel, then crush the leaves and store in an airtight container.
- To clarify sugared honey, remove the lid and microwave the jar on full power for 1 to 2 minutes. Stir well.
- To remove the last of the tomato sauce from the bottle, add a little orange juice, butter and wine. Microwave, without a lid, on full power for 2 minutes. Use for gravies or sauces.
- To warm a baby's bottle, invert the nipple, then microwave on full power for 1 minute. Make sure that no metal lids are used.
- To freshen soggy chips, pretzels or savoury biscuits, microwave on full power for 10 to 30 seconds. Stand for 1 minute.

How to use this book

Power levels

All the recipes in this book have been tested using microwave ovens with variable power levels. Each level serves a definite purpose, and recommended power levels should be used if possible. If your oven does not have the recommended settings, you may not achieve the same results, although some foods may be microwaved at a higher power than recommended as long as additional attention is given to stirring, turning or rotating them. Foods that require slow simmering or delicate dishes should not be attempted at high power settings.

The following chart gives the percentage of power at the various levels used in the recipes in this book. Consult your instruction book for similar power levels for your microwave oven.

Power level	Percentage of power used
Full power	100%
High	70%
Medium	50%
Defrost	25-30%
Low	15-20%

Full power is used to cook foods at a high temperature in a short time. The full power setting is used in many of the recipes given.

High power setting is used for foods that require more attention than those cooked at full power.

Medium power is used for slower cooking, such as when microwaving some sauces and meats.

Defrost is used not only to defrost foods, but also to cook delicate foods or dishes that need long, slow simmering.

Low power is used for extremely gentle cooking and for keeping foods warm before serving.

Hold setting: Some microwave ovens have a hold setting for use with the temperature probe. It is used to ensure that food is kept at a specific temperature for the required period of time.

Additional settings: You may find up to 10 power levels offered on some microwave ovens. This range gives greater flexibility in cooking a wide variety of foods. Check the instruction book for levels that correspond to the above chart.

Cooking times

The cooking times given for all recipes in this book are intended merely as a guide, since the amount of microwave energy required will differ according to the make of oven used, the size and type of container used, the food load, the temperature of the food before cooking, the depth of food in the container, and personal preferences where such foods as meats, poultry and casseroles are concerned.

Adapting recipe times

All the recipes in this book have been tested in microwave ovens with an output of 600 to 650 watts. Household current often varies from one part of the country to another and during periods of peak use such as early evening or in very cold weather. Always check food at the minimum cooking time to see whether it is done, then add more time if necessary.

If you are uncertain about the household current in your area, or if you wish to use the recipes in this book with microwave ovens of different wattage, you can check the timing and make adjustments to the recipe. To check timing, pour 250 mℓ iced water into a glass measuring jug. Place in the microwave oven and microwave on full power until the water reaches a good boil. Time the action carefully. If your oven takes 3¼ to 3¾ minutes, the recipes in this book should be correct for you. If your microwave oven takes considerably longer, add extra time to the cooking period, and if the water boils in less time, decrease the cooking time.

As a general rule, if you have a 500 watt microwave oven, add approximately 20 seconds to each minute of cooking time. If you have a 700 watt microwave, decrease the cooking time by about 15 seconds per minute.

Always check foods at the minimum suggested time

Breakfast

Traffic in your kitchen during the morning 'rush hour' can be kept to a minimum when the microwave is used to cook breakfasts. Eggs and egg dishes cook quickly with very little cleaning up for the cook. Hot beverages are almost instant and cooked cereals can be prepared either in one large dish or individually in serving bowls. Microwave cooking is ideal for weekend brunches too. The hostess can spend most of her time relaxing with her guests as she knows that each dish she plans to serve will be cooked or heated quickly and effortlessly. It is important to remember that because both egg and cheese dishes take a short time to microwave, care should be taken not to overcook them.

Microwaving eggs, cheese and cereals

Eggs are so versatile they can be prepared in a number of ways in the microwave oven. When frying, poaching or scrambling, it is important to remember that eggs are very delicate and will toughen when overcooked. Because the yolk of an egg contains more fat than the white, it will attract more microwave energy. If the egg is microwaved until the white is completely set, the yolk will then be overcooked. The times given in this chapter are to be used as a guideline only. Although personal preferences should be taken into consideration, always check eggs at the minimum cooking time. Remember that eggs continue to cook after being removed from the oven, so allow for standing time to complete the cooking process. When poaching or frying eggs in the microwave, always puncture the yolk membrane with a sharp skewer or toothpick to prevent it bursting during cooking. Do not try to cook an egg in its shell in the microwave as it expands during cooking and bursts the shell.

Cheese reacts to microwaving much as it does to conventional cooking, but faster because the high fat content attracts microwave energy and the cheese melts very quickly. When overcooked, cheese may become stringy and toughen, so check cheese dishes at the minimum suggested time. Processed cheese melts more smoothly than natural cheese, and very finely grated cheese added to casseroles or sauces takes only seconds to melt in the microwave. Some of the cheese dishes in this chapter also make good snacks, appetizers or even supper dishes.

Cereals and porridge are easily cooked in the microwave as it is not necessary to boil the water first, nor to stir constantly during cooking. Washing up is also easy as the cereals do not stick to the cooking dish. Personal preferences can always be accommodated as family members can microwave their favourite hot cereal in individual portions.

Microwaving breakfast cereals is a simple process. Mix the uncooked cereal with hot tap water in a container large enough to prevent the mixture boiling over. Microwave on full power, uncovered. Stir mixture halfway through the cooking time and, at the end of the time, let cereal stand a few minutes if desired.

Raisins, sultanas or currants can be stirred into the mixture before the last minute of cooking time. Other flavourings, such as fresh fruit, honey, butter, jam or marmalade, can be stirred into the mixture at the end of the cooking time, but before standing time.

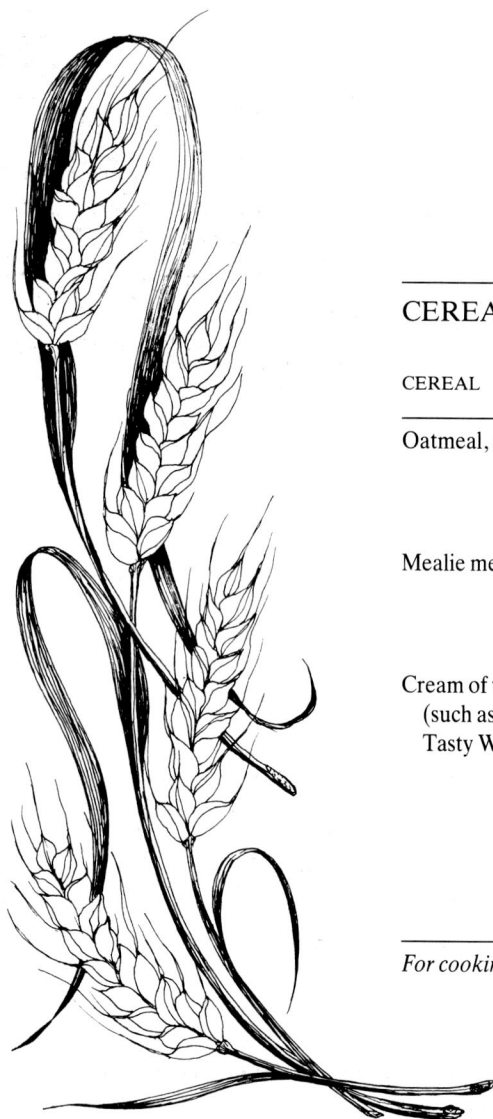

CEREAL MICROWAVE CHART – *For cooking cereals or porridge at full power*

CEREAL	SERVINGS	WATER	SALT	CEREAL	CONTAINER	COOKING TIME (MINUTES)
Oatmeal, quick	1	190 mℓ	2 mℓ	80 mℓ	large cereal bowl	1-2
	2	375 mℓ	3 mℓ	160 mℓ	1 litre bowl	2-3
	4	750 mℓ	4 mℓ	325 mℓ	2 litre bowl	5-6
Mealie meal	1	160 mℓ	2 mℓ	45 mℓ	large cereal bowl	1½-2
	2	330 mℓ	3 mℓ	80 mℓ	1 litre bowl	2½-3
	4	650 mℓ	4 mℓ	160 mℓ	2 litre bowl	4½-5
Cream of wheat (such as Tasty Wheat)	1	250 mℓ (or half milk)	2 mℓ	45 mℓ	large cereal bowl	2½-3
	2	450 mℓ (or half milk)	3 mℓ	80 mℓ	1 litre bowl	4½-5½
	4	825 mℓ (or half milk)	4 mℓ	160 mℓ	2 litre bowl	6½-8

For cooking instructions see cereals and porridge above.

Baked grapefruit and French toast (p. 34) with golden jelly marmalade (p. 142)

Breakfast fruit compote

Serve warm or cold

full power
5 minutes

1 x 410 g can apricot halves
60 mℓ water
4 whole cloves
1 cinnamon stick
2 oranges, peeled and segmented
1 punnet strawberries, sliced
2 x 2 cm slices pineapple, cut into chunks

Drain apricots, reserving syrup. Combine syrup, water, cloves and cinnamon in a 1 litre casserole dish, cover and microwave on full power for 3 minutes. Cut apricots in half and add to hot syrup. Microwave for 2 minutes more. Then let stand at room temperature until lukewarm. Add remaining fruit and chill if desired.

Serves 4 – 6

Baked grapefruit

full power
3 minutes

1 large grapefruit
30 mℓ apple juice
30 mℓ brown sugar
pinch cinnamon

Cut the grapefruit in half, remove pips and cut around each section to loosen. Place halves in individual bowls and spoon the apple juice over. Mix sugar and cinnamon together and sprinkle on top of the grapefruit halves. Microwave on full power for 2 – 3 minutes. Serve immediately. If necessary, rotate grapefruit halves a quarter turn after half the cooking time has elapsed.

Serves 2

VARIATION
For a delicious starter to a special brunch, replace apple juice with sherry or white rum.

Oatmeal with peachy sauce

Peachy sauce for oatmeal

full power
5 minutes

1 x 425 g can peach slices
30 mℓ brown sugar
10 mℓ cornflour
dash ground cinnamon
dash ground allspice
dash salt
125 mℓ orange juice
6 glacé cherries, chopped

Drain peaches, reserving syrup, then chop coarsely and set aside. Combine sugar, cornflour, ground cinnamon, ground allspice and salt in a 1 litre bowl. Stir in orange juice and reserved syrup. Microwave, uncovered, on full power for 2 minutes. Microwave for 3 minutes longer, stirring after each minute. Add chopped peaches and cherries. Spoon over hot oatmeal porridge.

Serves 4

Homemade yoghurt

full power
low
1¼ hours

500 mℓ milk
15 mℓ bought natural yoghurt
30 mℓ dried full-cream milk powder

Pour the milk into a large bowl. Cover with plastic wrap, and make two slits in the plastic to prevent 'ballooning' during cooking. Microwave for 6 minutes on full power. Uncover and cool over a basin of cold water until warm to the touch (about 45 °C). Add the yoghurt and the milk powder, and whisk to combine. Cover once more. Microwave on low for 70 minutes. Cool and refrigerate.

Makes 500 mℓ

Creamy yoghurt

low
1½ hours

90 g skim milk powder
675 mℓ warm water
175 mℓ evaporated milk
10 mℓ brown sugar
50 mℓ bought natural yoghurt

Combine skim milk powder and warm water in a large bowl. Add remaining ingredients and mix well. Cover with plastic wrap, and make two holes in the plastic to prevent 'ballooning' during cooking. Microwave on low for 1½ hours. Cool, then refrigerate.

Makes approximately 900 mℓ

Shirred eggs

Use individual glass custard cups or soufflé dishes to make perfect shirred eggs. Serve in the bowls in which they were cooked or turn out onto hot toast.

full power
medium
2½ minutes

10 mℓ butter or margarine
2 eggs
salt and pepper to taste

Place half the butter in each small dish and place the dishes on an ovenproof plate. Microwave on full power for about 30 seconds. Break 1 egg into each dish and gently pierce yolk. Cover and cook on medium for 1½ – 2 minutes, depending on how well done you like your eggs. Serve shirred eggs in glass custard cups or invert onto hot toast or toasted muffins.

Serves 2

Note: To increase the number of servings, increase the cooking time by 45 – 60 seconds per egg. If no turntable is used, rotate the plate half a turn halfway through the cooking time.

Creamy yoghurt is easily made in the microwave

Poached eggs

It is easy to poach eggs in the microwave. Poach individual eggs in glass custard cups, or several eggs at a time in a casserole dish.

full power
1½ minutes

For 1 or 2 eggs
60 mℓ hot water for each
2 mℓ white vinegar for each

Pour water into individual custard cups and add vinegar. Microwave on full power for 1 minute or until boiling. Carefully break egg into boiling water and prick egg yolk twice with a skewer. Cover with waxed paper and microwave on full power for 30 seconds. Stand in liquid for about 2 minutes. For firmer eggs, stand longer.

full power
or medium
8 minutes

For 3 or 4 eggs

Proceed as above with individual custard cups. The timing for boiling the water will be 3½ – 4 minutes. The timing for cooking the eggs is about 30 seconds per egg.
   To poach 3 or 4 eggs in a casserole dish, heat 500 mℓ water and 5 mℓ white vinegar to boiling by microwaving on full power for 5 – 6 minutes. Break eggs, one at a time, into a small bowl. Pierce the membrane of the yolk with a skewer twice, then tip gently into the boiling water. Cover and microwave on medium for 45 seconds per egg. Stand in liquid to become firm.

Fried eggs

full power
4 minutes

These sunny-side-up eggs are microwaved in a browning dish

20 mℓ butter or margarine
2 eggs
salt and pepper to taste
a little chopped parsley

Preheat a browning dish on full power for 2 – 3 minutes. Add butter to dish and allow to melt. Tilt dish to coat evenly with melted butter. Break eggs into dish and very gently pierce yolks with a needle or thin skewer. Season to taste. Cover and cook on full power for 30 – 60 seconds, depending on how well done you like your eggs. Serve sprinkled with a little chopped parsley.

Serves 2

Scrambled eggs

Eggs can be scrambled in a glass measuring jug or casserole dish

full power

For 1 – 3 eggs
5 mℓ butter per egg
15 mℓ milk per egg
salt and pepper to taste

Melt the butter in the measuring jug on full power for 30 seconds or until melted. Add eggs and milk and beat well. Season to taste. Microwave on full power for about 45 seconds per egg, stirring after every minute (after 25 seconds if only one egg is being cooked). Eggs should be very moist when removed from the oven, as they will continue to cook when left to stand. Let eggs stand for 1 – 1½ minutes before serving.

For 4 – 8 eggs
Using a larger container, follow the above instructions, but increase cooking times as follows:

4 eggs on full power   2½ – 3¼ minutes
6 eggs on full power   3½ – 4¼ minutes
8 eggs on full power   4½ – 5¼ minutes

VARIATION
Creamy scrambled eggs: Add 60 mℓ sour cream and 3 mℓ freshly chopped dill for every four eggs in the recipe for scrambled eggs.

Puffy omelette with mushroom filling

Puffy omelette

full power
medium
9 minutes

3 eggs, separated
45 mℓ mayonnaise
30 mℓ water
salt and pepper to taste
30 mℓ butter

Beat egg whites until soft peaks form. In a separate bowl, beat egg yolks, mayonnaise, water and seasonings. Gently pour yolk mixture over beaten whites and fold in. Place the butter in a 20 cm glass pie dish and microwave on full power for 1 minute. Swirl melted butter to coat the dish. Gently pour in egg mixture and spread evenly in the dish. Microwave on medium for 6 – 8 minutes, rotating dish if necessary, until mixture is set but still glossy on top. Let set 30 seconds to 1 minute, then run a spatula around sides of dish. Fold half of the omelette over and gently slide onto a serving plate.

Serves 1 – 2

Chicken sauce for puffy omelette

full power
5 minutes

15 mℓ butter or margarine
15 mℓ cake flour
salt and pepper to taste
190 mℓ cream
200 g cooked chicken
10 mℓ chopped chives
5 mℓ chopped fresh dill
10 mℓ chopped parsley
15 mℓ chopped green pepper
30 mℓ flaked almonds, toasted*

Microwave butter on full power in a glass measuring jug or bowl for 30 – 45 seconds. Stir in flour, salt and pepper. Add cream, mixing well. Microwave, uncovered, on full power for 2½ minutes, or until thickened and bubbly, stirring every minute. Add remaining ingredients and microwave on full power for about 2 minutes, or until heated through, stirring every minute. Spoon a little chicken sauce over half the cooked omelette, fold top over and slide gently onto a plate. Spoon more chicken sauce over, and serve immediately.

Serves 3 – 4

Cheese and chive omelette filling

full power
medium
30 seconds

60 g Cheddar cheese, finely grated
10 mℓ chopped chives

When omelette mixture is set, sprinkle with the cheese and microwave on medium for 30 seconds. Remove from oven, sprinkle with chives, fold omelette over and slide onto serving plate.

Serves 1 – 2

Mushroom omelette filling

full power
5 minutes

100 g mushrooms, sliced
½ small onion, chopped
30 mℓ chopped parsley
45 mℓ chopped green pepper
15 mℓ oil
salt and pepper to taste

Combine all ingredients in a casserole dish, cover and microwave on full power for 3 – 5 minutes, or until vegetables are tender. Stir after half the time. Spoon filling over half the cooked omelette and fold omelette over. Slide gently onto serving plate.

Serves 2

Eggs benedict

Elegant and easy, both the eggs and the hollandaise sauce are cooked in the microwave

4 slices cooked ham
butter or margarine
4 muffins
200 mℓ hollandaise sauce*
4 poached eggs*

Fry the cooked ham in a little butter or margarine until lightly browned on both sides. Split the muffins and toast. Spread with a little butter. Keep ham and muffins warm while making the hollandaise sauce. Keep sauce warm while cooking the eggs. To serve, place two muffin halves on each of four heated serving plates. Cover one muffin half with the cooked ham. Add one poached egg and spoon hollandaise sauce over. Serve immediately.

Serves 4

Cheese rarebit

A quick and delicious recipe to serve for brunch – or even supper

full power
medium
8 minutes

1 x 170 g jar Cheddar cheese spread
15 mℓ butter
salt and pepper to taste
2 mℓ dry mustard
3 mℓ Worcestershire sauce
dash cayenne pepper
80 mℓ cream
1 beaten egg yolk
hot toast
tomato wedges to garnish

Place cheese and butter in a casserole dish and microwave at full power for 2 – 3 minutes, stirring every minute until cheese has melted. Beat until smooth. Add salt and pepper, mustard, Worcestershire sauce and cayenne pepper and mix well. Stir in cream and egg yolk and microwave on medium for about 5 minutes, stirring every minute, until heated through. Serve over slices of toast and garnish with wedges of tomato.

Serves 2 – 3

VARIATIONS
Bacon rarebit: Stir in 45 mℓ cooked chopped bacon with the cream and egg yolk and continue as directed.
Chive rarebit: Stir in 30 mℓ chopped chives with the cream and egg yolk and continue as directed.
Egg rarebit: Stir in one chopped hard-boiled egg and 15 mℓ chopped parsley just before serving.

Mexican egg quiche

A crustless quiche to serve for a hearty breakfast or brunch

full power
16 minutes

30 mℓ butter
30 mℓ chopped green pepper
30 mℓ chopped onion
3 mushrooms, sliced
1 small tomato, peeled, seeded and chopped
5 eggs, lightly beaten
200 g Cheddar cheese, grated
250 g cottage cheese, well drained
60 mℓ cake flour
3 mℓ baking powder
salt and pepper to taste

Melt butter on full power in a 23 cm glass quiche dish for about 20 seconds. Add green pepper, onion and mushrooms and microwave on full power for 20 seconds. Combine all other ingredients in a bowl, mixing well. Season to taste and add sautéed vegetables, mixing well. Turn the mixture into the quiche dish and microwave on high for 12 – 15 minutes, or until set. If necessary, rotate dish a quarter turn every 3 minutes.

Serves 4

Cheesy egg and vegetable ring

full power
11 minutes

250 ml cauliflower florets
250 ml broccoli pieces
45 ml chopped onion
30 ml butter or margarine
6 eggs
80 ml milk
15 ml grated Parmesan cheese
salt and pepper to taste
250 ml cheese sauce*
parsley and tomatoes to garnish

Place vegetables and butter in a casserole dish, cover and microwave on full power for about 5 minutes, or until vegetables are just tender. Drain well and arrange vegetables in a greased ring mould. Combine eggs, milk, cheese, salt and pepper and beat well. Pour mixture over vegetables and microwave, uncovered, on full power for 4 – 6 minutes, or until almost set. Lift outer edges several times during the cooking to let uncooked mixture run under. Rotate dish if necessary. Let ring stand for 5 – 8 minutes.

To serve, turn out on a heated serving plate and pour half the cheese sauce over. Garnish with parsley and tomato wedges if desired, and serve with the remaining sauce.

Serves 4

Sausage and egg bake

full power
medium
18 minutes

250 g pork or beef sausage meat, crumbled
1 bunch spring onions, sliced
8 eggs
60 ml sour cream
60 ml milk
salt and pepper to taste
dash dry mustard
30 ml chopped parsley
100 g Swiss cheese, grated

Place crumbled sausage meat in a round baking dish and microwave, uncovered, on full power for 3 – 5 minutes, or until meat loses its pink colour. Stir once or twice during cooking. Drain meat well, set aside and keep warm. Place about 30 ml of the drippings in the baking dish. Add spring onions and microwave for 1 minute. Combine eggs, sour cream, milk, salt and pepper, mustard and chopped parsley in a bowl, mixing well. Pour over onion in the dish and microwave on full power for 5 – 7 minutes, or until eggs are almost set, stirring twice. Top the egg mixture with the sausage meat and sprinkle with grated cheese. Microwave on medium for 3 – 5 minutes just to melt cheese. Serve cut into wedges.

Serves 6

CHART FOR COOKING SAUSAGES AND BOEREWORS

TYPE	QUANTITY	PREHEAT TIME FOR BROWNING DISH (Full power)	COOKING TIME (Full power)
Sausages	2	4-6 minutes	35-45 seconds on each side
Sausages	4	5-6 minutes	1-1½ minutes on each side
Sausages	8 (500 g)	6-7 minutes	2 minutes on each side
Boerewors	1 piece (15 cm long)	4-5 minutes	35-45 seconds on each side
Boerewors	500 g	5-6 minutes	2 minutes on each side

SAUSAGES, BOEREWORS AND BACON

Sausages and boerewors microwaved in a browning dish look good and taste good. Let them stand for 2 – 3 minutes before serving.

Pork or beef sausages (500 g)
Microwave a browning dish on full power for 5 – 6 minutes. Brush sausages lightly with soy or Worcestershire sauce, prick them and arrange on the dish, allowing a small space between each one. Cover with greaseproof or parchment paper to prevent spattering. Microwave for 2 minutes. Turn sausages over and microwave for a further 2 minutes.

Boerewors (500 g)
The method used to microwave boerewors is exactly the same as for sausage. Arrange the boerewors in a circle in a browning dish. If cooking small pieces, arrange on the dish with a small space between each piece. Unless boerewors is extremely fatty, there is no necessity to prick it before microwaving.

Bacon
Bacon cooks very well in a microwave and there is less mess and shrinkage than if it is fried conventionally. A bacon rack is the ideal container for cooking bacon, as the fat drains off automatically. However, any flat, shallow dish will do. Drain bacon on paper towel before serving.

Place rashers of bacon, with or without rinds, on the rack. Cover with paper towel. Microwave on full power until cooked. Turn and rearrange bacon on rack to ensure even cooking.

To defrost bacon: Place a 250 g packet of bacon on a plate. Microwave on defrost for 3 – 4 minutes. Turn packet over after half the cooking time. Stand for 5 minutes.
• Do not defrost bacon in foil-lined packets.

2 – 3 rashers	2 – 3 minutes
4 – 6 rashers	4 – 5 minutes
7 – 10 rashers	6 – 8 minutes

Cook slightly longer for very crisp bacon.

Farmer's breakfast

Farmer's breakfast

full power
24 minutes

4 – 6 rashers bacon, rind removed
salt and black pepper
4 sheep's kidneys, cut in half
4 small pieces rump steak
4 large black mushrooms
2 tomatoes, sliced thickly
30 mℓ butter
4 eggs

Arrange rashers of bacon on a bacon rack. Microwave on full power for about 5 minutes, depending on size of rashers. Keep warm. Pour bacon fat into browning dish. Heat browning dish for 4 – 5 minutes. Season kidneys and steak lightly. Arrange steak and kidneys on dish, placing kidney on the inside. Microwave for 4 minutes, turning after 2 minutes. Microwave an extra 1 – 2 minutes if meat is preferred well done.

Brush mushrooms with a little of the dripping from the meat and season lightly. Season tomatoes, then arrange tomatoes and mushrooms on a plate. Microwave for 3 – 4 minutes. Keep warm.

Heat butter in a shallow casserole dish for 2 minutes. Carefully break eggs into dish. Pierce each yolk twice with the point of a skewer. Cover dish and microwave on full power for 2 minutes. Allow to stand for 1 minute. Microwave for approximately 1 minute more. The egg whites should be just set. Serve completed breakfast immediately.

Serves 4

Toasted cheese sandwich

Use a browning dish to 'toast' the bread

full power
7 minutes

2 slices wholewheat bread
a little French mustard
2 slices processed cheese
chopped spring onion or chives
1 slice cooked ham
butter or margarine

Spread one side of each slice of bread with a little mustard. Add 1 slice of cheese and sprinkle with a little chopped spring onion or chives. Add the ham and the remaining cheese. Top with remaining bread, mustard side down. Spread the outside of both slices with butter. Heat the browning dish on full power for 5 minutes. Place sandwich on browning dish. Flatten slightly and stand for about 25 seconds. Turn sandwich over and stand for 25 seconds. Microwave, uncovered, on full power for 30 – 45 seconds to melt the cheese. To make more than one sandwich at a time, increase time to 10 – 15 seconds per extra sandwich.

Serves 1

French toast

full power
6 minutes

2 eggs
45 mℓ milk
dash salt
few drops vanilla essence
90 g butter
6 slices bread

Mix together eggs, milk, salt and vanilla. Preheat browning dish on full power for 4 minutes. Add a third of the butter and heat for 30 seconds. Dip two bread slices in egg mixture and microwave in browning dish on full power for 30 – 40 seconds. Turn slices and microwave for 15 – 25 seconds. Serve topped with golden syrup or jam and cream. Repeat process with remaining bread slices, adding more butter as needed.

Serves 6

Hot tomato cocktail

A tasty wake-me-up for a winter morning

full power
10 minutes

750 mℓ tomato juice
1 x 298 g can beef consommé
3 mℓ celery salt
1 thin slice onion
1 bay leaf
4 whole cloves
a few drops Tabasco
thin lemon slices

In a 2 litre measuring jug, combine tomato juice, consommé, celery salt, onion, bay leaf, cloves and Tabasco. Cover and microwave on full power until the mixture boils, about 8 – 10 minutes. Stir twice. Strain and pour into four cups. Top each with a lemon slice.

Serves 4

Hot egg nog

Breakfast in a cup

full power
9 minutes

1 ℓ milk
50 mℓ sugar
5 mℓ vanilla essence
a few drops almond essence, if desired
dash salt
2 beaten eggs, plus 1 beaten egg yolk
1 egg white
30 mℓ icing sugar
ground cinnamon

In a 2 litre bowl, combine milk, sugar, vanilla, almond essence and salt. Microwave, uncovered, on full power until hot, but not boiling, 6 – 7 minutes. Stir. Combine eggs and egg yolk. Add 250 mℓ of the hot milk mixture to the beaten eggs, stirring constantly. Gradually add the egg mixture to the hot milk, stirring constantly. Return mixture

to oven and microwave, uncovered, for 2 minutes more, stirring once. Whisk egg white to soft peaks, then beat in icing sugar until stiff peaks form. Pour egg nog into mugs, top with egg white and sprinkle with ground cinnamon.

Makes 8 small or 4 large servings

Tea in a minute

full power
1½ minutes

180 mℓ water
1 teabag
sugar, milk or lemon, as desired

Microwave water in a cup or mug on full power to boiling, about 1½ minutes. Add teabag and steep to desired strength. Add milk, sugar or lemon, as desired.

Serves 1

Café au lait

full power
1½ minutes

10 mℓ instant coffee
160 mℓ milk
sugar

Combine coffee and milk in a cup or mug and microwave on full power for about 1½ minutes. Add sugar to taste.

Serves 1

Easy instant coffee

Use coffee mugs for heating the coffee in an instant

full power

For each cup
5 mℓ instant coffee
190 mℓ water

Spoon instant coffee granules into each mug and add the water. Microwave on full power until hot.

1 cup	1¼ minutes
2 cups	2 minutes
4 cups	3½ minutes

Hot chocolate

full power
7 minutes

60 mℓ cocoa powder
60 mℓ sugar
750 mℓ milk
5 mℓ grated orange rind
few drops almond essence, if desired
4 marshmallows

In a 1 litre glass measuring jug, combine cocoa, sugar and half the milk. Mix until smooth, then stir in remaining milk. Add orange rind and essence and microwave on full power for 6 – 7 minutes, stirring twice. Pour into cups and top with a marshmallow if desired.

Serves 4

Appetizers sandwiches & snacks

A variety of tempting appetizers from dips and patés to artichokes hollandaise are easily prepared in the versatile microwave oven. What is more, there need be no last-minute fuss if appetizers are made in advance. All that need be done just before serving is to place individual portions in separate dishes, set the timer, and reheating will take only a moment. Prepared this way, the appetizers will stay hot while your guests settle down.

Snacks and sandwiches are prepared quickly and easily at any time of the day. Store leftovers in the refrigerator and use for a variety of delicious fillings for bread and rolls. You can even microwave interesting fare in a matter of minutes for unexpected guests.

Garlic bread

high
2 minutes

1 long French bread
250 g garlic butter*
60 g Cheddar cheese, grated

Cut the French bread in half. Slice thickly at an angle, but do not cut completely through the slices. Spread bread thickly with garlic butter. To reshape, push slices together firmly. Spread a little of the butter along the top of the bread. Sprinkle cheese on top. Place each half of the bread in a cooking bag and tie ends with elastic bands or string. Microwave on high for 2 minutes. Serve immediately.

Makes 2 x 40 cm loaves

Note: Garlic bread freezes well for up to a month. To serve, place frozen bread in the microwave on defrost for 4 – 5 minutes. Microwave on high for 2 minutes, or until piping hot.

Bacon sticks

A savoury snack to serve with drinks

full power
12 minutes

10 rashers streaky bacon, rinds removed
20 grisini (Italian bread sticks)

Cut bacon strips in half lengthwise. Wrap one strip in a spiral around each bread stick. Place two paper towels on each of three paper plates and divide bread sticks among plates. Cover with another paper towel. Microwave each plate on full power for 3 – 4 minutes, or until bacon is cooked.

Makes 20 bacon sticks

Shrimp and dill dip

medium
5 minutes

250 g smooth cottage cheese
1 x 200 g can shrimps, drained
15 mℓ tomato sauce
15 mℓ finely chopped onion
5 mℓ English mustard
5 mℓ Worcestershire sauce
dash garlic salt
10 mℓ freshly chopped dill or 3 mℓ dried dill

Place cottage cheese in a 1 litre casserole dish and microwave on medium for 60 seconds. Stir in remaining ingredients and cover. Microwave for 3 – 3½ minutes, or until heated through. Stir before serving with savoury biscuits or toast.

Makes about 350 mℓ

Hot cheese dip

full power
5 minutes

1 x 170 g jar cheese spread
250 g smooth cottage cheese
60 mℓ dry white wine
30 mℓ milk
15 mℓ chopped chives
2 mℓ dry mustard
few drops Tabasco, if desired

In a covered 1 litre casserole dish, heat cheese spread until bubbly, 2 – 3 minutes on full power. Stir in cottage cheese and remaining ingredients. Microwave to heat through, 1 – 2 minutes. Add a little more milk if mixture becomes too thick. Serve with potato crisps or biscuits. If mixture cools during serving, reheat for about 1 minute.

Makes 500 mℓ

Tangy crab dip

medium
4½ minutes

250 g smooth cottage cheese
1 x 170 g can crab meat, drained
15 mℓ milk
30 mℓ finely chopped onion
20 mℓ lemon juice
20 mℓ dry sherry
8 – 10 mℓ grated lemon rind
5 mℓ prepared horseradish
salt and pepper to taste

Place cottage cheese in a 1 litre casserole and microwave on medium for 1 minute. Stir in remaining ingredients and microwave, covered, for 3 – 3½ minutes, or until heated through. Stir before serving with savoury biscuits or toast.

Makes about 350 mℓ

Mexican bean spread

full power
medium
11 minutes

2 – 3 rashers bacon
1 x 410 g can baked beans
10 mℓ vinegar
10 mℓ Worcestershire sauce
salt and cayenne pepper
dash garlic salt
50 g Cheddar cheese, grated

Place the rashers of bacon on a bacon rack. Microwave on full power for 4 minutes, or until crisp. Crumble and set aside. Combine all the remaining ingredients in a blender or processor and blend until smooth. Add bacon, turn into a bowl and cover. Microwave on medium for 7 minutes before serving. Serve as a dip with crisps or biscuits, or use as a spread over hot dogs. If the consistency is a little too thick, thin with a small quantity of milk.

Makes about 500 mℓ

Potted shrimp

Serve in one bowl as a spread, or in individual ramekins as a starter

full power
7 minutes

250 g small shelled shrimps, thawed
230 g butter
8 ml fresh dill or 4 ml dried dill
dash pepper
lemon slices to garnish

Place shrimps in a small bowl. Cover and microwave on full power for 30 seconds. Stand for 1 minute, then microwave again for 1 minute. Put 160 g of the butter in a glass measuring jug and microwave for about 3 minutes, or until melted. Process shrimps, melted butter, dill and pepper in a food processor or blender until the mixture is smooth. Spoon mixture into a serving dish or into six individual ramekins and press down well. Melt remaining butter in the microwave for about 2 minutes, then spoon over top of shrimp mixture. Chill, covered, for several hours or overnight. Serve garnished with lemon slices.

Serves 6

Chicken liver paté

full power
high
7 minutes

100 g butter	30 ml water
1 clove garlic, crushed	10 ml lemon juice
250 g chicken livers, cleaned and cut up	30 ml cream
salt and black pepper	15 ml whisky
1 ml thyme	parsley, slices of gherkin and slices of lemon to garnish
1 slice white bread	

Place butter in a shallow casserole dish. Microwave on full power for 3 minutes. Add garlic and chicken livers, toss in butter. Microwave, uncovered, on high for 4 minutes. Turn livers at least once during cooking time. Add seasonings and thyme. Soak the bread in water for a few minutes. Squeeze out excess water. Add moist bread to livers. Add remaining ingredients and blend until smooth. Taste for seasonings. Pour into a small prepared mould, an earthenware crock or small individual pottery containers. Refrigerate for 3 – 4 hours. Turn out mould onto a platter and garnish, or decorate individual servings with a small sprig of parsley and slices of gherkin and lemon. Serve with plenty of Melba toast.

Serves 4 – 6

Creamy chicken liver paté

Cognac adds an elegant touch to this paté

full power
8 minutes

30 ml butter
1 onion, chopped
1 small clove garlic, crushed
500 g chicken livers, trimmed and cut up
dash ground allspice
dash nutmeg
salt and freshly ground black pepper to taste
60 ml cognac (or brandy)
250 g smooth cottage cheese
30 ml chopped parsley
15 ml chopped chives

Melt butter in a large casserole dish on full power for 1 minute. Add onion, garlic and chicken livers. Microwave, covered, on full power for 5 – 6 minutes, stirring halfway through the cooking time. Add allspice, nutmeg, salt and pepper, and cognac. Cover and heat for 1½ minutes. Spoon half the mixture into work bowl of food processor, purée with half the cottage cheese and set aside. Repeat with remaining liver mixture and cheese. Stir in parsley and chives and spoon into serving bowl. Chill for several hours or overnight before serving with bread or savoury biscuits.

Makes about 750 ml

Clockwise: fish pâté (p. 38), creamy chicken liver pâté and potted shrimp

Fish paté

full power
12 minutes

250 g hake
125 g haddock
1 small onion, sliced
bay leaf
a few peppercorns
100 mℓ milk
100 mℓ water
50 mℓ white wine
200 g butter
45 mℓ lemon juice
5 mℓ dried dill
50 mℓ cream
salt and black pepper
lettuce, slices of lemon and sprigs of parsley or fresh dill to garnish

Place the hake, haddock, onion, bay leaf, peppercorns, milk, water and white wine in a shallow casserole dish. Cover and microwave on full power for 6 minutes. Drain fish, reserving onion and cooking liquid. Remove skin and bones from fish, and flake. Place butter, lemon juice and dill in a bowl. Microwave on full power for 4 minutes. Add fish, then cover with plastic wrap, making two slits to prevent 'ballooning' during cooking. Microwave on full power for 2 minutes. Stir in cream. In a food processor or blender, purée the fish mixture with the onion and 50 mℓ of the cooking liquid. Season to taste. Pour into a container or prepared mould and refrigerate for at least 6 hours. If using a mould, turn out onto a bed of lettuce. Decorate with slices of lemon and chopped parsley or sprigs of fresh dill. If not using a mould, place scoops of paté on crisp lettuce leaves, then garnish with lemon and parsley. Serve with hot toast, or Melba toast.

Serves 6

Savoury mushrooms

A tasty appetizer to serve with drinks

full power
3 minutes

30 mℓ softened butter
15 mℓ dry red wine
1 clove garlic, chopped
45 mℓ grated Cheddar cheese

5 mℓ soy sauce
10 mℓ chopped parsley
90 mℓ dry breadcrumbs
12 mushrooms, about 3 cm in diameter

Mix together butter, red wine, garlic, grated cheese, soy sauce, parsley and breadcrumbs, blending well. Remove stems from mushrooms and reserve for another use. Divide breadcrumb mixture evenly among upturned mushroom caps, mounding it up and pressing it lightly into shape. Place a double layer of paper towel on a flat plate and arrange stuffed mushrooms in a circle on the plate. Microwave, uncovered, on full power for 2½ – 3 minutes, rotating the plate twice during cooking if necessary. Let mushrooms stand for about 3 minutes before serving.

Makes 12 appetizers

Avocado Ritz

Avocado Ritz

full power
defrost
medium
13 minutes

24 prawns with shells
50 mℓ water
50 mℓ white wine
salt and black peppercorns
10 mℓ lemon juice
1 clove garlic, peeled
3 avocados
little lemon juice
lettuce, shredded or whole
   leaves, chopped parsley and
   lemon twists to garnish

For the sauce
2 eggs
125 mℓ oil
2 mℓ mustard
salt and cayenne pepper
Fondor
20 mℓ tomato sauce
50 mℓ cream, beaten until thick
lemon juice to taste

Place prawns, water, wine, salt, peppercorns, lemon juice and whole cloves of garlic in a shallow casserole dish. Cover and microwave on full power for about 8 minutes. Cooking time will vary considerably, depending on the size of the prawns. Prawns are cooked when they start to turn pink and become opaque. Do not overcook. Drain prawns, and allow to cool slightly before removing shells.

   Meanwhile, make the sauce. Place eggs in a bowl and whisk lightly. Microwave on defrost for 1 minute. Whisk in oil and seasoning. Microwave on medium for 4 minutes. Whisk well after each minute of cooking time. Cool slightly, then add tomato sauce, cream and lemon juice to taste. Set aside to cool further before adding to prawns. Cut prawns into small pieces, saving six whole prawns for decoration. Combine cooled sauce and prawns. Refrigerate for at least 30 minutes before serving.

To serve, cut avocados in half and brush with a little lemon juice. Place avocado half on lettuce and fill cavity with prawn mixture. Garnish with a whole prawn, chopped parsley and a twist of lemon.

Serves 6

Avocado Waldorf

full power
8 minutes

2 avocados	50 g walnuts, chopped
few drops lemon juice	125 mℓ smooth cottage cheese
½ apple, peeled and chopped	15 mℓ mayonnaise
1 stick celery, chopped	15 mℓ vermouth
125 mℓ seedless green grapes, halved	dash salt to taste

Cut avocados in half and remove stones. Sprinkle each half with a little lemon juice and arrange in a microwave dish with the narrow end toward the centre. Mix together the remaining ingredients, season to taste with a little salt and set aside. Place avocados in oven and microwave, covered, on full power for 5 – 7 minutes, depending on size and ripeness of avocados. Uncover avocados and divide apple mixture among the four halves. Heat in microwave just to warm apple mixture, about 1 minute. Serve hot, garnished with a little parsley if desired.

Serves 4

Fresh asparagus with eggs and caviar

full power
7 minutes

1 packet fresh asparagus, cooked (see p. 94)
45 mℓ butter
20 mℓ chopped onion
6 eggs
5 mℓ finely chopped fresh dill or 3 mℓ dried dill
60 mℓ cream
lemon pepper and salt to taste
red lumpfish caviar and fresh parsley to garnish

Arrange cooked asparagus spears on a serving platter, cover and keep warm. Microwave butter in a glass jug for 45 – 60 seconds on full power. Add onion and microwave for 1½ minutes. In a mixing bowl, combine eggs, dill, cream, pepper and salt, mixing well. Add the butter and onion and microwave on full power for 4 – 5 minutes, stirring well after each minute. Eggs should still be slightly 'runny' in texture as they will continue to cook after having been taken from the oven. Stand for 1 – 2 minutes, then gently spoon over the asparagus. Garnish with parsley and caviar. Serve warm.

Serves 4 – 6

Fresh asparagus with eggs and caviar

Artichokes retain their full flavour when cooked in the microwave

Artichokes hollandaise

full power
high
25 minutes

4 medium-sized globe artichokes
100 mℓ water
50 mℓ white wine
2 mℓ salt
1 slice lemon
1 clove garlic, peeled
few black peppercorns
5 mℓ oil
200 mℓ hollandaise sauce*

Wash artichokes and trim off the stalk, lower leaves and tips. Place in a cooking bag or covered casserole. Combine all remaining ingredients except the hollandaise sauce, and pour over artichokes. Microwave on full power for 18 – 20 minutes. Rearrange artichokes halfway through cooking time. To test if artichokes are cooked, remove one of the lower leaves. The leaf should peel off easily. Drain upside down and cool. Carefully lift out the middle portion and set aside. Using the handle end of a teaspoon, scrape away the hairy choke. Replace leaves and level base so that artichoke can be served upright. To serve, arrange in a dish, cover and reheat on high for 4 – 5 minutes. Serve artichokes on individual plates with plenty of hollandaise.

Serves 4

Note: Artichokes may also be served cold with a French dressing* or a suitable sauce.

Pickled prawns with avocado

full power
7 minutes

400 g prawns, shelled and deveined
2 avocados
15 mℓ chopped coriander leaves
few sprigs fresh coriander to garnish

For the spiced vinegar
250 mℓ white wine vinegar
1 onion, sliced
2 whole cloves
5 mℓ black peppercorns
2 mℓ salt
dash cayenne pepper
15 mℓ sugar

In a large bowl, combine all the ingredients for spiced vinegar. Microwave on full power for 6 minutes. Add prawns, then microwave for 1 minute. Allow mixture to cool. Cover and chill for a few hours.
   Halve avocados lengthwise, remove stones and, using a melon baller, scoop out balls of avocado. Carefully stir into prawn mixture. Stir in chopped coriander. Using a slotted spoon, drain prawns and avocado and place in individual glasses. Garnish with sprigs of coriander.

Serves 6

Chicken salad sandwiches

These open sandwiches take only a minute to heat. Make up the mixture in advance and keep on hand for a really quick snack.

full power
2 minutes

250 g cooked chicken, chopped
1 large dill pickle, finely chopped
8 stuffed olives, finely chopped
30 mℓ finely chopped onion
5 mℓ prepared mustard
60 mℓ mayonnaise, to moisten
80 g Cheddar cheese, grated
salt and pepper to taste
4 slices rye bread or wholewheat bread

Mix all ingredients except bread, and season to taste. Refrigerate until needed. To heat, spread a quarter of the mixture on each slice of bread. Place two slices on a serving plate and heat on full power for about 1 minute, or until cheese is melted and mixture is hot. Repeat with remaining mixture and bread, and serve at once.

Serves 4

Ham salad sandwiches

Another open sandwich to make in minutes

full power
4 minutes

400 g cooked ham, chopped
1 stick celery, finely chopped
1 gherkin, finely chopped
15 mℓ finely chopped onion
5 mℓ English mustard
60 mℓ mayonnaise, to moisten
100 g Cheddar cheese, grated
a little pepper
6 – 8 slices rye bread or wholewheat bread

Mix all ingredients except bread and season with a little pepper. Refrigerate until needed. To heat, spread mixture on slices of bread and heat two at a time on full power for about 1 minute, or until mixture is hot and cheese has melted.

Serves 6 – 8

Tuna salad sandwiches

full power
2 minutes

1 x 200 g can tuna, drained and flaked
2 hard-boiled egg yolks, chopped
15 mℓ chopped onion
30 mℓ chopped dill pickle or gherkin
salt and pepper to taste
5 mℓ lemon juice
45 – 60 mℓ mayonnaise, to moisten
75 g Cheddar cheese, grated
4 slices rye bread or wholewheat bread

Mix all ingredients except bread, and refrigerate until needed. To heat, spread mixture on slices of bread and heat, two at a time, on full power for about 1 minute, or until cheese melts and mixture is hot.

Serves 4

Salmon rolls

full power
4 minutes

6 – 8 small crisp dinner rolls
1 x 200 g can red salmon, drained and flaked
30 mℓ finely chopped onion
20 stuffed olives, coarsely chopped
3 – 4 small mushrooms, chopped
few drops Tabasco
pepper to taste
15 mℓ chopped parsley
100 g Cheddar cheese, grated
90 – 125 mℓ cream

Cut tops from rolls and remove soft centres, leaving hollow shells. Save centres for breadcrumbs. Place salmon in a mixing bowl, add onion, olives, mushrooms, Tabasco and pepper. Stir in parsley and about three quarters of the

cheese. Add enough cream to moisten well and spoon mixture into rolls. Sprinkle with remaining cheese and replace tops. Place in a circle on a flat plate and microwave at full power for 3 – 4 minutes, depending on number and size of rolls. Rotate halfway through cooking if necessary. Serve hot. Use tiny rolls for snacks or appetizers and larger ones for starters.

Serves 6 – 8 as a starter

Sloppy Joes

Make this mixture in advance and keep on hand for quick sandwiches

full power
6 minutes

500 g minced beef
½ small onion, chopped
250 mℓ tomato sauce
30 mℓ prepared mild mustard
salt and pepper to taste
15 mℓ brown sugar
10 mℓ vinegar
dash curry powder, if desired
50 g Cheddar cheese, grated

Break up minced beef and place in a 1 litre casserole dish. Add onion and microwave on full power for 4 minutes. Stir to break up meat, then microwave until meat is cooked, 1 – 2 minutes. Drain off excess moisture. Add tomato sauce, mustard, salt and pepper, brown sugar, vinegar, curry powder and cheese. Mix well, then cover and refrigerate until needed. To serve, spoon about 80 mℓ of the mixture between roll halves and microwave on full power, timing about 1 minute a roll.

Makes enough for 8 sandwiches

Sloppy Joe

Easy pizza served with salad

Easy pizza

full power
5 minutes

120 g cake flour	*For the topping*
2 mℓ cream of tartar	350 mℓ tomato topping*
1 mℓ bicarbonate of soda	100 g Cheddar cheese, grated
1 mℓ oregano	½ x 56 g can flat anchovy fillets
30 mℓ margarine	few sliced stuffed olives
60 mℓ milk	

To make the base, sift the dry ingredients. Add the oregano and margarine, and rub in. Mix to a moist scone dough consistency with the milk. Grease a 20 cm plate or pizza plate and press the dough to fit. Microwave on full power for 2 minutes. Spread tomato mixture over the dough. Sprinkle with cheese and arrange anchovy fillets in a lattice design. Place a slice of stuffed olive in each 'diamond'. Microwave on full power for 3 minutes. Stand for at least 2 minutes before serving.

Serves 4 – 6

Italian pizza

full power
defrost
25 minutes

120 mℓ warm water
10 g fresh yeast
4 mℓ sugar
250 g cake flour
4 mℓ salt
30 mℓ oil
700 mℓ tomato topping*
400 g mozzarella cheese, thinly sliced
1 x 56 g can anchovies, sliced lengthwise

Combine the water, yeast and sugar in a small bowl. Sprinkle 45 mℓ of measured flour onto the yeast mixture, but do not stir in. Cover with plastic wrap. Microwave for 30 seconds on full power. Allow to stand until bubbly. Sift cake flour and salt into a mixing bowl. Add oil to yeast mixture, then add this liquid to the flour. Mix to a firm dough and knead until smooth. Shape into a ball and brush it with a little extra oil to prevent a skin from forming. Place in a large bowl and cover tightly with plastic wrap. Microwave on defrost for 15 seconds. Rest for 5 minutes. Repeat this 3 – 4 times, until the dough has doubled in size.

Divide risen dough into four portions and knead each piece lightly. Roll each portion into a 20 cm round. Grease four plates and dust lightly with flour. Cover plates with dough. Microwave each round of dough on defrost for 15 seconds, then rest for 4 minutes. Repeat at least twice, or until dough has doubled in size.

Divide the tomato topping between the four pizzas, and spread over the dough. Cover with slices of cheese, and finally with slices of anchovy. Microwave pizzas, uncovered, one at a time on full power for 5 minutes. Stand for at least 3 minutes before serving.

Serves 4

VARIATIONS

Seafood pizza: 1 x 200 g can shrimps, drained, 1 x 225 g can mussels, drained, 15 mℓ chopped parsley. Arrange on top of cheese.

Mushroom pizza: 350 g mushrooms, sliced, 30 mℓ oil, 2 mℓ dried thyme. Combine all the ingredients. Add to pizza, on top of cheese.

Artichoke pizza: 1 x 410 g can artichokes, drained and sliced, 30 mℓ chopped parsley, 30 mℓ capers. Add to pizza, on top of cheese.

Salami pizza: 20 thin slices salami. Arrange salami around the edges of pizza, on top of cheese.

Ham pizza: 100 g ham, diced, 30 mℓ chopped parsley, paprika. Combine ham and parsley, add to pizza on top of cheese and sprinkle with paprika.

Tuna pizza: 1 x 200 g can tuna, drained and flaked, 10 mℓ lemon juice, 2 sticks celery, chopped. Combine all the ingredients. Add to pizza, on top of cheese.

For a really special pizza use a combination of two or more of these variations.

Chicken curry crêpes

full power
medium
22 minutes

45 mℓ butter
1 small onion, chopped
2 sticks celery, chopped
1 clove garlic, crushed
30 mℓ cake flour
375 mℓ chicken stock
30 mℓ tomato paste
5 mℓ curry paste
300 g cooked chicken, diced
100 mℓ chutney
1 apple, diced
60 mℓ raisins
salt and black pepper
60 mℓ peanuts
approximately 12 crêpes*

Place the butter in a shallow casserole dish. Microwave on full power for 1 minute. Add onion, celery and garlic. Toss in butter. Microwave on full power for 4 minutes. Stir once during the cooking time. Stir in the flour. Pour in the chicken stock and stir well. Add tomato paste and curry paste. Cover and microwave on full power for 7 minutes. Stir three times during the cooking time. In a bowl, combine chicken, chutney, apple and raisins. Season well. Add a little of the sauce to bind the mixture. Place a little chicken mixture along one end of a crêpe and roll up. Arrange crêpes in a greased shallow ovenproof dish. Coat with the remaining sauce. Sprinkle with peanuts. Cover and microwave on medium for 8 – 10 minutes. Serve hot.

Serves 4 – 6

Asparagus lunch dish

full power
medium
19 minutes

5 slices white bread, crusts removed
butter
a little English mustard
90 g Cheddar cheese, grated
1 x 410 g can asparagus cuts
250 mℓ milk
3 eggs
15 mℓ chopped parsley
1 mℓ thyme
salt and black pepper
15 mℓ oil
1 small onion, chopped
125 mℓ cornflakes

Butter bread, then spread on a little mustard. Cut each slice into three. Butter base of a shallow 1 litre casserole dish. Arrange bread, butter side up, on the base and up the edges. Sprinkle half the cheese over the bread. Drain asparagus and reserve juice. Add asparagus to casserole dish. Combine milk, eggs, 100 mℓ reserved asparagus juice, parsley, thyme and seasoning.
   Place oil in a small bowl and microwave on full power for 1 minute. Add onion and toss well. Microwave for 2 minutes. Add to egg mixture. Stir to combine and pour over asparagus. Combine remaining cheese with cornflakes and sprinkle on top. Cover with plastic wrap and make two slits in plastic to prevent 'ballooning' during cooking. Microwave on medium for about 16 minutes. The centre should still be slightly soft. Stand for 5 minutes before serving.

Serves 6

VARIATIONS

Add any one of the following to the basic recipe:

– 4 rashers bacon, cut up and sautéed for 2 minutes extra with the onion
– 100 g diced ham to the mixture
– 100 g diced, cooked chicken to the mixture
– 2 medium-sized, peeled and chopped tomatoes to the mixture

Cheese and onion quiche

full power
medium
17 minutes

1 x 23 cm shortcrust pastry shell*
5 mℓ Worcestershire sauce
1 egg yolk

For the filling
15 mℓ butter
1 onion, chopped
5 mℓ mixed herbs
120 g Cheddar cheese, grated
4 eggs
125 mℓ cream
125 mℓ milk
dash Tabasco
salt and pepper to taste
10 mℓ chopped parsley to garnish

Brush pastry shell with mixture of Worcestershire sauce and egg yolk. Microwave on full power for 2 minutes, then cool. For the filling, microwave butter on full power for 30 seconds, add onion, toss to coat and microwave for 2 minutes. Add mixed herbs. Sprinkle three quarters of the cheese over bottom of the pastry and top with onion mixture. Combine eggs, cream, milk, Tabasco and salt and pepper to taste. Pour over onion and cheese and microwave on medium for 11 – 13 minutes, rotating dish if necessary. Sprinkle quiche with remaining cheese during last minute of cooking, then allow to stand for 5 minutes before serving. Garnish with parsley.

Serves 6 – 8

VARIATIONS

Italian quiche: Use mozzarella cheese instead of Cheddar, and basil instead of mixed herbs. During last minute of cooking time, arrange sliced tomatoes on top.

Ham or bacon quiche: Add 100 g cooked, chopped ham or 8 cooked, crumbled rashers of bacon to the quiche after adding the onion.

Soups, sauces & butters

Delicious hot or cold soups are simple to make in a microwave. Not only are cooking times considerably reduced, but the kitchen remains free of strong soup odours. Bones, seasonings, water and a few soup vegetables microwaved together make a perfect stock which can be used as a basis for many soups. Once prepared, these may be frozen in individual portions, offering each member of the family a soup of his choice. At first glance, it appears that making a sauce in the microwave takes almost as long as one made conventionally. However, microwave cooking offers a number of advantages as there are no scorched messy pans to wash up, and there is no need to stir the sauce continuously. Other ingredients may be added to the sauce once it has been made, and reheating takes only a few seconds.

Crab soup

full power
19 minutes

20 mℓ butter
1 onion, chopped
400 mℓ milk
200 mℓ chicken stock
½ x 112 g packet instant mashed potato
8 – 10 crab sticks, thickly sliced
150 mℓ white wine
5 mℓ dried tarragon
salt and black pepper
125 mℓ cream
10 mℓ chopped parsley to garnish

Using a large bowl, microwave butter on full power for
1 minute. Add onion and toss in butter. Microwave for
5 minutes. Stir in milk, chicken stock and instant mashed
potato. Microwave on full power for 7 minutes, stirring
once during the cooking time. Now add crab, white wine,
tarragon and seasonings. Microwave for 4 minutes. Stir in
cream and microwave for 2 minutes. Sprinkle with parsley
and serve. This soup may also be served chilled.

Serves 6

Cold Senegalese soup

full power
7 minutes

30 mℓ butter
30 mℓ chopped onion
10 mℓ curry powder
15 mℓ cake flour
1 ℓ chicken stock
4 egg yolks
500 mℓ cream
100 g cooked chicken, finely chopped

In a large casserole dish, microwave butter on full power
for 30 seconds. Add onion and microwave for 2 minutes.
Stir in curry powder and flour and microwave for 1 minute.
Stir until smooth, then gradually stir in chicken stock.
Microwave, covered, for 3 minutes, then remove from the
oven and stir. Beat egg yolks lightly, then add a little hot
soup and beat well. Return yolk mixture gradually to the
soup, stirring constantly. Microwave soup, covered, for
30 seconds, then stir very well. Pour soup through a sieve
into a serving bowl and chill well. Add cream and cooked
chicken just before serving. Serve very cold.

Serves 6

Curried apple soup

full power
medium
32 minutes

45 mℓ oil
5 sticks celery, chopped
2 onions, chopped
1 leek, chopped
45 mℓ butter
45 mℓ cake flour
5 mℓ curry powder
1 ℓ chicken stock
2 medium apples
black pepper
125 mℓ cream
5 mℓ lemon juice
10 mℓ whisky
paprika and apple slices to garnish

Pour oil into a large casserole dish. Microwave on full
power for 1 minute. Add celery, onion and leek.
Microwave on full power for 5 minutes and set aside. Place
butter in a large jug. Microwave on full power for 1 minute.
Stir in flour and curry powder. Microwave for 30 seconds.
Stir in half the stock. Cover and microwave on full power
for 10 minutes, stirring every 2 minutes. Pour over sautéed
vegetables, and add remaining stock. Peel, core and dice
apples, and add to soup. Season with black pepper. Cover
and microwave on full power for 10 minutes. Stir in cream,
lemon juice and whisky. Microwave on medium for
5 minutes. Garnish with paprika and slices of apple. Serve
hot or cold.

Serves 6

French-style onion soup

full power
33 minutes

60 g butter or margarine
3 large onions, peeled and sliced
5 mℓ sugar
30 mℓ cake flour
1 ℓ beef stock
salt and pepper to taste
60 mℓ sherry
6 slices French bread, toasted
90 g Cheddar cheese, grated

Microwave butter in a large casserole dish on full power for
30 – 45 seconds, or until melted. Add onion and microwave
for 4 – 5 minutes. Stir in sugar and flour, and gradually stir
in beef stock. Season to taste with salt and pepper. Cover
and microwave for 22 – 25 minutes, or until onions are very
tender. Stir in the sherry. To serve, spoon soup into
individual serving dishes and top with toasted French
bread. Sprinkle with grated cheese and microwave for
about 2 minutes to melt cheese. The cheese can also be
melted under the grill. Serve hot.

Serves 6

Spiced carrot soup

Spiced carrot soup

full power
medium
32 minutes

15 mℓ oil
15 mℓ butter
6 medium carrots, sliced
2 onions, chopped
2 small turnips, sliced
1 mℓ curry powder
pinch ground cloves
pinch ground nutmeg
800 mℓ chicken stock
45 mℓ rice, uncooked
salt and black pepper
buttermilk
carrot curls to garnish

Microwave the oil and butter in a large casserole dish on full power for 1 minute. Add vegetables, toss in oil and cover. Microwave on full power for 6 minutes, stirring twice. Add curry powder, spices, stock, rice, salt and black pepper. Cover and microwave on full power for 15 minutes, stirring twice. Liquidize the soup in batches. Add buttermilk until soup has a pouring consistency. Reheat in microwave on medium for 10 minutes. Serve garnished with carrot curls. To make curls, use a vegetable peeler to shave off pieces of carrot lengthwise. Drop into iced water for a few minutes before using.

Serves 6 – 8

Cream of vegetable soup

Using one basic recipe, you can make a variety of delicious creamy soups

full power
16 minutes

For the basic soup
60 g butter
1 large onion, chopped
1 large potato, peeled and chopped
750 mℓ chicken stock
10 mℓ cornflour
250 mℓ milk
125 mℓ cream
salt and pepper to taste

Place butter in a 2 litre casserole dish and microwave on full power for 30 – 45 seconds to melt. Add onion and potato and microwave, covered, for 3 minutes. Add stock, cover and microwave for 10 minutes. Transfer mixture to a blender and purée. Mix cornflour with milk and gradually stir into the purée. Return to casserole dish and microwave, covered, for 2 minutes, stirring after 1 minute. Stir in cream and season to taste. Serve hot or chilled.

Serves 4 – 6

Cream of celery soup

cream of vegetable soup*
6 sticks celery, chopped
30 mℓ chopped parsley

Add chopped celery to basic soup mixture with the stock. Proceed as for basic soup, increasing cooking time by 1 or 2 minutes if necessary. Add chopped parsley with the cream and mix well. Serve hot.

Serves 6

Cream of mushroom soup

cream of vegetable soup*
300 g fresh mushrooms, sliced

Add sliced mushrooms to basic soup mixture with the stock. Proceed as for basic soup. Serve hot.

Serves 4 – 6

Cream of cauliflower soup

cream of vegetable soup*
1 small cauliflower, broken into florets
10 mℓ fresh dill or 5 mℓ dried dill
125 mℓ sour cream *instead of* 125 mℓ cream

Add cauliflower to basic soup mixture with the stock. Proceed as for basic soup, increasing cooking time by 1 or 2 minutes if necessary. Add the dill to the purée along with the cornflour and milk. When the soup is cooked, stir in sour cream instead of fresh cream. Serve hot.

Serves 6

46

Cream of leek soup

cream of vegetable soup*
30 mℓ butter
300 g leeks, thinly sliced

Melt butter for basic soup, add an extra 30 mℓ butter, then the potato and onion from the basic recipe. Now add the leeks. Microwave for 4 – 4½ minutes on full power. Add stock and proceed as for basic soup. Serve hot or cold.

Serves 4 – 6

Cream of carrot soup

cream of vegetable soup*
450 g carrots, peeled and sliced

Add the carrots to the basic soup mixture with the stock. Proceed as for basic soup, increasing cooking time by 1 or 2 minutes if necessary. Serve hot or cold.

Serves 6

Cream of broccoli soup

cream of vegetable soup*
450 g fresh broccoli, or frozen and thawed

Add the broccoli to the basic soup mixture with the stock. Proceed as for basic soup, increasing cooking time by 1 or 2 minutes if necessary. Serve hot or cold.

Serves 6

Goulash soup

full power
medium
1¼ hours

60 mℓ oil
250 g stewing beef, diced
60 mℓ cake flour
salt and black pepper
1 onion, chopped
1 green pepper, chopped
1 clove garlic, crushed
2 large potatoes, diced
2 large tomatoes, peeled and chopped
60 mℓ tomato purée
5 mℓ vinegar
1 ℓ beef stock
30 mℓ paprika
5 mℓ caraway seeds
1 small chilli, chopped (optional)

Pour half the oil into a browning dish. Microwave on full power for 4 minutes. Toss meat in flour and seasonings. Place in browning dish and microwave on full power for 4 minutes, stirring twice during the cooking time. Pour remaining oil into a large casserole dish and microwave on full power for 1 minute. Add onion, green pepper and garlic. Microwave on full power for 5 minutes. Now add meat, and all remaining ingredients. Cover and microwave on medium for 1 hour. Stir occasionally during cooking time. Serve with crusty bread.

Serves 6 – 8

Prawn bisque

full power
18 minutes

200 g butter
1 onion, chopped
1 carrot, chopped
20 medium prawns, cleaned but not shelled
1 sprig thyme
1 small bay leaf
3 sprigs parsley
salt and pepper to taste
dash cayenne pepper
75 mℓ brandy
250 mℓ white wine
1 ℓ fish stock
50 g cake flour, dissolved in a little cold fish stock

In a large casserole dish, microwave 50 g butter on full power for 30 seconds to melt. Add onion and carrot and microwave for 3½ – 4 minutes. Add prawns, thyme, bay leaf, parsley, salt and pepper, and cayenne pepper. Cover and microwave for 3 – 3½ minutes or until prawns are very red. Add brandy and wine, then cover and microwave for 2 minutes.
  Remove prawns and peel, reserving the flesh. Process prawn shells and heads in food processor with metal blade until finely chopped. Add 100 g butter and chop again until well mixed.
  Mix fish stock and dissolved flour into the vegetable mixture in the casserole dish. Cover and microwave for 3 minutes, stirring after each minute. Add shell and butter mixture to stock and microwave for 3 minutes, stirring after each minute. Pass soup through a fine sieve, pressing to extract all the juices. Add remaining butter and microwave, covered, for 2 minutes. Strain soup again and add reserved prawns.

Serves 5 – 6

Hearty mussel soup

Creamy mussel soup

full power
18 minutes

30 mℓ butter
10 mℓ chopped onion
4 sticks celery, chopped
2 x 225 g cans mussels
350 mℓ milk
salt and black pepper
100 mℓ white wine
125 mℓ cream
10 mℓ cornflour
30 mℓ chopped parsley

Using a large casserole dish, microwave butter on full power for 1 minute. Add onion and celery, and toss in butter. Microwave on full power for 4 minutes. Add mussels and liquid, milk and seasonings. Cover and microwave on full power for 5 minutes. Add white wine, cover and microwave for a further 5 minutes. Combine cream and cornflour. Stir into soup, cover and microwave on full power for 2 – 3 minutes. Stir in parsley and serve with crisp croûtons or Melba toast.

Serves 6

Hearty mussel soup

full power
36 minutes

30 mℓ oil
1 – 2 cloves garlic, crushed
1 onion, chopped
1 carrot, diced
2 sticks celery, chopped
1 ℓ chicken stock
30 mℓ tomato paste
1 x 410 g can whole peeled tomatoes, chopped
250 g white fish
3 mℓ sugar
salt and black pepper
3 mℓ dried basil
1 x 810 g can mussels with shells
125 mℓ frozen peas

Pour oil into a large bowl. Microwave on full power for 1 minute. Add garlic, onion, carrot and celery. Cover and microwave on full power for 5 minutes. Stir in chicken stock, tomato paste and peeled tomatoes. Microwave, covered, on full power for 10 minutes. Add fish, sugar, seasonings and basil. Microwave, covered, for 10 minutes. Discard fish, then add mussels and peas. Cover and return to microwave for 10 minutes.

Serves 8

Basic white sauce

full power
4 minutes

30 mℓ butter or margarine
30 mℓ cake flour
salt and pepper to taste
250 mℓ milk

Place butter in a 1 litre glass jug and microwave on full power for about 30 seconds to melt. Stir in flour, salt and pepper. Microwave for 45 seconds. Stir, then slowly whisk in milk, blending well. Microwave for about 2 minutes, stirring twice. Remove from oven and stir well. Serve hot.

Makes about 250 mℓ

VARIATIONS

Make up the basic sauce, then try one of the following:

Cheese sauce: Stir in 50 – 100 g grated mature Cheddar cheese. Mix until cheese melts and sauce is smooth. If cheese has not completely melted, microwave on full power for about 30 seconds and stir again. Add 3 mℓ prepared mustard if a tangy cheese sauce is desired.

Dill sauce: Stir in 15 mℓ freshly chopped dill or 5 mℓ dried dill, and 10 mℓ lemon juice. Mix until smooth.

Mornay sauce: Add 50 g grated Swiss or Parmesan cheese to the sauce, mixing until cheese has melted and sauce is smooth. Add a dash of cayenne pepper and mix in.

Curry sauce: Add 3 – 5 mℓ curry powder or to taste, and 5 mℓ lemon juice. Stir until smooth.

Horseradish sauce: Add 5 – 10 mℓ prepared horseradish or to taste, and mix well.

Thick white sauce: Use 45 mℓ flour instead of 30 mℓ in the basic recipe.

Mild mustard sauce

This sauce is delicious with ham, beef or pastrami, and makes an excellent dip for cocktail sausages

defrost
medium
4 minutes

2 eggs
20 mℓ English mustard
30 g castor sugar
salt and pepper
1 mℓ dried dill
100 mℓ oil
45 mℓ white vinegar

Place eggs in a bowl and whisk lightly. Add mustard, sugar, seasonings and dill. Microwave, uncovered, on defrost for 1 minute. Slowly beat in oil. Microwave on medium for 3 minutes, whisking well after each minute of cooking time. Lastly, whisk in vinegar. Serve hot or cold.

Makes 175 mℓ

Béchamel sauce

high
full power
10 minutes

300 mℓ milk
1 thick slice onion
1 small carrot, cut up
1 sprig parsley
2 cloves
1 blade mace
few black peppercorns
1 bay leaf
45 mℓ margarine
75 mℓ cake flour
salt

Place milk, onion, carrot, parsley, cloves, mace, peppercorns and bay leaf in a jug. Microwave, uncovered, on high for 3 minutes. Remove from oven, allow to stand for 15 minutes, then strain. Using a large jug or bowl, heat margarine on full power for 2 minutes. Stir in flour. Add half the infused milk and stir well. Stir in remaining milk. Microwave for about 5 minutes, stirring every minute during cooking time. Add a little salt and use as required.

Makes 300 mℓ

Piquant sauce

A sweet and sour sauce for meat, poultry and hamburgers

full power
6 minutes

100 g sugar
30 mℓ cornflour
60 mℓ water
1 x 410 g can crushed pineapple
½ green pepper, seeded and chopped
60 mℓ chopped pimento (canned red pepper)
1 clove garlic, finely chopped
125 mℓ white vinegar
30 mℓ soy sauce
salt to taste
few drops Tabasco

Place sugar, cornflour and water in a 2 litre casserole dish and mix well. Add pineapple, green pepper, pimento, garlic, vinegar, soy sauce, salt and Tabasco. Microwave on full power for 5 – 6 minutes, stirring every 2 minutes. The sauce should be thickened and clear. Stand for 10 minutes before serving.

Makes about 450 mℓ

Clockwise: sherry mushroom sauce, dill sauce (p. 49), mild mustard sauce (p. 49) and braai sauce

Sherry mushroom sauce

full power
medium
10 minutes

60 g butter
200 g mushrooms, sliced
60 mℓ water
60 mℓ sherry
15 mℓ cornflour
salt and pepper to taste

Place butter in a 1 litre casserole dish and microwave on full power for about 1 minute, until melted. Add mushrooms and microwave, covered, for 2½ – 3 minutes. Combine water, sherry and cornflour, mixing until smooth. Slowly stir into mushroom mixture. Cover and microwave on medium for 4 – 5 minutes until mixture thickens, stirring at least twice. Season to taste and microwave for 1 minute more. Serve with steaks or chops.

Makes about 375 mℓ

Braai sauce

full power
8 minutes

15 mℓ butter
½ onion, chopped
15 mℓ finely chopped green pepper
2 cloves garlic, chopped
250 mℓ seasoned tomato sauce (not ketchup)
30 mℓ brown sugar
30 mℓ lemon juice
5 mℓ Worcestershire sauce
salt and freshly ground black pepper to taste
2 mℓ paprika
2 mℓ dry mustard
dash cayenne pepper
dash ground turmeric

Place butter in a 2 litre container and microwave on full power for about 30 seconds to melt. Add onion, green pepper and garlic. Microwave for 3 minutes, then stir in remaining ingredients. Cover and microwave for 4 – 5 minutes, until sauce is bubbly. Brush sauce over steaks, chops or ribs on the braai. The sauce can be kept in the refrigerator, but should be covered.

Makes about 300 mℓ

Bearnaise sauce

full power
7 minutes

45 mℓ dry white wine
15 mℓ tarragon vinegar
2 spring onions, chopped
2 mℓ dried tarragon
few black peppercorns
3 egg yolks
125 g butter
salt

Place white wine, tarragon vinegar, spring onion, dried tarragon and peppercorns in a flat dish. Microwave, uncovered, on full power for 4 minutes, until liquid has reduced to at least half. Strain and set aside. Using a food processor fitted with a metal blade, process egg yolks until light in colour. Microwave butter for 3 minutes (butter must be very hot). With machine running, pour hot butter onto yolks. Process for about 45 seconds. Add strained liquid and a little salt. Process to combine. Serve hot with beef, lamb, chicken or fish.
    To reheat the sauce, microwave, covered, on defrost for 2 – 4 minutes, depending on how cold the sauce is. Whisk well and serve.

Makes about 175 mℓ

VARIATIONS

Avocado bearnaise: Follow directions for making bearnaise sauce, substituting wine vinegar for tarragon vinegar. Finally, fold in 1 puréed avocado. Serve with beef, chicken or fish.

Pineapple bearnaise: Follow directions for making bearnaise sauce, substituting pineapple juice for dry white wine. Finally, stir in 60 mℓ crushed pineapple. Serve with beef or chicken.

Tomato topping

full power
18 minutes

15 mℓ oil
½ onion, chopped
1 clove garlic, crushed
1 x 410 g can whole peeled tomatoes, chopped
15 mℓ tomato paste
1 mℓ oregano
1 bay leaf
salt and black pepper
2 mℓ sugar

Use a deep bowl to prevent excess splashing in the oven. Pour oil into bowl and add onion and garlic. Microwave on full power for 4 minutes. Add remaining ingredients. Microwave, uncovered, on full power for 14 minutes, stirring every 3 minutes. The tomato mixture should be fairly thick. Microwave for 1 – 2 minutes more if necessary.

Makes 350 mℓ

Marmalade sauce

This tasty accompaniment to pork, ham or tongue can also be served as a dip for cocktail sausages

full power
10 minutes

3 mℓ dry mustard
10 mℓ brown sugar
1 mℓ ground ginger
salt
pinch cloves
200 mℓ sweet red wine
60 mℓ raisins
30 mℓ apple jelly
7 mℓ orange rind
15 mℓ cornflour
30 mℓ orange juice
15 mℓ lemon juice

Place all ingredients except cornflour and fruit juices in a bowl. Cover and microwave on full power for 6 minutes. Meanwhile, blend cornflour with orange and lemon juices. Add a little of the boiling liquid to the cornflour mixture, then return to the bowl. Stir well. Microwave, uncovered, for 4 minutes, stirring once during cooking time. Serve hot or cold.

Makes 250 mℓ

Hollandaise sauce

full power
3 minutes

125 g butter
2 egg yolks
15 mℓ lemon juice
3 mℓ dry mustard
dash salt and pepper

Place butter in a glass measuring jug and microwave on full power for 2½ – 3½ minutes until hot and bubbly. Place remaining ingredients in a blender or food processor. When butter is ready, turn blender or processor to highest speed and slowly add hot butter, mixing until sauce is creamy and thickened.

Makes about 175 mℓ

Easy spaghetti sauce

full power
20 minutes

30 mℓ oil
1 large onion, coarsely chopped
1 stick celery, thinly sliced
10 mushrooms, sliced
½ green pepper, seeded and coarsely chopped
2 – 3 cloves garlic, finely chopped
250 g minced beef
1 x 410 g can whole peeled tomatoes, chopped
15 mℓ tomato paste
30 mℓ chopped fresh parsley
3 mℓ dried basil
10 mℓ lemon juice
salt and black pepper

Place oil in a 2 litre casserole dish. Add onion, celery, mushrooms, green pepper and garlic. Cover and microwave on full power for 5 minutes, stirring once. Break up minced beef and add to the vegetables. Microwave for 3 minutes, stirring after each minute. Blend in chopped tomatoes and juice, tomato paste, parsley, basil and lemon juice. Season to taste. Cover and microwave on full power until the sauce is slightly thickened, about 12 minutes, stirring 3 or 4 times.

Makes about 900 mℓ

Lemon butter sauce

Serve with fish or vegetables such as asparagus and broccoli

full power
3 minutes

60 mℓ lemon juice
125 g butter, cut into pieces
dash salt
10 mℓ freshly chopped parsley

Place lemon juice in a glass measuring jug and microwave on full power until juice is bubbly, 30 – 45 seconds. Remove from oven and whisk in about a third of the butter. Return to oven for 30 – 45 seconds, then whisk in another third of the butter. Microwave for 30 – 45 seconds and finally whisk in remaining butter. Stir in salt and parsley. Heat again until bubbly, about 45 seconds. Serve hot.

Makes 150 mℓ

Reduced cream

full power
medium
10 minutes

Place 250 mℓ cream in a deep 1,5 litre casserole dish or jug. Microwave on full power for 2 minutes. Stir, then microwave for a further 2 minutes. Stir again. Reduce power to medium, and microwave for 6 minutes more, stirring every 2 minutes. Various flavourings can be added to the reduced cream, such as wine, lemon juice, salt and pepper, grated cheese, savoury butter, mustard. This makes a rich, smooth sauce to serve with vegetables, meat or fish, depending on the flavouring.

Makes 200 mℓ

Seasoned butter

low
45 seconds

Place 250 g butter in a glass measuring jug and microwave on low for 30 – 45 seconds just to soften. Then flavour with ingredients of your choice, and beat with an electric mixer until light and fluffy. Transfer to a suitable container or shape into a roll. Keep refrigerated until needed and serve with roast meat, fish or vegetables.

VARIATIONS

Herbed butter: Add 10 mℓ freshly chopped parsley, 10 mℓ lemon juice, salt and pepper to taste and 3 – 5 mℓ dried thyme, tarragon or rosemary, as desired.

Garlic butter: Add 2 – 3 crushed cloves of garlic, 10 mℓ lemon juice and 2 mℓ dry mustard. For parsley garlic, add 80 mℓ chopped parsley to the butter mixture.

Dill butter: Add 20 mℓ freshly chopped dill, salt and pepper to taste and the sieved yolk of 1 hard-boiled egg.

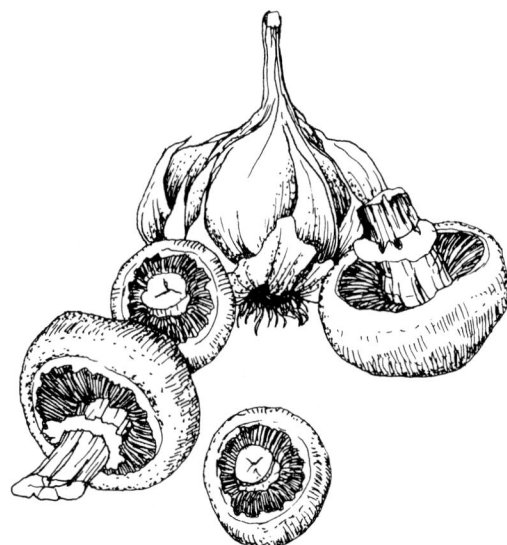

Salads & dressings

Whether a starter to a rich meal, an interesting accompaniment to a hot or cold spread, or even a light main course, create a salad for every season and every occasion with freshly blanched, crisp vegetables. Moulded salads make an imposing centrepiece for a cold buffet – and are quick to prepare in the microwave. For the perfect salad toss an interesting selection of salad ingredients with just the right dressing.

To blanch vegetables

Place vegetables in a cooking bag or covered casserole dish with only a drop of water, microwave for a few minutes, then plunge into cold water. Blanching produces crisp, brightly coloured vegetables with maximum flavour. Remember, vegetables for salads should still be crunchy so take care not to overcook them.

French dressing

Although not made in a microwave, this classic dressing is used in many of the following recipes

100 mℓ oil
60 mℓ vinegar (white, wine or tarragon)
salt and black pepper to taste
dash cayenne pepper
2 mℓ dry mustard
2 mℓ sugar

Combine all ingredients well and use as required. French dressing may be kept in the refrigerator for a few days. The vinegar flavour will become stronger if it is stored for a longer period.

Makes 160 mℓ

Boiled salad dressing

full power
low
4 minutes

10 mℓ cake flour
15 mℓ sugar
dash salt
5 mℓ prepared English mustard
75 mℓ white vinegar
60 mℓ water
15 mℓ margarine
1 egg
little cream or milk

Combine the dry ingredients in a medium-sized bowl. Add the mustard, vinegar and water. Stir well to remove lumps. Microwave, uncovered, for 3 minutes on full power. Stir every minute. Remove from oven, add margarine and then pour onto the lightly beaten egg, mixing well. Return to oven and microwave on low for 1 minute. Beat well, then allow to cool. Dilute to desired consistency with cream or milk.

Makes 175 mℓ

Beetroot salad

full power
33 minutes

6 medium beetroots	300 mℓ white vinegar
1 onion, sliced	2 mℓ salt
45 mℓ water	2 mℓ black peppercorns
15 mℓ sugar	sprigs of parsley to garnish

Top and tail beetroot. Arrange in a circle in a shallow casserole dish. Add enough water to cover bottom of casserole, about 200 mℓ. Cover and microwave on full power for 29 – 33 minutes, depending on the size of beetroot. Uncover and allow to cool. Peel and slice thinly. Place beetroot in a glass jar in layers, adding a little onion between each layer. Place water and sugar in a container and microwave for 30 seconds. Combine remaining ingredients and pour onto beetroot. Stand overnight before serving. To serve, drain beetroot, place in a serving bowl. Garnish with sprigs of parsley. This beetroot salad will keep for about 1 month in the refrigerator.

Serves 12

Marinated mushrooms

full power
3½ minutes

400 g button mushrooms, wiped clean
250 mℓ French dressing*
30 mℓ chopped chives
20 mℓ chopped parsley
30 mℓ white vinegar

Place cleaned mushrooms in a large glass bowl. Combine dressing, chives, parsley and vinegar in a casserole dish. Cover and microwave on full power for 3 – 3½ minutes. Pour over mushrooms, cover, and place in refrigerator for several hours or overnight. Drain dressing and serve mushrooms on lettuce leaves, if desired.

Serves 4 – 6

Potato salad

full power
28 minutes

6 potatoes	*For the dressing*
3 rashers bacon, rinds removed	100 mℓ white vinegar
150 g mushrooms, sliced	5 mℓ dry mustard
1 small onion, chopped	salt and black pepper
30 mℓ chopped chives	cayenne pepper
30 mℓ chopped parsley	5 mℓ sugar
1 gherkin, chopped	
mayonnaise	
lettuce and parsley to garnish	

Wash potatoes and wipe dry. Pierce each with a skewer or fork. Place in a circle on a plate and microwave on full power for 20 minutes. Test that they are ready and cook for 1 or 2 minutes longer if necessary. Allow to cool slightly. Peel and dice, then place in a bowl. Combine all the ingredients for the dressing in a jug. Microwave on full power for 1 minute. Pour over potato and allow to cool.

Microwave bacon on full power for 4 – 6 minutes. Remove bacon, reserving fat, then drain on paper towel. Chop bacon and add to potato. Toss mushrooms in the reserved bacon fat. Microwave on full power for 1 minute. Cool, then add to potato. Add onion, chives, parsley and gherkin. Carefully mix in enough mayonnaise to bind the potato mixture. Turn into a salad bowl. Garnish with a few lettuce leaves and parsley.

Serves 6 – 8

VARIATION

Use a mixture of mayonnaise and sour cream to bind salad, and add a few caraway seeds.

Chef's spinach salad

full power
3 minutes

4 leeks, white portion only
100 mℓ chicken stock
1 bunch spinach
1 small lettuce
200 g chicken, diced
150 g ham, diced
60 g feta or Gruyère cheese, diced
250 mℓ croûtons
2 tomatoes, sliced

For the dressing
150 mℓ oil
60 mℓ red wine vinegar
20 mℓ French mustard
salt and black pepper
dash cayenne pepper
5 mℓ sugar

Place leeks in a small casserole dish, add chicken stock and cover. Microwave on full power for 3 minutes. Uncover and cool leeks in the stock. Drain and slice thickly. Wash, dry and break spinach and lettuce into bite-sized pieces. Place in a salad bowl. Add leeks, chicken, ham, cheese and croûtons. Toss well, and add tomato slices.

To make dressing, combine all ingredients and mix well. Pour dressing over salad, toss again and serve.

Serves 4 – 6

Minted corn and baby marrow salad

full power
9 minutes

6 – 8 baby marrows
30 mℓ oil
1 onion, chopped
45 mℓ wine vinegar
5 mℓ fresh oregano, or 2 mℓ dried oregano
15 mℓ finely chopped mint
1 x 410 g can corn kernels, drained
salt and black pepper
fresh sprigs of mint to garnish

Cut ends off baby marrows and slice thickly. In a shallow casserole dish, microwave oil on full power for 2 minutes. Add the marrows and onion. Toss in the oil. Microwave, covered, for 5 minutes. Stir once during the cooking time. Add wine vinegar, oregano, mint, corn and seasoning. Cover and microwave for 2 minutes. Allow to cool, then chill. Serve garnished with sprigs of mint.

Serves 4 – 6

Minted corn and baby marrow salad

Salad Irma

Salad Irma

full power
7 minutes

250 g prawns, heads removed
45 mℓ water
salt
15 mℓ lemon juice
250 g green beans
lettuce leaves
1 avocado, peeled and sliced
200 g mushrooms, sliced
15 mℓ chopped parsley

For the dressing
75 mℓ oil
15 mℓ lemon juice
30 mℓ tarragon vinegar
5 mℓ fresh tarragon, chopped
2 mℓ sugar
salt and black pepper

Place the prawns in a shallow dish. Add half the water, salt and 5 mℓ lemon juice. Cover and microwave on full power for 3 – 4 minutes, depending on the size of the prawns. Cool slightly. Peel prawns and cut into chunks. Reserve four for garnishing.

String the beans and cut in half. Place beans in a shallow dish. Add remaining water and a little salt. Cover and microwave on full power for 3 minutes. Drain and refresh in plenty of cold water. Allow to cool.

Line a shallow salad platter with lettuce leaves. Brush the avocado slices with a little lemon juice. Carefully arrange beans and avocado on the lettuce. Top with mushrooms and prawns. Combine all the ingredients for the dressing and pour over the salad. Sprinkle with chopped parsley.

Serves 4

Caesar salad

medium
4 minutes

1 lettuce
75 mℓ sunflower seed oil
1 egg
1 mℓ dry mustard
salt and black pepper
5 anchovy fillets, mashed
3 mℓ Worcestershire sauce
10 mℓ lemon juice
30 mℓ wine vinegar
250 mℓ small croûtons, cooled
45 mℓ grated Parmesan cheese
few black olives

Wash and dry lettuce, break into bite-sized pieces and place in a salad bowl. In a jug, combine oil, egg, mustard, salt, black pepper, anchovy fillets, Worcestershire sauce, lemon juice and vinegar. Place in microwave, uncovered, and cook on medium for 4 minutes. Stir once during cooking time. Mix well and cool slightly. Add croûtons, cheese and olives to lettuce. Pour dressing over, toss and serve immediately.

Serves 4 – 6

Chunky vegetable salad

full power
22 minutes

1 small bunch carrots, sliced	*For the dressing*
45 mℓ water	120 mℓ oil
salt	120 mℓ brown vinegar
200 g green beans, sliced	45 mℓ sugar
4 baby marrows, sliced	3 mℓ thyme
45 mℓ water	1 x 410 g can concentrated
30 mℓ oil	tomato soup
1 onion, chopped	
1 green pepper, chopped	
30 mℓ chopped almonds	

Place the carrots, water and a little salt in a shallow casserole dish. Cover and microwave on full power for 7 – 8 minutes, stirring once or twice during cooking time. The carrots should still be crisp. Drain and refresh in cold water. Place the green beans and baby marrows in the shallow casserole dish, add 45 mℓ water and a little salt. Cover and microwave on full power for 4 minutes. Drain and refresh in cold water.

Pour oil into a small dish, microwave on full power for 1 minute. Add onion and green pepper, and toss in oil. Microwave on full power for 4 minutes. Drain all the vegetables well, combine in a bowl and set aside.

In a glass jug, combine all ingredients for the dressing. Cover and microwave on full power for 5 minutes, stirring twice during cooking time. Pour hot dressing over the vegetables. Chill and serve very cold. Before serving, sprinkle with almonds.

Serves 8 – 10

Seasonal salad

full power
4 minutes

¼ medium cauliflower or a few florets broccoli
4 baby marrows, thickly sliced
30 mℓ water
1 medium lettuce
100 g mushrooms, sliced
1 kohlrabi, thinly sliced
2 – 3 tomatoes, cut into wedges
1 small onion, sliced
30 mℓ chopped parsley
a few black olives
60 g feta cheese, cubed
1 avocado, cut up
100 mℓ French dressing*

Wash the cauliflower well and cut into small florets. Add the baby marrows. Place in a shallow casserole dish. Add water and cover. Microwave on full power for 4 minutes. Drain and refresh in cold water. Cool completely. Wash and dry the lettuce. Break into bite-sized pieces and place in a salad bowl. Add all the vegetables, parsley, olives and feta cheese. Cover and refrigerate until required. At the last minute add avocado. Pour the dressing over the salad, toss well and serve.

Serves 6 – 8

Hot potato salad

full power
24 minutes

4 large potatoes
6 rashers bacon, diced
30 mℓ cake flour
45 mℓ sugar
8 – 10 mℓ salt
pepper to taste
250 mℓ water
125 mℓ vinegar
1 stick celery, finely chopped

Wash potatoes and wipe dry. Pierce with a skewer or fork. Microwave potatoes on full power for 10 – 12 minutes, turning them after 4 minutes. Remove from oven, cool slightly, then peel and cut into bite-sized pieces. Keep warm. Place diced bacon in a deep casserole dish and microwave on full power for 5 – 6 minutes, stirring after 2 minutes. Remove bacon with a slotted spoon and keep warm. Add flour, sugar, salt and pepper to bacon fat in the casserole dish, mixing well. Microwave for 1 minute, stir well, then microwave 1 minute more. Stir until smooth. Combine water and vinegar and gradually stir into flour mixture. Add chopped celery and microwave for 3½ – 4 minutes, stirring after each minute. Remove from oven and stir well. Add potatoes and bacon, and mix well. Cover and stand for a few minutes before serving.

Serves 6

Pasta salad

full power
7 minutes

½ medium cauliflower
90 mℓ water
4 baby marrows, sliced thickly
½ English cucumber, julienned
250 g ham or tongue, julienned
3 tomatoes, peeled and diced
1 bunch spring onions, chopped
30 mℓ chopped parsley
30 mℓ pine nuts or almonds, chopped
salt and black pepper
100 mℓ French dressing*
15 mℓ tomato sauce
150 mℓ mayonnaise
250 g noodles, cooked

Wash the cauliflower well and cut into small florets. Place in a casserole dish with 45 mℓ water, cover and microwave on full power for 4 minutes. Drain and refresh in plenty of cold water. Place the baby marrow in the casserole dish and add the remaining water. Cover and microwave on full power for 3 minutes. Drain and refresh in cold water. Using a large bowl, combine all the ingredients. Toss well and chill before serving.

Serves 4 as a main course

Spicy three bean salad

This dish is delicious with a braai

full power
21 minutes

15 mℓ oil
2 rashers bacon, cut up
2 medium onions, chopped
1 green pepper, chopped
2 cloves garlic, crushed
10 mℓ chopped fresh ginger
5 mℓ curry paste
1 x 810 g can whole peeled tomatoes, chopped
salt and black pepper
2 mℓ sugar
1 bay leaf
1 x 410 g can baked beans
1 x 410 g can butter beans, drained
1 x 410 g can kidney beans
parsley to garnish

Use a large, deep casserole dish for this. Microwave oil on full power for 1 minute. Add bacon, onion, green pepper, garlic, ginger and curry paste. Toss in oil. Microwave on full power for 5 minutes. Add tomatoes, seasonings, sugar and bay leaf. Microwave, uncovered, on full power for 15 minutes. Stir from time to time. Remove the bay leaf. Add all the beans. Decorate with sprigs of parsley. Serve hot or cold.

Serves 12

Sweet and sour bean salad

full power
13 minutes

5 rashers bacon, diced
100 g sugar
15 mℓ cornflour
salt and pepper to taste
150 mℓ vinegar
5 mℓ prepared mustard
1 x 410 g can green beans, drained
1 x 410 g can red kidney beans, drained
1 x 410 g can butter beans, drained
1 onion, sliced

Place bacon in a large, deep casserole dish. Microwave on full power for about 4 minutes, or until bacon pieces are crisp. Remove bacon with slotted spoon and drain on paper towel. Add sugar, cornflour, salt and pepper, vinegar and mustard to bacon fat in the casserole, mixing well. Microwave for 3 minutes, stirring after each minute. The mixture should be thick. Add all the drained beans and the onion. Mix gently to coat all ingredients. Cover and microwave for 6 minutes, stirring after 3 minutes. Stir at the end of cooking time, then let salad stand, covered, for about 10 minutes before serving. Sprinkle bacon over beans and serve.

Serves 6

Spicy three bean salad

Bean and bacon salad

full power
6 minutes

3 – 4 rashers bacon, rinds removed
1 x 410 g can red kidney beans, drained
1 small cucumber, diced
1 small onion, chopped
1 clove garlic, crushed
15 mℓ chopped chives
salt and black pepper
few drops Tabasco
60 mℓ French dressing*
1 hard-boiled egg, sliced

Place the bacon on a rack and microwave on full power for 4 – 6 minutes. Drain on paper towel. When cool, crumble. In a bowl combine the beans, cucumber, onion, garlic, chives, salt and pepper, and Tabasco. Pour the French dressing over and toss lightly. Turn into a salad bowl. Top with crumbled bacon and slices of egg.

Serves 4

Pepper, brinjal and tomato salad

full power
25 minutes

1 medium-sized brinjal
salt
oil
1 green pepper, cut into chunks
1 onion, sliced
2 tomatoes, sliced
30 mℓ lemon juice
1 clove garlic, crushed
black pepper
2 mℓ dried basil
15 mℓ chopped parsley and black olives to garnish

Wash brinjal and slice into rings without peeling. Sprinkle with a little salt, and set aside for 30 minutes. Pat dry with paper towel, then brush with oil. Microwave a browning dish on full power for 6 minutes. Add 15 mℓ oil to the dish and microwave for 1 minute. Arrange brinjal slices in browning dish, press down firmly for 30 seconds to sear, then microwave for 1 minute. Turn and repeat. Drain on paper towel. Cut each slice into four. Repeat with remaining brinjal by reheating browning dish for 2 minutes before searing and microwaving. Add more oil to browning dish if necessary.
  Heat browning dish for 3 minutes, add a little oil and the green pepper. Microwave 1 minute on each side. Drain on paper towel. Repeat with onion rings. Place tomato slices on browning dish without reheating it. Microwave 1 minute on each side and set aside.
  Add lemon juice, garlic, black pepper and basil to dish. Stir to mix. Arrange cooked salad ingredients in a shallow dish and pour lemon mixture over. Cover and chill well. Before serving, sprinkle with chopped parsley and a few black olives.

Serves 4 – 6

Hot tuna salad

Makes a good starter or a main course for supper

high
8 minutes

2 x 200 g cans tuna in water, drained
5 sticks celery, chopped
500 mℓ croûtons
250 mℓ mayonnaise
50 g flaked almonds, toasted*
30 mℓ finely chopped onion
10 mℓ capers, drained
15 mℓ lemon juice
salt and pepper to taste
60 g Cheddar cheese, grated

In a 2 litre casserole dish, combine tuna, celery, half the croûtons, mayonnaise, almonds, onion, capers and lemon juice. Season to taste and mix well. Cover and microwave on high for 7 minutes, stirring after 3 minutes. Sprinkle remaining croûtons over casserole and top with grated cheese. Microwave on high for 1½ minutes or until cheese melts.

Serves 6 as a main course or serves 8 as a starter

Lettuce salad with a difference

full power
6 minutes

4 rashers streaky bacon, diced
60 mℓ white vinegar
10 mℓ sugar
salt and pepper to taste
pinch mixed herbs
1 stick celery, finely chopped
15 mℓ chopped chives
1 head lettuce, broken into pieces
1 orange, peeled and segmented
50 g walnuts, coarsely chopped

Microwave bacon in a deep casserole dish on full power for 3 minutes, or until crisp. Remove bacon with a slotted spoon and drain on paper towel. Add vinegar, sugar, salt, pepper and herbs to the casserole dish and mix well with bacon fat. Microwave on full power for 2 – 2½ minutes. Stir well, then mix in celery and chives. Microwave for 30 seconds. Add lettuce pieces, a few at a time, to the hot dressing, tossing to coat pieces. When all have been added and lettuce is slightly limp, gently stir in orange segments and walnuts. Serve immediately.

Serves 8

Moulded apple salad with chive cream

full power
2 minutes

300 mℓ water
1 x 90 g packet lemon jelly
150 mℓ apple juice or Appletiser
3 sticks celery, chopped
1 apple, sliced
½ small cucumber, thinly sliced

For the chive cream
250 g low fat cottage cheese
60 mℓ milk
45 mℓ chopped chives
60 g chopped walnuts
cucumber slices (optional)

Microwave 150 mℓ water on full power for 1 – 1½ minutes, until boiling. Pour over lemon jelly powder, stirring to dissolve. Return to microwave and heat for 20 seconds. Remove from oven and add remaining water and apple juice. Pour a third of the jelly into a ring mould and sprinkle with chopped celery. Chill until set. Pour in half the remaining jelly and let set slightly. Arrange apple slices around the ring. Chill until set, then add remaining jelly and place cucumber slices around, making sure all slices are submerged in the jelly. Chill until set.

To make the chive cream, beat cottage cheese with milk, stir in chives and nuts. Turn apple salad mould out onto serving plate, fill centre with chive cream and garnish with walnuts, chives or cucumber slices.

Serves 4 – 6

Fruity slaw

high
6 minutes

½ head cabbage, shredded
water
60 mℓ seedless raisins
1 apple, cored and sliced
1 x 312 g can mandarin oranges, drained
125 mℓ seedless grapes, halved
60 mℓ chopped nuts
1 stick celery, sliced

For the dressing
75 mℓ honey
45 mℓ lemon juice
5 mℓ sesame seeds
3 mℓ dry mustard
dash paprika
2 mℓ salt
125 mℓ oil

Place cabbage in a large bowl, sprinkle with 90 mℓ water. Cover and microwave on high for 3 minutes. Refresh in cold water and drain well. Place raisins in a measuring jug, add enough water to just cover and microwave on high for 1½ minutes. Drain and cool. Place cabbage in a large bowl, add raisins, fruits, nuts and celery. Toss to mix.

To make the dressing, combine honey, lemon juice, sesame seeds, dry mustard, paprika and salt in a measuring jug. Microwave on high for 1 minute, stir, then microwave for 30 seconds more. Turn mixture into a blender or food processor and, with machine running, slowly add the oil. Blend until slightly thickened, then pour over cabbage mixture. Toss well. Chill for at least 2 hours, stirring occasionally.

Serves 6 – 8

Moulded green vegetable salad

Moulded green vegetable salad

full power
3 minutes

250 mℓ water
1 x 90 g packet lime jelly
3 sticks celery, chopped
1 small green pepper, chopped
15 mℓ chopped chives
250 mℓ chopped cucumber
250 g cottage cheese
250 mℓ mayonnaise

Microwave water on full power for 2 – 2½ minutes, until boiling. Pour over lime jelly and stir to dissolve. Return mixture to microwave and heat on full power for 30 seconds. Remove jelly from oven and cool until partially set. With an electric mixer, beat jelly, then add vegetables, cottage cheese and mayonnaise, mixing well. Spoon into a serving bowl or ring mould and chill until set, about 3 hours.

Serves 6 – 8

Fish

Fish does not enjoy the popularity it deserves, possibly because this delicate food is easily over-cooked. To make use of the wide variety of fish available in South Africa, whether fresh or frozen, cook it correctly in the microwave. Fish not only has an excellent flavour and texture, but it has a good appearance too. Little or no extra liquid is used when fish is cooked in the microwave, and this guarantees a delicious result. In addition, more vitamins and mineral salts are retained than when conventional cooking methods are used. Shellfish can also be cooked successfully in the microwave and the tender flesh remains moist and succulent.

When cooking fish

- Cover the fish tightly during cooking.
- Large whole fish should have 2 to 3 slits cut in the skin to prevent them from bursting.
- Defrost frozen fish before cooking in the microwave. Pieces should be separated during defrosting time.
- Do not deep-fry fish in the microwave oven.
- Arrange fish so that the thicker sections are towards the outside.
- Shield the narrow tail end of a large whole fish with a strip of aluminium foil.
- Always undercook rather than overcook fish. Check whether it is ready after the minimum cooking time.
- Brush the fish with melted butter to prevent it from drying out.
- Pierce the bag before microwaving 'boil in the bag' fish.

FISH DEFROSTING AND COOKING CHART

FISH	DEFROST TIME	COOKING TIME (Full power)
Fillets of white fish, kingklip, hake, kob, etc., 500 g	5-7 minutes, stand 5 minutes	5-6 minutes
Haddock, 500 g	5 minutes, stand 5 minutes	4-5 minutes
Salmon steaks, 500 g	5 minutes, stand 5 minutes	5-7 minutes
Trout, 2 medium	5-7 minutes, stand 5 minutes	5-6 minutes
Sole, 2 large	5-6 minutes, stand 5 minutes	4-5 minutes
Kipper fillets and 'boil in the bag' fish, 300 g	3-4 minutes, stand 5 minutes	3-4 minutes
Prawns, 500 g		
large, with shells and heads	7-8 minutes, stand 5 minutes	4-5 minutes
small, peeled and deveined	4-5 minutes, stand 5 minutes	2-4 minutes

Pickled fish

full power
21 minutes

500 g firm white fish	15 mℓ sugar
60 mℓ cake flour	15 mℓ chutney
salt and black pepper	15 mℓ apricot jam
60 mℓ oil	200 mℓ white vinegar
2 onions, sliced	60 mℓ water
15 mℓ curry powder	2 bay leaves
2 mℓ turmeric	slices of lemon and parsley
1 small green chilli, chopped	or celery leaves to garnish

Cut fish into small portions and pat dry. Sprinkle with flour, salt and black pepper. Heat 30 mℓ oil in browning dish for 4 minutes on full power. Microwave the fish for 5 minutes, turning once during cooking time. Drain on paper towel. Place the fish in an earthenware or glass dish.

In a shallow casserole dish, microwave remaining oil for 2 minutes. Add onion, curry powder, turmeric and green chilli. Toss the vegetables in hot oil and microwave for 3 minutes, stirring at least once during cooking time. Add sugar, chutney, jam, vinegar, water and bay leaves, cover and microwave for 3 minutes. Stir, then microwave,

uncovered, for 4 minutes. Pour hot sauce over fish. Cover and allow to stand for 2 days before serving. Serve cold. Garnish with slices of lemon and parsley or celery leaves.

Serves 4

Herbed angel fish

full power
10 minutes

1 angel fish, about 750 g
oil
salt and black pepper
45 mℓ chopped chives
45 mℓ chopped parsley
10 mℓ chopped fresh basil
1 clove garlic (optional)
45 mℓ butter
75 mℓ white wine

Wipe fish and pat dry. Oil a flat dish well. Brush fish with oil and season lightly. Combine chives, parsley and basil. Sprinkle a little on the base of the dish. Place fish on top and cover with remaining herb mixture. Combine garlic and butter, and dot on top of fish. Add white wine. Cover with plastic wrap and make two slits in the plastic to prevent 'ballooning' during cooking. Microwave on full power for 8 – 10 minutes. Let stand for 4 minutes before serving. To serve, lift fish off bone in portions. Spoon a little of the cooking liquid onto each serving.

Serves 4

Note: Make sure the fish has been properly scaled before preparing this dish.

Baked salmon steaks

full power
8 minutes

4 salmon steaks, 2 cm thick
30 mℓ butter
30 mℓ lemon juice
salt and freshly ground black pepper
5 mℓ chopped fresh dill or fennel
1 small onion, sliced
4 lettuce leaves, rinsed
lemon wedges to garnish

Arrange salmon steaks in a glass casserole dish with narrow ends toward the centre. Microwave butter in a glass measuring jug on full power for 30 – 45 seconds. Add lemon juice and pour mixture evenly over salmon. Sprinkle with salt and pepper to taste, and with dill or fennel. Top with onion slices. Arrange a damp lettuce leaf over each salmon steak. Microwave on full power for 5 – 7 minutes, rotating dish halfway through cooking time if necessary. Let stand for 5 minutes before serving. Serve with lemon wedges.

Serves 4

Salmon pie

full power
high
25 minutes

500 mℓ water
1 x 48 g packet chicken noodle soup
30 mℓ margarine
30 mℓ cake flour
200 mℓ milk
2 x 220 g cans pink salmon, drained and flaked
3 hard-boiled eggs, chopped
500 mℓ cooked rice
30 mℓ chopped parsley
black pepper
125 mℓ fruit chutney

Combine the water and soup in a bowl. Cover and microwave on full power for 5 minutes. Stir, replace cover and microwave on high for 4 minutes. Place the margarine in a jug or bowl. Microwave on full power for 1 minute. Stir in cake flour. Add milk and stir well. Microwave on full power for 3 minutes, stirring every minute. Add cooked soup, microwave for 2 minutes more. The sauce should boil for at least 1 minute. Stir once more. Add all the remaining ingredients, except the chutney. Pour into a greased casserole dish and dot spoonfuls of chutney on top. Cover and microwave on high for 10 minutes. Serve hot.

Serves 6 – 8

Salmon steaks de luxe

full power
low
17 minutes

4 salmon steaks, 2,5 cm thick	1 small carrot, sliced
100 mℓ water	1 mℓ salt
100 mℓ white wine	1 blade mace
15 mℓ lemon juice	60 g butter
1 bay leaf	60 mℓ cream
1 slice onion	chopped parsley and slices
few peppercorns	of lemon to garnish

Wipe salmon steaks, pat dry and set aside. Place water, wine, lemon juice, bay leaf, onion, peppercorns, carrot, salt and mace in a large, shallow casserole dish. Cover and microwave on full power for 3 minutes. Add salmon and dot with butter. Replace cover and microwave for 6 minutes, or until the fish starts to turn opaque. Transfer fish to a serving dish, cover and keep warm. Strain the liquid and return to the casserole dish. Microwave, uncovered, for 5 minutes. Whisk in the cream, then microwave on low for 3 minutes. Pour over fish and serve immediately, garnished with chopped parsley and slices of lemon.

Serves 4

Salmon steaks ready for baking in the microwave

Marinated butterfish kebabs

Marinated butterfish kebabs

full power
8 minutes

800 g butterfish, or any other firm white fish
10 mℓ finely chopped fresh ginger
2 cloves garlic, crushed
150 mℓ plain yoghurt
100 mℓ sour cream
10 mℓ soy sauce
4 mℓ curry powder
juice of ½ lemon
salt and black pepper
15 mℓ chopped parsley

Remove skin from butterfish. Cut fish into 2 cm cubes and set aside. Combine all remaining ingredients, except parsley. Add fish to marinade and mix to coat all the cubes. Cover and refrigerate for 2 hours. Divide fish between six wooden kebab sticks and arrange on a plate. Microwave on full power for about 8 minutes. Spoon a little of the marinade over each kebab. Sprinkle with chopped parsley and serve immediately.

Serves 6

VARIATION

To add extra flavour, alternate cubes of fish with pieces of green pepper and a few blanched baby onions.

Tuna-topped spaghetti Italiano

full power
9 minutes

230 g spaghetti
30 mℓ oil
1 clove garlic, chopped
1 x 56 g can anchovy fillets, drained and chopped
60 mℓ tomato purée
1 x 425 g can whole tomatoes
5 mℓ sugar
2 mℓ dried oregano
pinch dried basil
salt and black pepper to taste
1 x 200 g can tuna, drained and broken into chunks
20 ripe olives, pitted and halved
30 mℓ chopped parsley

Cook spaghetti and keep warm. Microwave oil in a large casserole dish on full power for 30 – 45 seconds. Add garlic and anchovy, and microwave for 1½ – 2 minutes. Stir in tomato purée, tomatoes with liquid, sugar, oregano and basil, and season with salt and pepper. Microwave for 3 – 4 minutes to blend flavours. Stir in tuna, olives and parsley and microwave on full power for 2 – 2½ minutes. Add half the tomato sauce to the spaghetti and toss gently to mix well. Turn spaghetti onto a large warmed platter and spoon remaining sauce over.

Serves 4

Savoury crêpes Newburg

full power
medium
10 minutes

230 g butter or margarine
15 mℓ chopped spring onion
60 mℓ Madeira
250 mℓ cream
3 egg yolks, beaten
450 g cooked lobster or crayfish
15 mℓ tomato paste
salt and pepper to taste
8 crêpes*
125 mℓ cream, lightly whipped
15 mℓ brandy

Microwave butter in a deep casserole dish on full power for 1 – 1½ minutes. Add onion and microwave, covered, for 1 minute. Add Madeira, replace cover and microwave for 1½ – 2 minutes. Add cream to butter mixture and mix well. Microwave, covered, for a further 1½ – 2 minutes. Gradually add some of the cream mixture to beaten egg yolks, stirring constantly. Now stir egg yolks into the cream mixture. Add lobster and tomato paste, and season to taste. Spoon a little lobster mixture into each crêpe, roll up and place in a casserole dish. Combine whipped cream and brandy and spoon over crêpes. Microwave, covered, on medium for 3 – 4 minutes, or until heated through.

Serves 4

Baked stuffed kingklip

Baked stuffed kingklip

full power
high
26 minutes

1 kg whole kingklip, on the bone, or any other firm white fish	*For the stuffing*
	60 g butter
salt and black pepper	4 leeks
oil	250 mℓ cooked brown rice
2 leeks, including green portion	1 x 225 g can mussels, drained
	1 egg
	30 mℓ chopped parsley
	5 mℓ lemon rind
	salt and black pepper
	1 mℓ thyme

First make the stuffing. Microwave butter in a bowl for 1 minute on full power. Slice the white portion of leeks thinly, add to the butter and toss well. Microwave for 3 minutes. Add rice, mussels, egg, parsley, lemon rind, salt, black pepper and thyme, and stir to combine.

Wipe and pat dry the fish. Remove fins, but do not skin. Split fish along stomach to within 5 cm of the tail. Starting at the thick end of the fish, remove backbone by slicing horizontally, just above and just below the bone. Cut bone away 5 cm before the tail. Brush a sheet of parchment paper with oil. Season fish lightly, place on paper and open up. Place stuffing on bottom portion of fish and replace top portion. Brush top of fish with oil.

Wash two leeks well, but do not dry. Microwave on full power for 2 minutes, then refresh in cold water. Peel off each layer of leek. Starting at the large end of the fish, wrap leek leaves around fish and tuck the ends under. Brush with a little oil. Roll long edges of parchment paper together until the fish has been sealed inside, and tie ends with string or elastic bands. Place fish on a large plate and microwave on high for 18 – 20 minutes, depending on the thickness of the fish. Let stand for a few minutes before serving. Open parchment paper carefully and transfer the fish to a serving platter. Cut fish crosswise, following the lines of the leek leaves.

Serves 4 – 6

Seafood bake

full power
high
16 minutes

60 g butter or margarine
2 sticks celery, thinly sliced
½ onion, finely chopped
1 small green pepper, chopped
250 mℓ white sauce*
15 mℓ Worcestershire sauce
230 g cooked crab meat or crab sticks, chopped
230 g cooked shrimps or small peeled prawns
250 mℓ mayonnaise
15 mℓ lemon juice
15 mℓ chopped parsley
500 mℓ cooked rice
250 mℓ crushed potato crisps

In a shallow casserole dish, microwave butter on full power for 1 minute. Add celery, onion, green pepper and toss to coat. Cover and microwave for 3 minutes, stirring once. Add vegetables to white sauce, along with Worcestershire sauce, crab meat, shrimps, mayonnaise and lemon juice. Stir in chopped parsley. Press cooked rice gently into bottom of a buttered, 2 litre casserole dish. Top with seafood mixture, smooth over and sprinkle crushed crisps on top. Microwave on high for 10 – 12 minutes.

Serves 6 – 8

Fish bake with tomato salsa

This is a Spanish dish from the La Dorado restaurant, where succulent Mediterranean sea bass is served. The success of this dish, however, depends on the quality of the fish – it should be absolutely fresh. Fish baked this way can also be served with hollandaise sauce or, for those on diet, with just a wedge of lemon.

high
18 minutes

1 kg whole, firm white fish, rock cod, red roman, kingklip, etc.
coarse salt

For tomato salsa
2 ripe tomatoes, chopped
2 half-green tomatoes, chopped
1 onion, chopped
1 small green chilli, chopped
10 mℓ lemon juice

To make tomato salsa, combine all the ingredients and let stand for 1 hour before serving.

Wipe the cleaned fish and pat dry. Cover base of a shallow container with a 6 mm layer of coarse salt, place fish on top and cover with another 6 mm layer of salt. Cover container with plastic wrap in which two slits have been cut to prevent 'ballooning' during cooking. Microwave on high for 15 – 18 minutes. Cooking time will depend on the thickness of the fish used. Remove plastic wrap and lift fish onto a board. Carefully scrape away crust and skin from top of fish. Lift off flesh in portions. Turn fish over and repeat. Serve immediately with tomato salsa or hollandaise sauce.

Serves 4 – 6

Scallops with cream sauce

Poached trout with tarragon cream

full power
high
20 minutes

4 medium-sized trout
salt and black pepper
120 mℓ white wine
30 mℓ water
1 slice onion
2 slices lemon
15 mℓ chopped tarragon
few sprigs parsley
100 mℓ cream
45 mℓ plain yoghurt
4 lemon twists and sprigs of parsley to garnish

Rinse trout and pat dry with paper towel. Season well. Place in a rectangular shallow casserole dish. Add wine, water, onion, lemon slices, 5 mℓ tarragon and a few sprigs parsley. Cover with plastic wrap and make two slits in the plastic to prevent 'ballooning' during cooking. Microwave fish on full power for 8 – 10 minutes, depending on size. Drain fish and keep warm. Microwave cooking liquid for 6 minutes to reduce. Whisk in cream and yoghurt, then microwave on high for 4 minutes. Coat trout with a little sauce and sprinkle with remaining tarragon. Serve remaining sauce separately. Garnish with twists of lemon and sprigs of parsley.

Serves 4

French fish fillets

full power
6 minutes

500 g fish fillets (hake or kingklip)
75 mℓ French dressing*
200 mℓ savoury biscuit crumbs or seasoned cornflake crumbs
paprika
salt

Dip fillets in French dressing, then roll in crumbs. Arrange in a greased baking dish and sprinkle with paprika and salt. Cover with waxed paper and microwave for 5 – 6 minutes on full power, until fish flakes easily. Turn dish halfway through cooking time.

Serves 3 – 4

Scallops with cream sauce

Apple juice and a dash of whisky add interesting flavour to these scallops

full power
high
16 minutes

150 mℓ apple juice	salt and pepper to taste
30 mℓ whisky	30 mℓ butter
30 mℓ lemon juice	30 mℓ cake flour
1 small onion, chopped	60 mℓ cream
1 kg frozen scallops, thawed	50 g Parmesan cheese, grated
10 mℓ fresh parsley	lemon and parsley to garnish

Combine apple juice, whisky, lemon juice and onion in a casserole dish. Microwave for 1½ – 2 minutes on full power. Add scallops, parsley, salt and pepper. Microwave on high for 5 – 7 minutes, or until scallops are opaque and feel firm when touched. Remove from the oven. With a slotted spoon, transfer scallops to a serving platter, cover and keep warm. Reserve cooking liquid.

In a large glass jug, microwave butter for 30 – 45 seconds on full power. Stir in flour and microwave for 30 seconds. Stir well, then gradually stir in cooking liquid from scallops. Microwave on full power for 2½ – 3½ minutes, stirring every 45 seconds, until the mixture is thick and bubbly. Stir in cream and microwave on high for 30 seconds to heat through. Pour sauce over scallops, sprinkle with cheese and microwave for 1½ – 2 minutes to melt cheese. Garnish with lemon and parsley and serve hot.

Serves 6

Caramelized duck

Caramelized duck

full power
high
58 minutes

1 duck, approximately 1,5 kg	*For the sauce*
salt and black pepper	10 mℓ cornflour
1 onion, peeled	10 mℓ gravy powder
1 apple, quartered	150 mℓ giblet stock (see opposite)
15 mℓ butter	100 mℓ orange juice
2 mℓ ginger	100 mℓ strained cooking liquid
45 mℓ honey	15 mℓ van der Hum
45 mℓ brown sugar	
45 mℓ van der Hum	
2 oranges	
30 mℓ butter	

Rinse duck and pat dry with paper towel. Scrape the skin very well with a knife to remove any feathers. Season inside and outside. Place onion and apple in the cavity. Tie duck into shape with string and shield wings with small strips of foil. Secure neck skin with a toothpick. Place duck, breast side down, on a roasting rack or in a cooking bag. To calculate the cooking time, allow 14 – 15 minutes per 500 g. Microwave on full power for 10 minutes. Drain off excess fat. Combine 15 mℓ butter and ginger, and spread over breast and thighs. Return duck to rack, breast side down. Microwave for approximately half the remaining cooking time on high. Drain off excess fat and turn duck over. Microwave for 5 minutes.

Combine honey, brown sugar and van der Hum. Spread this mixture over duck and microwave for the remaining time, basting with glaze once or twice. Remove string and toothpick and keep the duck warm. Let stand for 10 – 15 minutes.

Remove zest from oranges, peel them and slice thickly. Microwave 30 mℓ butter on full power in a shallow casserole dish for 1 minute. Add orange slices, turn slices over immediately, then microwave for 2 – 3 minutes. Keep warm. Place zest and 100 mℓ water in a bowl. Microwave on full power for 4 minutes, then drain.

To make the sauce, combine cornflour, gravy powder, giblet stock and orange juice in a bowl. Add cooking liquid, orange zest and van der Hum, and stir to combine. Microwave on full power for 5 minutes, stirring every minute. Arrange orange slices along duck breast, and spoon a little sauce over. Serve remaining sauce separately. Garnish with cress, if desired.

Serves 3 – 4

Giblet stock

full power
medium
12 minutes

1 set giblets, duck or chicken, cleaned
1 thick slice onion
1 small carrot, cut up
1 sprig parsley
salt and black pepper
1 bay leaf
200 mℓ water

Combine all ingredients in a bowl. Cover and microwave on full power for 5 minutes. Reduce power to medium, microwave for a further 7 minutes. Strain and use as required.

Makes 200 mℓ

Meat

It is often said that meat makes the meal, and the microwave cooks meat and meat dishes to perfection. Microwaved meats become tender and juicy in a third to half the time it takes to cook them conventionally. Many meats can be cooked on full power, but a lower power setting will cook tougher, more economical cuts until they are tender and full of flavour. Larger joints brown naturally during the cooking process, but small cuts cook too quickly to do so. The addition of a browning agent (see page 22) or basting with a marinade or glaze improves both the appearance and taste of these meats. Hints for cooking meats successfully as well as a defrosting and cooking guide have also been included.

MEAT DEFROSTING AND COOKING CHART

MEAT	DEFROST TIME Per 500 g (On defrost)	COOKING TIME Per 500 g (Full power)	METHOD
BEEF			
Steak	3-4 minutes, stand 5-10 minutes	3-5 minutes, stand 1 minute	Separate pieces as soon as possible. Microwave in browning dish.
Boned and rolled	8-12 minutes, stand 1 hour	*rare* 8-10 minutes *medium* 9-12 minutes *well done* 10-13 minutes	Defrost wrapped for half the time. Unwrap, shield warm sections, and lie meat on its side.
Large joints on the bone	10-14 minutes, stand 1 hour	*rare* 8-10 minutes *medium* 9-12 minutes *well done* 10-13 minutes, stand 10 minutes	Defrost wrapped for half the time, then shield bone. Turn meat over after half the defrosting time, then again after half the cooking time.
Minced beef, lamb or pork	9-12 minutes, stand 5 minutes	use as required	Break up during defrosting. Remove thawed pieces.
Stewing beef, lamb or pork	10-12 minutes, stand 15 minutes	use as required	Separate pieces during defrosting. Remove thawed sections.
LAMB OR VEAL			
Leg	8-10 minutes, stand 30 minutes	8-11 minutes, stand 15 minutes	Shield bone-end during defrosting and halfway through cooking.
Shoulder or loin	7-8 minutes, stand 30 minutes	8-11 minutes	Shield thin portion during defrosting and three quarters of the way through cooking time.
Chops	3-5 minutes, stand 5-10 minutes	8-10 minutes, stand 1 minute	Separate chops during defrosting. Microwave in browning dish, turn after 2½ minutes.
PORK			
Leg	8-9 minutes, stand 1-1½ hours	11-14 minutes, stand 20 minutes	Select a joint with a uniform shape. Tie into shape if necessary.
Loin	6-8 minutes, stand 30 minutes	8-11 minutes, stand 10 minutes	Shield bone-end during defrosting and halfway through cooking time.
Chops	3-5 minutes, stand 10-15 minutes	10-12 minutes, stand 2 minutes	Separate chops during defrosting. Microwave in browning dish. Turn after 3 minutes.
OFFAL			
Liver and kidney	8-10 minutes, stand 5 minutes	3-5 minutes, stand 1 minute	Separate pieces during defrosting. Use browning dish for cooking. Turn after 2 minutes.
SAUSAGES			
Sausages and boerewors	6-8 minutes, stand 10 minutes	8-10 minutes, stand 3-4 minutes	Prick skins before cooking. Using browning dish if desired. For added colour, brush with a browning agent.

Note: When microwaving large pieces of meat, or less tender cuts, the power may be reduced so that the cooking period is longer. Meat should be microwaved on high for half the cooking time, then the power reduced to medium to complete the cooking process.

Example: 1,5 kg rolled beef – rare

Full power method: Microwave for 24 – 30 minutes on full power. Stand for 10 minutes.

Alternative method: Microwave for 15 – 18 minutes on high. Microwave on medium for about 20 – 22 minutes. Stand for 10 minutes.

Cover all meat before placing it in the microwave. Joints of meat should be placed in a cooking bag, a microwave roasting dish, or a shallow dish before cooking. When using a browning dish, meat should be covered with paper towel to prevent spattering.

When cooking meat
- Defrost the meat completely for best results and even cooking.
- Joints of meat cook more evenly if they are symmetrical – that is, boned or rolled.
- Thin parts or bone-ends should be shielded with small strips of aluminium foil during the first half of the cooking time to prevent overcooking.
- Seasoning meats such as roast joints before cooking may dry them out and toughen the meat.
- When preparing casseroles or stews, cut the ingredients to uniform size to promote even cooking.
- Prevent spattering when cooking sausages, bacon or other fatty meats by covering with waxed paper or paper towel.
- To improve the natural browning of meat, microwave in a covered glass casserole dish or in a pierced roasting bag fastened with an elastic band or string.
- Reduce liquid in recipes such as casseroles as there is little evaporation during microwave cooking.
- Shape meat mixtures into individual loaves, ring shapes or flat round shapes rather than one large loaf so that the meat will cook quickly and evenly.
- Arrange such foods as meatballs in a circle to promote even cooking. Meats such as chops or steaks should have the narrow end towards the centre of the oven.

Ham mousse

A make-ahead dish for a cool summer lunch

medium
1 minute

150 mℓ unsweetened pineapple juice
15 mℓ gelatine
dash ground cloves
15 mℓ French mustard
125 mℓ parsley leaves
230 g cooked ham, finely chopped
1 egg white
125 mℓ cream

Combine pineapple juice and gelatine. Let stand for 5 minutes, then microwave on medium for 1 minute. Stir in cloves and mustard, mixing well. Chop parsley finely with blender or food processor, then set aside in refrigerator. Stir ham into gelatine mixture. Beat egg white until stiff and fold into ham mixture. Beat cream to soft peaks and fold into ham mixture. Place mixture in a 750 mℓ mould and chill for at least 3 hours, or until set. To serve, unmould and sprinkle with chopped parsley. Serve with brown bread or savoury biscuits.

Serves 6 as a main course, 10 as an appetizer

Cannelloni

full power
high
55 minutes

30 mℓ oil
1 onion, chopped
1 clove garlic, crushed
½ green pepper, chopped
2 chicken livers, cut up
2 sticks celery, chopped
500 g minced beef
½ x 410 g can peeled tomatoes
60 mℓ tomato purée
100 mℓ tomato paste
5 mℓ oregano
1 bay leaf
5 mℓ Worcestershire sauce
5 mℓ sugar
salt and black pepper
1 bunch spinach
60 mℓ cream
2 eggs
50 g Parmesan cheese, grated
10 – 12 large lasagne noodles, cooked

For the sauce
60 g margarine
100 mℓ cake flour
300 mℓ milk
salt and black pepper
2 mℓ dry mustard
a little extra Parmesan cheese

Pour the oil into a large casserole dish. Microwave on full power for 1 minute. Add onion, garlic, green pepper, chicken livers and celery. Toss in oil. Microwave on full power for 5 minutes. Add minced beef and microwave on full power for 5 minutes, stirring once during the cooking time. Add tomatoes, tomato purée, tomato paste, oregano, bay leaf, Worcestershire sauce, sugar and seasonings. Microwave, uncovered, for 15 minutes on full power, stirring every 5 minutes. Set aside.

Wash spinach and remove stem ends. Place in a bowl with only the water that clings to the leaves. Cover and microwave on full power for 6 minutes. Drain and chop. Combine spinach, cream, eggs and cheese. Season lightly.

To make the sauce, place the margarine in a bowl. Microwave on full power for 2 minutes. Stir in flour. Add half the milk and stir well. Stir in remaining milk. Microwave for 6 minutes, whisking well at the end of every minute. Season to taste. Cover and set aside.

To assemble cannelloni, cut the lasagne noodles into 7 cm lengths, place a little of the spinach mixture along one edge and roll up. Arrange in a greased shallow dish. Repeat until the spinach mixture and the noodles have been used up. Pour the sauce over the top, followed by the meat mixture. Sprinkle liberally with Parmesan cheese. Cover and microwave on high for 15 minutes. Serve hot.

Serves 6 – 8

Lasagne

full power
high
42 minutes

45 mℓ oil
1 onion, chopped
2 rashers bacon, cut up
1 small green pepper, chopped
1 – 2 cloves garlic, crushed
1 small carrot, grated
300 g minced beef
1 x 410 g can peeled tomatoes
15 mℓ tomato paste
salt and black pepper
1 bay leaf
2 mℓ dried oregano
75 mℓ red wine
150 g ribbon noodles, cooked
400 mℓ béchamel sauce*
80 g Cheddar cheese, grated
little Parmesan cheese

Pour the oil into a large casserole dish. Microwave on full power for 1 minute. Add the onion, bacon, green pepper, garlic and carrot. Toss in oil. Microwave for 6 minutes on full power, stirring twice during cooking time. Add the meat, microwave for a further 5 minutes. Stir from time to time. Add tomatoes, tomato paste, seasonings, bay leaf, oregano and red wine. Microwave, uncovered, on full power for 20 minutes, stirring from time to time. Remove the bay leaf.

Use a casserole dish deep enough to hold two layers of lasagne. Pour half the meat mixture into the casserole, cover with half the noodles and a little sauce. Sprinkle with a little Cheddar cheese. Repeat the layers, ending with sauce and cheese on the top. Dust with a little Parmesan. Cover and microwave on high for 10 minutes.

Serves 6

Moussaka

full power
high
59 minutes

2 medium brinjals, sliced	2 mℓ oregano
salt	3 mℓ cinnamon
oil	salt and black pepper
1 onion, chopped	3 potatoes
2 cloves garlic, crushed	40 g Cheddar cheese, grated
500 g minced beef	2 eggs
1 x 410 g can peeled tomatoes	300 mℓ béchamel sauce*
30 mℓ tomato paste	15 mℓ Parmesan cheese

Sprinkle the brinjals with a little salt and set aside for 30 minutes. Drain and pat dry. Toss in a little oil. Arrange the brinjal slices on the bottom of a large shallow dish, overlapping them slightly if necessary. Cover and microwave on full power for 6 minutes. The brinjal should not be completely cooked. Drain on paper towel.

Pour a little oil into a casserole dish and microwave on full power for 1 minute. Add onion and garlic and toss in oil. Microwave for 5 minutes. Add meat and microwave for a further 5 minutes. Stir at least once during the cooking time. Now add the tomatoes, tomato paste, oregano, cinnamon and seasonings. Cook, uncovered, on full power for 12 minutes, stirring from time to time.

Place washed potatoes on a plate. Microwave for 8 – 10 minutes. Potatoes should be only partially cooked. Peel potatoes and slice thickly.

Fill a large greased casserole dish with layers of meat mixture, brinjal and potato. Add half the Cheddar cheese

Moussaka served with seasonal salad (p. 57)

and the eggs to the sauce and mix well. Pour over the top layer of potatoes. Sprinkle with the remaining Cheddar and Parmesan cheese. Microwave, uncovered, on high for 15 – 20 minutes. The mixture should be very hot and the tomatoes bubbling round the sides of the casserole. Traditionally, moussaka is served warm and not piping hot.

Serves 6

Cheese-topped meat loaf

full power
12 minutes

360 g lean minced beef
½ x 62 g packet thick white onion soup mix
90 mℓ tomato sauce
10 mℓ prepared mustard
1 egg
pepper to taste
75 mℓ crushed wheatbran flakes
100 g Cheddar cheese, grated
45 mℓ tomato sauce

Mix beef with soup, 90 mℓ tomato sauce, mustard, egg, pepper, wheatbran flakes and 75 g of the grated cheese. Press into a lightly greased, 20 cm deep glass baking dish and spread with 45 mℓ tomato sauce. Sprinkle remaining cheese on top and microwave on full power for 12 minutes. Cut in wedges or squares to serve.

Serves 6 – 8

Pork spareribs

medium
1¾ hours

1,5 kg pork ribs	45 mℓ brown sugar
500 mℓ hot water	30 mℓ lemon juice
1 onion, sliced	15 mℓ prepared mustard
1 lemon, sliced	60 mℓ tomato paste
salt and pepper	15 mℓ Worcestershire sauce
	2 mℓ basil
For the sauce	2 mℓ marjoram
60 mℓ peach chutney	30 mℓ finely chopped onion
45 mℓ vinegar	300 mℓ tomato juice

Place ribs, bone side up, in a large dish. Add the water, cover and microwave on medium for 40 minutes. Turn ribs over, cover with onion and lemon slices, and sprinkle with salt and pepper. Cover and microwave on medium for another 40 minutes. Drain ribs, discarding onion and lemon, and keep warm.

To make the sauce, combine all ingredients, mixing well. Cover and microwave on medium for 6 minutes, stirring after 3 minutes. Pour over ribs, cover and refrigerate until ready to serve. To reheat, microwave ribs and sauce, loosely covered, on medium for 10 – 15 minutes. These ribs are delicious heated on the braai.

Serves 3 – 4

From top to bottom: blue cheese burger, plain hamburger and cheese and wine burger

Hamburgers

This chart is for cooking lean minced beef patties in a browning dish. Each hamburger patty should weigh about 125 g. Use full power and turn hamburgers after half the cooking time. Season the patties after turning.

Number of patties	Preheat browning dish	Cooking time
1	4 minutes	2-3 minutes
2	6 minutes	3-4 minutes
3	6 minutes	4-5 minutes
4	8 minutes	5-6 minutes

To cook hamburgers in a glass dish, increase the cooking time by about 20 seconds per patty. To add good colour to hamburgers not cooked in a browning dish, brush with barbecue or braai sauce, soy sauce, Worcestershire sauce or sprinkle each side with a little brown onion soup powder. The length of cooking time depends on how well done you like your hamburgers.

Blue cheese burgers

A double beefburger with a cheesy filling

full power
17 minutes

750 g minced beef
1 egg, lightly beaten
5 mℓ salt
3 mℓ freshly ground black pepper
4 hamburger buns, lightly toasted

For the filling
120 g Blaauwkrantz cheese, crumbled
5 mℓ dry mustard
30 mℓ mayonnaise
15 mℓ Worcestershire sauce

Mix beef with beaten egg, salt and pepper. Shape into eight slim patties. Mix ingredients for the filling and top four of the beef patties with the mixture, leaving a 1 cm margin around the edges for sealing. Cover filling with remaining patties and seal edges well.
   Preheat browning dish for 8 minutes on full power. Arrange burgers and microwave, covered, on full power for 5 minutes. Turn patties and microwave, covered, for another 3 – 4 minutes. Serve on toasted hamburger buns.

Serves 4

Cheese and wine burgers

Mix the cheese and wine with the beef, and top with extra cheese

full power
14 minutes

500 g minced beef
45 mℓ tomato sauce
60 mℓ dry red wine
90 g cheese, such as Cheddar, grated
salt and black pepper to taste
30 mℓ chopped onion
4 slices cheese
4 hamburger buns, lightly toasted

Combine beef, tomato sauce, wine, cheese, salt and pepper and chopped onion. Mix well and shape into four patties. Preheat browning dish on full power for 7 – 8 minutes. Place patties in dish, cover and microwave on full power for 2½ minutes. Turn patties, cover and microwave for 2½ minutes more. Top each patty with a slice of cheese and microwave for 1 minute. Serve on toasted hamburger buns.

Serves 4

Tasty meatballs

full power
low
40 minutes

15 mℓ oil
1 onion, chopped
1 green pepper, chopped
500 g minced beef
5 mℓ Tabasco
100 mℓ fresh white breadcrumbs
1 egg
2 mℓ mixed herbs
salt and black pepper
200 mℓ uncooked rice
1 x 410 g can peeled tomatoes, chopped
350 mℓ boiling water
10 mℓ beef stock powder
10 mℓ soy sauce

Pour the oil into a small casserole dish. Microwave on full power for 1 minute. Add onion and green pepper and toss in the oil. Microwave on full power for 4 minutes. In a large bowl, combine onion, green pepper, mince, Tabasco, breadcrumbs, egg, mixed herbs and seasonings. Form into small meatballs. Roll meatballs in rice and place in a deep casserole dish. Combine all the remaining ingredients and pour over the meatballs. Finally, add any remaining rice, cover and microwave on full power for 15 minutes, then on low for 20 minutes. Serve hot.

Serves 6

Easy beef stroganoff

full power
medium
19 minutes

500 g beef, cut into thin strips
1 stick celery, thinly sliced
½ small onion, chopped
100 g mushrooms, sliced
salt and pepper
3 mℓ mixed herbs
125 mℓ smooth cottage cheese
30 mℓ tomato sauce
45 mℓ beef stock
90 mℓ cream
10 mℓ lemon juice
2 mℓ paprika
100 g cheese, grated

Microwave browning dish for 4 minutes on full power. Place meat in dish with celery, onion and mushrooms. Season with salt and pepper and mixed herbs. Cover and microwave on full power for 5 – 6 minutes, stirring frequently. Drain. Meanwhile, mix together cottage cheese, tomato sauce, beef stock, cream, lemon juice and paprika. Stir in half the cheese. Microwave on full power for 45 seconds. Stir well and add to drained beef. Mix well, spoon into a casserole dish and cover. Microwave on medium for about 6 minutes. Uncover, sprinkle remaining cheese over meat and microwave for 1½ – 2 minutes. Serve with hot buttered noodles or rice.

Serves 4 – 6

Monkeygland steak

full power
21 minutes

750 g rump steak, cut into four pieces
15 mℓ oil
1 onion, chopped
2 cloves garlic, crushed
100 mℓ tomato sauce
60 mℓ water
15 mℓ brown vinegar
45 mℓ fruit chutney
5 mℓ dry mustard
10 mℓ soy sauce
black pepper
salt

Place steaks on a flat dish. Pour oil into a shallow casserole dish. Microwave on full power for 1 minute. Add onion and garlic. Toss in oil. Microwave, uncovered, for 2 minutes. Add all the ingredients, except salt and steak. Stir well. Microwave, uncovered, for 3 minutes. Cool. Pour over steaks. Allow to marinate for at least 1 hour.

Remove meat from sauce, drain well and pat dry with paper towel. Microwave browning dish for 6 minutes. Wipe dish with either a small piece of rump fat or a little oil. Microwave meat for 4 – 6 minutes, turning only once during cooking time. The cooking time will vary according to thickness of steaks, and how well done you wish to cook them. Remove steaks and keep warm on a serving dish. Microwave sauce for 3 minutes, stirring every minute during cooking time. Add salt to taste. Pour over steaks and serve immediately.

Serves 4

Hawaiian pork chops

full power
17 minutes

4 thick pork chops
125 mℓ crushed pineapple, drained
½ small onion, chopped
60 mℓ brown sugar
45 mℓ cider vinegar
1 clove garlic, chopped
5 mℓ salt
3 mℓ grated orange rind
5 mℓ freshly grated ginger
lemon pepper to taste
dash Tabasco

Preheat a browning dish on full power for 5 minutes. Place chops in dish and microwave, covered, on full power for 5 minutes, turning chops halfway through cooking time. Drain off fat. Combine remaining ingredients in a blender and process until smooth. Pour mixture over chops and microwave, covered, for 6 – 7 minutes, rotating dish once. Let stand for 5 minutes before serving.

Serves 4

Sweet and sour kassler chops

full power
22 minutes

1 kg kassler chops
15 mℓ oil
1 onion, sliced
1 green pepper, sliced
2 sticks celery, sliced
1 x 400 g can pineapple chunks, drained, juice reserved
black pepper
15 mℓ cornflour
30 mℓ water

For the marinade
60 mℓ white vinegar
30 mℓ honey
15 mℓ soy sauce
1 clove garlic, crushed
30 mℓ brown sugar
150 mℓ pineapple juice

Place chops in a flat dish. Combine all ingredients for marinade. Pour over chops and stand for at least 1 hour. Drain chops, place in a shallow casserole dish and cover. Microwave on full power for 10 minutes. Keep warm. In another shallow dish, heat oil on full power for 1 minute. Add onion, green pepper and celery. Microwave on full power for 4 minutes, stirring once during cooking time. Add pineapple chunks and marinade. Season with black pepper. Cover and microwave on full power for 4 minutes. Combine cornflour and water. Add a little of the hot liquid to the cornflour and then return this mixture to the sauce. Stir, then cover and microwave for a further 3 minutes. Pour over meat and serve immediately.

Serves 4

Sweet and sour kassler chops

Lamb curry

full power
high
medium
1 – 1¼ hours

750 g stewing lamb, cubed
30 mℓ cake flour
salt and black pepper
60 mℓ oil
2 medium onions, chopped
1 green pepper, chopped
2 cloves garlic, crushed
15 mℓ curry powder or blended curry spices
3 tomatoes, skinned and chopped
10 mℓ apricot jam
250 mℓ combined beef and chicken stock
10 mℓ biryani spices
15 mℓ curry leaves

Toss lamb in flour, salt and pepper. Microwave browning dish on full power for 5 – 6 minutes. Add half the oil and microwave for 2 minutes. Add lamb and stir to coat with oil. Microwave for 3 – 4 minutes, stirring twice during cooking time. Pour remaining oil into a 2,5 – 3 litre casserole dish and microwave on full power for 2 minutes. Add onions, green pepper, garlic and curry powder. Stir to combine. Microwave on full power for 4 minutes, stirring once during cooking time. Add browned meat, tomatoes, jam and stock, and stir to combine. Tie the spices and curry leaves in a small piece of muslin and add to curry. Cover, then microwave for 5 minutes on full power. Reduce power to high and microwave for 15 minutes. Stir. Uncover and reduce power to medium, then microwave for 30 minutes, stirring once or twice. Remove the spices and allow curry to stand for 10 – 15 minutes. Serve with rice and a selection of sambals.

Serves 4 – 6

Suggested sambals: poppadums, roti, onion and tomato, sliced banana, cucumber with mint and yoghurt, chopped green pepper, sliced pineapple, lime pickle, chutney, Bombay duck.

Apricot-glazed ham

full power
medium
24 minutes

125 g dried apricots
100 mℓ van der Hum
25 mℓ water
1 x 900 g can cooked ham
200 mℓ smooth apricot jam
1 mℓ ground ginger
30 mℓ orange juice
pecan nuts
few whole cloves

Soak apricots in van der Hum and water for 30 minutes. Drain the ham well and pat dry with paper towel. Place on a meat rack. Combine apricot jam, ginger and orange juice. Brush thickly over ham. Microwave on full power for 6 minutes. Baste with apricot glaze. Place fruit and liquid in

Roast lamb with savoury topping, served with garlic mushrooms (p. 103), stuffed tomatoes (p. 100) and green beans almondine (p. 100)

a bowl. Cover and microwave for 3 minutes. Arrange rows of apricots on top of ham, leaving a space between each row large enough for a row of pecans. Fill the spaces with pecans and a few cloves. Brush the fruit and nuts with some of the apricot glaze. Microwave on medium for 15 minutes. Brush at least twice during the cooking time with glaze. Serve hot or cold.

Serves 6

Roast lamb with savoury topping

full power
33 minutes

1,5 kg leg of lamb
2 slices brown bread, crumbed
15 mℓ brown sugar
10 mℓ freshly chopped rosemary or 3 mℓ dried rosemary
30 – 45 mℓ French mustard
salt and pepper to taste
45 mℓ chopped onion
30 mℓ brandy
15 mℓ melted butter

Dry leg of lamb with paper towel. Combine remaining ingredients and pat over surface and sides of lamb before roasting. Place in a cooking bag or covered casserole and microwave for 24 – 33 minutes (8 – 11 minutes per 500 g), depending on how well done you like your meat. Shield bone-end with a strip of foil halfway through cooking. Stand for 15 minutes before serving.

Serves 6

Marinated glazed lamb chops

full power
medium
19 minutes

6 lamb chops	pinch sugar
250 mℓ red wine	1 mℓ dried rosemary
60 mℓ chopped spring onion	1 mℓ dried basil
3 mℓ dry mustard	15 mℓ cornflour
salt and pepper to taste	a little red wine
5 mℓ soy sauce	fresh rosemary or parsley to garnish

Place chops in a glass microwave dish. Combine red wine, spring onion, dry mustard, salt and pepper, soy sauce, sugar, rosemary and basil. Mix well and pour over chops. Cover and marinate for at least 2 hours, turning chops at least once. Microwave chops in marinade on full power for 4 minutes. Reduce heat to medium and microwave for 5 – 6 minutes. Pour off marinade. Turn chops over and keep warm. Combine cornflour with a little red wine and stir into the marinade. Microwave on full power for 3 – 4 minutes, stirring every minute. Pour sauce over chops and microwave, covered, on medium for 4 – 5 minutes until chops are nicely glazed. Garnish with rosemary or parsley and serve with hot cooked rice.

Serves 6

French beef stew with wine

French beef stew with wine

full power
low
1½ hours

6 rashers bacon, chopped
1 kg stewing beef, cut into 2 cm pieces
4 carrots, peeled and sliced
180 g baby onions, peeled
1 clove garlic, peeled and chopped
45 mℓ tomato paste
250 mℓ beef stock

250 mℓ wine
200 g mushrooms, cleaned
5 mℓ mixed herbs
salt and pepper to taste
15 mℓ cornflour
a little extra wine
chopped parsley to garnish

Place bacon in a large casserole dish and microwave on full power for 3 minutes. Add beef, carrots, onions, garlic, tomato paste, beef stock and wine. Cover and microwave on full power for 5 – 8 minutes or until liquid boils. Reduce power to low and microwave, covered, for 30 minutes. Add mushrooms and mixed herbs, then microwave, covered, for 30 – 40 minutes more or until meat is tender and vegetables cooked. Season to taste. Combine cornflour with a little wine and stir into the cooked stew, mixing thoroughly. Microwave, covered, on full power for 3 – 4 minutes. Stir after 2 minutes and again before serving. Garnish with chopped parsley, and serve with hot noodles or rice.

Serves 6 – 8

84

Pork delight

full power
high
medium
1 hour

30 mℓ oil
30 mℓ butter
750 g stewing pork, cubed
45 mℓ cake flour
salt and black pepper
5 mℓ dried sage
1 large onion, chopped
400 mℓ chicken stock
60 mℓ tomato purée
60 mℓ sherry
15 mℓ soy sauce
2 bay leaves
300 g button mushrooms
250 mℓ peas
1 x 410 g can artichoke hearts, drained

Place oil and butter in a large casserole dish. Microwave on full power for 3 minutes. Toss cubes of pork in flour, salt, pepper and sage. Add to oil. Microwave for 5 minutes, stirring twice. Add onion, stir to combine, then microwave for 2 minutes. Stir in stock, purée, sherry, soy sauce and bay leaves. Cover and microwave on high for 15 minutes. Let stand for 10 minutes. Uncover, then microwave on medium for 30 minutes, stirring from time to time. Add whole mushrooms and peas, then stir. Microwave for 2 minutes. Cut artichokes into quarters and stir in. Microwave for 2 minutes. Let casserole stand for 5 minutes before serving.

Serves 4 – 6

Picnic loaf

Serve hot straight from the oven, or chill and take along on a picnic

high
26 minutes

1 round bread loaf, unsliced
100 mℓ milk
45 mℓ chopped parsley
1 small tomato, peeled and chopped
2 eggs
8 mℓ salt
pepper to taste
2 mℓ oregano
2 mℓ basil
500 g lean minced beef
250 g lean minced veal
45 mℓ grated cheese
30 mℓ finely chopped onion

Slice a small lid from the top of the bread. Pull enough soft bread out of the centre of the loaf to leave a 1 cm shell. Crumb the bread and place 250 mℓ in a large mixing bowl. Stir in milk and chopped parsley. Add all remaining ingredients to the bread mixture and combine well. Pack the mixture into the bread loaf and replace the lid. Place loaf in a cooking bag and wrap tightly. Make 2 or 3 slits in the bag near the top. Place loaf in a dish and microwave on high for 22 – 26 minutes. Internal temperature should be 57 °C. Remove loaf from oven and stand for at least 10 minutes before serving. To serve, cut in wedges and serve with mustard or tomato sauce. To serve cold, stand for 20 minutes to cool. Do not unwrap, just refrigerate until needed.

Serves 6 – 8

Pepper steak flambé

Use fillet, rump or rib eye steaks

full power
high
12 minutes

4 beef steaks, about 120 g each
Worcestershire sauce
10 mℓ freshly crushed black peppercorns
salt

For the sauce
30 mℓ brandy
125 mℓ cream
15 mℓ lemon juice

Brush the steaks with Worcestershire sauce, and press crushed peppercorns into both sides of each steak. Preheat a browning dish for 7 minutes on full power. Sprinkle the dish with a light layer of salt and add steaks. Microwave on full power for 2 minutes. Turn steaks and microwave for another 2 minutes. Remove from oven and keep warm. In a small jug, microwave brandy on high for 30 seconds. Pour over steaks and ignite. When flame subsides, stir in cream and lemon juice and microwave on high for 30 – 60 seconds, until heated through. Serve immediately.

Serves 4

Note: The above timing will give a medium steak. Microwave 30 – 60 seconds less for rare or 30 – 60 seconds longer for well done.

Glazed stuffed roast pork

full power
46 minutes

1,5 kg pork roast, boned

For the stuffing	*For the glaze*
3 slices brown bread, broken into pieces	45 mℓ brown sugar
½ apple, cored and peeled	30 mℓ butter
½ small onion	15 mℓ brandy
10 mℓ fresh sage or 3 mℓ dried sage	
salt and pepper to taste	
15 mℓ brown sugar	
20 mℓ brandy	
30 mℓ butter	

Remove rind from pork, leaving a layer of fat. To make the stuffing, place bread, apple, onion, sage and salt and pepper in a food processor with a metal blade and process until bread is finely crumbed, and apple and onion are chopped. Add brown sugar, brandy and soft butter and mix well. Use mixture to stuff cavities of the pork, then reshape pork and tie securely. Place pork in a roasting dish.
   To make the glaze, combine brown sugar and butter in

Picnic loaf

a jug and microwave on full power for 1 minute. Stir well, add brandy and microwave for 30 seconds more. Brush meat with glaze. Cover with waxed paper and microwave on medium for 39 – 45 minutes (13 – 15 minutes per 500 g). Internal temperature should be 56 °C. Brush frequently with glaze. Stand for 10 minutes before serving.

Serves 6

Veal Milanese

full power
medium
26 minutes

6 veal schnitzels	3 mℓ oregano
45 mℓ cake flour	50 g ham, chopped
salt and black pepper	125 mℓ chicken stock
2 mℓ paprika	250 mℓ white sauce*
15 mℓ oil	3 mℓ mustard
15 mℓ butter	60 g Cheddar cheese, grated
1 onion, chopped	60 g Swiss cheese, grated
1 clove garlic, crushed	1 tomato, sliced
100 g mushrooms, sliced	sprigs of parsley to garnish
45 mℓ tomato purée	

Toss meat in flour seasoned with salt, pepper and paprika. Microwave a browning dish on full power for 6 minutes. Add oil and butter, and microwave for 1 minute. Place 2 – 3 schnitzels in the browning dish and press down firmly for 30 seconds to sear. Turn meat over, press down firmly again, then microwave for 1 minute. Remove meat from the dish. Reheat browning dish for 2 minutes. Cook remaining meat, 2 – 3 pieces at a time. Place meat in a shallow casserole dish.
   Add onion and garlic to the browning dish and stir to coat with oil. Stir in any remaining flour, the mushrooms, tomato purée, oregano, ham and stock. Pour over meat. Cover and microwave on full power for 4 minutes. To the white sauce, add mustard and half of each of the cheeses, then stir well. Pour over meat mixture. Sprinkle remaining cheese on top and cover with slices of tomato. Microwave on medium for 8 – 10 minutes. Garnish with parsley and serve immediately.

Serves 4 – 6

Casseroles pasta & rice

Casseroles are ideal to serve for any occasion – be it a family meal or a special celebration. Included in this chapter are many casseroles which can be made in moments, as well as some which require a longer cooking period. There are also those which can be made in advance and are ideal for reheating. Fish and canned foods have been used to provide a wide variety of recipes.

When making casseroles in the microwave, use slightly less liquid as there is very little evaporation. Cut meat and vegetables into similar-sized pieces to ensure even cooking. Remember that tougher, more economical cuts of meat will become more tender if the casserole is allowed to cool after cooking. Just reheat for a few minutes before serving.

Microwaving pasta and rice

The preparation of pasta and rice may be the most controversial issue of microwave cooking. Both foods must be re-hydrated during the cooking process, and the microwave oven does not speed up the re-hydration to any great extent. Those who cook pasta and rice in the microwave maintain the flavour is better and the texture is firmer or 'al dente'. Others insist that, because pasta and rice take almost the same amount of time to cook in the microwave as on the stove, these two items should be cooked conventionally, leaving the microwave free to cook sauces or toppings, or other foods. However, everyone agrees that pasta and rice can be reheated in the microwave with excellent results – a freshly cooked flavour and firm texture. To reheat pasta or rice, just place in a suitable container, cover tightly and microwave for 1 to 3 minutes on full power, depending on quantity. A chart for cooking pasta and rice follows, but most of the casserole recipes in this chapter include cooked pasta or rice.

PASTA AND RICE COOKING CHART

PASTA/RICE	COOKING TIME (On full power)	PREPARATION
Egg noodles and tagliatelle, 250 g	7-9 minutes, stand 5 minutes	Add 600 mℓ boiling water, 3 mℓ salt, 10 mℓ oil
Spaghetti, 250 g	14-16 minutes, stand 5 minutes	Add 900 mℓ boiling water, 3 mℓ salt, 10 mℓ oil
Macaroni, 250 g	10-12 minutes, stand 5 minutes	Add 600 mℓ boiling water, 3 mℓ salt, 10 mℓ oil
Lasagne, 250 g	14-16 minutes	Add 1 ℓ boiling water, 3 mℓ salt, 10 mℓ oil
Pasta shells, 250 g	18-20 minutes, stand 5 minutes	Add 1 ℓ boiling water, 3 mℓ salt, 10 mℓ oil
Rice, 200 g	12-15 minutes, stand 20 minutes	Add 500 mℓ boiling water, 3 mℓ salt, 5 mℓ oil. Keep rice sealed during standing time.
Brown rice, 200 g	25-30 minutes, stand 20 minutes	Add 600 mℓ boiling water, 3 mℓ salt, 5 mℓ oil. Keep rice sealed during standing time.

Sausage and almond bake

full power
31 minutes

500 g pork sausage meat
1 large onion, chopped
60 mℓ chopped green pepper
2 sticks celery, chopped
500 mℓ cooked brown rice
1 x 410 g can cream of celery soup
125 mℓ tomato sauce
5 mℓ mixed herbs
190 mℓ water
200 g flaked almonds, toasted*

Preheat browning dish on full power for 4 minutes. Break up sausage meat and place in dish with onion, green pepper and celery. Microwave, covered, for 5 – 6 minutes on full power, stirring frequently to break up meat. Remove from oven and drain off excess fat. Stir in rice, soup, tomato sauce, herbs, water and half the almonds. Place in a casserole dish and microwave, covered, on full power for 17 – 20 minutes, stirring twice and rotating dish if necessary. Uncover, sprinkle with remaining almonds and microwave 1 minute more. Let stand for 10 minutes before serving.

Serves 6 – 8

Corned meat and asparagus casserole

full power
12 minutes

120 g noodles
30 mℓ butter
½ small onion, finely chopped
30 mℓ chopped green pepper
1 x 300 g can corned meat, chopped
120 g sweetmilk cheese, grated
1 x 410 g can asparagus salad cuts, drained
1 x 410 g can mushroom soup
125 mℓ evaporated milk
salt and pepper to taste
250 mℓ crushed potato crisps

Cook noodles according to packet directions and drain well. Microwave butter on full power for about 30 seconds to melt. Add onion and green pepper and microwave on full power for 2 – 2½ minutes. Place corned meat, grated cheese, asparagus cuts and noodles in a mixing bowl and add sautéed onion and green pepper. Mix together mushroom soup and evaporated milk, season with salt and pepper and stir gently into corned meat mixture. Place mixture in a lightly greased 1,5 litre casserole dish and top with crisps. Microwave, uncovered, on full power for 7 – 9 minutes to heat through.

Serves 4 – 6

Club chicken casserole

full power
19 minutes

60 g butter
60 mℓ cake flour
300 mℓ chicken stock
300 mℓ evaporated milk
salt and pepper to taste
750 mℓ cooked rice
400 g cooked chicken, diced
100 g mushrooms, sliced
60 mℓ chopped pimento (canned red pepper)
60 mℓ chopped green pepper
1 x 420 g can whole sweet corn, drained
50 g flaked almonds, toasted*

Microwave butter in a 1 litre glass bowl on full power for 45 – 60 seconds. Stir in flour, mixing well. Microwave for 30 seconds. Slowly beat in chicken stock and evaporated milk, blending well. Microwave for about 3 minutes, stirring every minute. Remove from oven and stir very well. Add salt and pepper, rice, chicken and vegetables. Pour into a greased baking dish, cover and microwave on full power for 12 – 14 minutes. Uncover, sprinkle with toasted almonds and microwave for 30 seconds. Let stand for 8 – 10 minutes before serving.

Serves 8

Macaroni cheese and ham bake

Macaroni cheese and ham bake

high
15 minutes

250 mℓ cheese sauce*
200 g Cheddar cheese, grated
4 eggs, beaten
30 mℓ cake flour
1 x 410 g can cream of mushroom soup
200 g cooked ham, chopped
60 g mushrooms, sliced
30 mℓ chopped spring onion
30 mℓ chopped parsley
45 mℓ chopped stuffed olives
60 mℓ mayonnaise
375 g macaroni, cooked

Combine cheese sauce with three quarters of grated cheese. Mix in eggs, flour and mushroom soup, beating well. Add ham, mushrooms, spring onion, parsley and olives. Stir in mayonnaise, then fold in cooked macaroni. Turn into a 2 litre casserole dish. Microwave, covered, on high for 10 – 13 minutes, or until mixture is almost set. Uncover, sprinkle with remaining cheese and microwave on high for about 2 minutes to melt cheese. Let casserole stand for 8 – 10 minutes before serving.

Serves 6 – 8

Seafood creole

Almost a soup, but served with hot buttered rice it makes a hearty meal

full power
high
30 minutes

30 mℓ oil

1 small brinjal, peeled and cut into cubes	15 mℓ soy sauce
2 small baby marrows, sliced	5 mℓ dried oregano
6 – 8 mushrooms, sliced	3 mℓ dried mixed herbs
½ small onion, chopped	2 mℓ dried basil
½ small green pepper, sliced	pinch dried sage
1 stick celery, sliced	pepper to taste
1 clove garlic, chopped	1 x 190 g can shrimps, drained
1 x 410 g can whole tomatoes	60 mℓ sliced stuffed olives
125 mℓ dry red wine	30 mℓ capers
	1 x 200 g can tuna, drained

Pour oil into a deep casserole dish and microwave on full power for 45 seconds. Add brinjal, baby marrow, mushrooms, onion, green pepper, celery and garlic. Toss lightly to coat, then microwave on full power for about 8 minutes, stirring occasionally. Add undrained tomatoes, wine, soy sauce, herbs and pepper. Microwave, covered, on high for 12 – 15 minutes. Add shrimps, olives and capers. Cover and microwave on high for 3 minutes. Stir in tuna, and microwave for a further 2 – 3 minutes to heat through. Serve in bowls with hot cooked rice.

Serves 4 – 6

Salmon lasagne

full power
13 minutes

30 mℓ butter
½ onion, chopped
½ green pepper, chopped
190 mℓ tomato purée
5 mℓ cornflour
45 mℓ dry white wine
45 mℓ water
15 mℓ lemon juice
salt and pepper to taste
3 mℓ basil
1 mℓ oregano
2 x 200 g cans salmon, drained and flaked
120 g lasagne noodles, cooked
120 g mozzarella cheese, thinly sliced
60 g Parmesan cheese, grated

Microwave butter in a casserole dish on full power for 45 – 60 seconds. Add onion and green pepper, and toss to coat. Microwave, covered, on full power for 3 minutes. Combine tomato purée, cornflour, wine, water and lemon juice, mixing well. Season with salt and pepper, basil and oregano. Add the salmon and mix in gently. Layer noodles, salmon mixture and the cheeses in a 23 cm casserole dish, ending with a layer of cheese. Microwave on full power for 7 – 9 minutes. Let stand for 5 – 8 minutes before serving.

Serves 6

Crab and artichoke casserole

It's a bit expensive, but really delicious

full power
9 minutes

1 x 400 g can artichoke hearts
30 mℓ butter
230 g cooked crab meat or crab sticks, chopped
1 x 280 g can sliced mushrooms, drained
250 mℓ white sauce*
5–8 mℓ Worcestershire sauce
60 mℓ dry sherry
1 egg yolk
salt and pepper to taste
45 mℓ grated Parmesan cheese
45 mℓ grated Cheddar cheese

Drain artichoke hearts and arrange in the bottom of a greased 23 cm baking dish. In a glass bowl, microwave butter on full power for 30 seconds to melt. Add crab meat and mushrooms and toss lightly. Spread crab mixture over artichoke hearts. Mix together white sauce, Worcestershire sauce, sherry and egg yolk and season to taste with salt and pepper. Spoon over crab mixture. Sprinkle with Parmesan and Cheddar cheeses and microwave on full power for 7–9 minutes to heat through.

Serves 4–6

Note: This recipe can be prepared in individual flan dishes. Microwave two at a time on full power for 3–4 minutes.

Crab and artichoke casserole

Salmon and pasta bake

full power
medium
27 minutes

45 mℓ oil
2 onions, chopped
1 green pepper, chopped
200 g mushrooms, sliced
2 x 220 g cans salmon, drained and flaked
1 x 410 g can tomato purée
10 mℓ Worcestershire sauce
30 mℓ tomato sauce
5 mℓ dry mustard
salt and black pepper
250 g pasta shells, cooked
120 g Cheddar cheese, grated
15 mℓ butter

Pour the oil into a large casserole dish and microwave on full power for 2 minutes. Add onions and green pepper and toss well in oil. Microwave for 4 minutes. Stir in the sliced mushrooms and microwave for 2 minutes. Add fish, tomato purée, Worcestershire sauce, tomato sauce, mustard and seasonings, and stir well. Microwave for 4 minutes. Stir in pasta shells and half the cheese. Sprinkle remaining cheese on top of the pasta mixture. Dot with butter, cover and microwave on medium for 15 minutes. Serve hot.

Serves 6

Asparagus and tuna casserole

full power
medium
15 minutes

30 mℓ margarine
60 mℓ cake flour
125 mℓ evaporated milk
60 mℓ mayonnaise
1 x 410 g can asparagus cuts, drained and liquid reserved
salt and black pepper
Fondor
30 mℓ chopped chives
1 x 200 g can tuna, drained and flaked
90 g Cheddar cheese, grated
15 mℓ cornflake crumbs
1 x 30 g packet plain crisps, crushed
sprigs of parsley to garnish

Place margarine in a bowl and microwave on full power for 1 minute. Stir in flour. Add evaporated milk, mayonnaise and 125 mℓ asparagus liquid and stir to remove lumps. Microwave for 4 minutes, stirring every minute. Season well. Add asparagus, chives, tuna and half the cheese. Pour into a greased shallow casserole dish. Combine remaining cheese, cornflake crumbs and crisps. Sprinkle on top of casserole. Microwave, covered, on medium for 10 minutes. Serve hot. Garnish with parsley.

Serves 4

Tuna and mushroom lasagne

full power
medium
22 minutes

75 g margarine
1 onion, chopped
3 sticks celery, chopped
1 small green pepper, chopped
200 g mushrooms, sliced
75 mℓ cake flour
350 mℓ milk
15 mℓ lemon juice
salt
Tabasco
60 mℓ cream
2 x 200 g cans tuna, drained and flaked
30 mℓ chopped parsley
100 g Cheddar cheese, grated
5 mℓ paprika
250 g ribbon noodles, cooked

Place margarine in a large casserole dish and microwave, uncovered, on full power for 2 minutes. Add onion, celery and green pepper, and toss in margarine. Microwave for 3 minutes. Add the mushrooms and stir to combine ingredients. Microwave for 1 minute. Stir in cake flour. Now add milk and stir well. Microwave, uncovered, for 4 minutes, stirring every 30 seconds. Add lemon juice, seasonings, cream, tuna, parsley and half the cheese. Stir well. Combine remaining cheese with paprika and set aside. Arrange noodles in a shallow casserole dish, pour tuna sauce over and sprinkle cheese on top. Cover and microwave on medium for about 12 minutes until cheese has melted and the edges begin to bubble.

Serves 6 – 8

Seafood spaghetti

full power
high
23 minutes

30 mℓ oil
1 onion, chopped
1 green pepper, chopped
2 cloves garlic, crushed
30 mℓ cake flour
75 mℓ tomato purée
1 x 410 g can whole peeled tomatoes
10 mℓ fresh thyme
1 bay leaf
salt and black pepper
75 mℓ white wine
150 g prawns, peeled and deveined
1 x 290 g can clams, undrained
1 x 225 g can mussels, undrained
250 g spaghetti, cooked
Parmesan cheese

Pour the oil into a deep casserole dish. Microwave on full power for 2 minutes. Add onion, green pepper and garlic, toss in oil and microwave on high for 5 minutes. Stir in flour, tomato purée, peeled tomatoes, thyme, bay leaf and seasonings. Microwave, uncovered, on full power for 10 minutes, stirring at least twice during the cooking time. Add wine and prawns. Cover and microwave on full power for 3 minutes. Stir in the clams and mussels. Cover and microwave on full power for 3 minutes. Serve with piping hot spaghetti and plenty of Parmesan cheese.

Serves 4 – 6

Tuna and mushroom lasagne

Sunday's rice

Sunday's rice

full power
16 minutes

60 mℓ oil	3 tomatoes, peeled and chopped
1 onion, chopped	8 mushrooms, sliced
1 green pepper, chopped	100 mℓ frozen peas
100 g ham, diced	salt and pepper to taste
1 ℓ cooked rice	80 g Cheddar cheese, grated
45 mℓ soy sauce	4 – 6 eggs

In a large shallow casserole dish, microwave the oil on full power for 2 minutes. Add onion and green pepper and toss in the oil. Microwave for 3 minutes. Stir in ham, rice and soy sauce. Microwave, uncovered, for 4 minutes, stirring after 2 minutes. Add tomatoes, mushrooms and peas and season well. Cover and microwave for 4 minutes, stirring once during the cooking time. Remove the lid and stir in the cheese. Make small hollows to hold the eggs. Carefully break the eggs into the hollows. Prick the yolks very carefully. Cover and microwave for 2 – 3 minutes. Allow to stand, covered, for 1 – 2 minutes before serving. The whites should be set. If not, microwave for a further 30 seconds. Serve immediately.

Serves 4 – 6

Chilli con carne

full power
medium
high
36 minutes

30 mℓ oil
1 onion, chopped
1 small green pepper, chopped
1 clove garlic, crushed
500 g minced beef
1 x 48 g packet tomato vegetable soup
chilli powder to taste
salt and black pepper
500 mℓ boiling water
1 x 410 g can baked beans in tomato sauce

Microwave oil in a shallow casserole dish on full power for 2 minutes. Add onion, green pepper and garlic. Toss in oil. Microwave, uncovered, for 3 minutes. Add meat and break up with a fork. Microwave for 4 minutes, stirring every minute. Add soup, chilli powder, salt and black pepper, and boiling water. Stir to combine. Microwave, covered, for 5 minutes. Stir again. Reduce power to medium and microwave, uncovered, for about 20 minutes or until soup is completely cooked. Stir at least twice during the cooking time. Finally, stir in baked beans and microwave on high for 2 minutes. Stir and serve hot.

Serves 4 – 6

Farmhouse frankfurters

full power
medium
29 minutes

5 – 6 potatoes
2 medium onions, sliced
salt and black pepper
150 mℓ milk
150 mℓ water
4 mℓ chicken stock powder
2 mℓ mixed herbs
5 mℓ grated orange rind
375 g packet German frankfurters
15 mℓ oil
60 g Cheddar cheese, grated
3 mℓ paprika

Peel potatoes and slice thickly. Grease a shallow square or rectangular dish. Arrange potato and onion slices in layers. Sprinkle with salt and pepper. Combine milk, water, stock powder, herbs and orange rind and pour over potato and onion mixture. Cover with plastic wrap and make two slits in the plastic to prevent 'ballooning' during cooking. Microwave on full power for 16 – 18 minutes.

Meanwhile, cut sausages into 1 cm lengths. Microwave oil for 2 minutes. Add the sliced sausage and stir to coat. Microwave for 2 minutes. Sprinkle half the cheese over the potato mixture. Add sausages. Combine remaining cheese with paprika, and sprinkle on top of sausages. Microwave, uncovered, on medium for 5 – 7 minutes, or until cheese has melted. Serve immediately.

Serves 4 – 6

FRESH VEGETABLE COOKING CHART

VEGETABLE	QUANTITY	WATER ADDED	COOKING TIME (On full power)	PREPARATION
Artichokes, globe	4	150 mℓ	15-20 minutes	Wash and trim lower leaves
Asparagus, green	250 g	45 mℓ	6-8 minutes	Trim ends, leave whole
Asparagus, white	250 g	45 mℓ	8-10 minutes	Trim ends, leave whole
Baby marrow	450 g	30 mℓ water or stock	6-8 minutes	Trim ends and slice
Beans, broad	450 g	45 mℓ	9-11 minutes	Remove from pods
Beans, green	450 g	45 mℓ	8-10 minutes	String and slice, or cut
Beetroot	6 medium	150 mℓ	28-32 minutes	Trim tops, prick
Brinjal	2 medium	45 mℓ	8-10 minutes	Slice, sprinkle with salt. Stand 30 minutes, rinse and dry
Broccoli	450 g	45 mℓ	8-12 minutes	Trim ends, cut into even-sized lengths
Brussel sprouts	450 g	45 mℓ	12-15 minutes	Remove outer leaves, trim
Butternut	1 medium	45 mℓ	12-15 minutes	Cut in half, remove membranes and seeds. Cook cut side down. Turn halfway through cooking
Cabbage	450 g	15 mℓ	7-9 minutes	Shred or chop
Carrots, whole new	450 g	45 mℓ	7-9 minutes	Scrape
Carrots, sliced large	450 g	45 mℓ	8-10 minutes	Peel, slice in rings or long strips
Cauliflower, whole	1 medium	45 mℓ	9-11 minutes	Trim outside leaves and stem
Cauliflower, cut into florets	1 medium	45 mℓ	7-9 minutes	Cut into medium-sized florets
Celery	450 g	45 mℓ	10-12 minutes	Trim and slice
Leeks	4 medium	45 mℓ	7-11 minutes	Trim and slice or cook whole if small
Marrow	450 g	15 mℓ	8-10 minutes	Cut into slices and quarter. Add 30 mℓ butter with water
Mealies	4 ears	–	7-8 minutes	Rotate halfway through cooking time
Mushrooms	250 g	30 mℓ water or stock, or 30 mℓ butter	4-6 minutes	Wipe and slice or cook whole
Onions, whole	4-6	30 mℓ butter or oil	8-10 minutes	Peel
Onions, sliced	4-6	30 mℓ butter or oil	7-9 minutes	Peel and slice
Parsnips	450 g	45 mℓ	9-11 minutes	Peel and slice
Peas, shelled	250 g	30 mℓ	8-10 minutes	Add a sprig of mint
Potatoes, new	450 g	30 mℓ	12-13 minutes	Scrub well and prick
Potatoes, baked	4 medium	–	12-16 minutes	Scrub well and prick
Potatoes, mashed	4 medium	45 mℓ	16-18 minutes	Peel and cut into cubes
Pumpkin	450 g	45 mℓ	8-10 minutes	Peel and dice
Spinach	450 g	–	6-9 minutes	Cook with water that clings to the leaves. Remove thick stalks
Squash, gem	2-3	–	11-15 minutes	Cut in half and remove membranes. Cook cut side down and turn over halfway through cooking time
Squash, hubbard	450 g	45 mℓ	8-10 minutes	Peel and dice
Sweet potatoes	4 medium	45 mℓ	12-15 minutes	Peel and slice
Tomatoes, sliced	4 medium	–	4-5 minutes	Slice, dot with butter
Tomatoes, stewed	4 medium	15 mℓ	6-8 minutes	Peel and chop roughly
Turnips	3 medium	30 mℓ	10-12 minutes	Peel and dice

When cooking vegetables

- Cut vegetables into even-sized slices or pieces.
- If using a cooking liquid, add salt to the liquid. If not, add a little salt to the vegetable after it has been microwaved. Remember when vegetables are cooked in the microwave, far less salt is needed.
- Cooking time will vary depending on size, thickness and age of the vegetable. Always check vegetables after the minimum time stated on the chart.
- Allow 2 to 4 minutes standing time before serving vegetables as they continue to cook for some time after being removed from the microwave. Vegetables should still be firm or crisp when cooking time is up. If they are overcooked, they dehydrate.
- Arrange vegetables in a circle if they are being cooked whole, for example potatoes. Also arrange vegetables with woody stems, such as broccoli, with the stem end towards the outside. Vegetables which have an irregular shape, such as whole baby marrows, should be arranged with the thin end towards the middle of the dish. Rearrange or stir vegetables halfway through cooking time to ensure even cooking.
- When possible, cook vegetables with their skins on. Simply pierce the skin to allow steam to escape.
- Cover vegetables before cooking. Use a lid or plastic wrap, with two slits cut in the plastic to prevent 'ballooning' during cooking. When uncovering cooked vegetables, uncover from the edge farthest away from you because the escaping steam may cause a bad burn. Vegetables may also be cooked in a cooking bag or can be individually wrapped in plastic wrap.
- All vegetables are microwaved on full power, unless otherwise stated.

94

- Microwave time increases with the amount of food cooked. If the quantity of vegetables given on the chart opposite is altered in a recipe, the cooking time must be adjusted accordingly. Allow one third to one half extra time if the amount is doubled.

To cook frozen vegetables

There is no need to thaw frozen vegetables before microwaving, nor to add any extra water. Just place them in a suitable container, even a boilable plastic container or a cooking bag. Before microwaving, frozen vegetables should always be covered and cooking bags or plastic wrap must be pierced to prevent steam from building up. Microwave frozen vegetables for approximately two thirds of the time required for fresh vegetables. Refer to the chart given opposite.

Dried vegetables

Pulses – dried peas, beans and lentils – require soaking before being cooked in the microwave. Soak, in plenty of cold water, for at least eight hours. If this is impossible, cover pulses with cold water. Microwave on full power until the water boils. Continue boiling for 3 to 4 minutes. Allow them to stand, covered, for 1 to 2 hours, then drain and rinse in plenty of cold water before using.

To cook pulses, select a large bowl or casserole dish, remembering that these vegetables absorb a great deal of liquid and will swell during the cooking process. Cover with boiling water, add salt and bring vegetables and water back to the boil in the microwave oven on full power. Continue cooking on high for approximately 1 hour, or until tender. Remember, it may be necessary to add extra water during the cooking time. Stir occasionally during the cooking time.

Smaller pulses, lentils and split peas (250 g)	when boiling, microwave on high for 30-35 minutes.
Larger pulses, haricot and sugar beans (250 g)	when boiling, microwave on high for 60-70 minutes.

Allow pulses to stand for 10 minutes before serving.

Stir-frying vegetables

Vegetables stir-fried in the microwave are not only bright in colour and look good, but they are also crisp in texture and have a far higher vitamin and mineral salt content than boiled or steamed vegetables. Create your own stir-fry combinations by using whatever vegetables are in season, and for interesting variations add thin slivers of meat or a few prawns.

Choose from the following selection of ingredients:

4 – 5 broccoli spears, cut into small florets
peas (use 'sugar snap' in their shells, when available)
2 – 3 carrots, sliced
100 g button mushrooms, whole
100 g bean sprouts
3 – 4 baby marrows, sliced
100 g meat, sliced thinly (beef or pork)
    or 100 g prawns, peeled and deveined
oil
salt and black pepper

Prepare vegetables carefully. Slice long stems and roots at an angle to produce a long oval shape. Cut meat into paper-thin slices (semi-frozen meat cuts perfectly). Brush meat

and vegetables lightly with oil. Toss to coat. Place mixture in a shallow casserole dish and microwave on full power for a few minutes. The time will depend on the quantity of vegetables being used. Stir vegetables every 2 – 3 minutes. Season lightly and serve.

Baked potatoes

Wash potatoes and pat dry, then pierce with a skewer or fork. Place potatoes on paper towel on the microwave shelf, making sure they are at least 2 cm apart. If microwaving several potatoes, arrange them in a circle. Turn and rearrange potatoes after half the cooking time.

Quantity	Time	Power level
1	4-6 minutes	full power
2	6-8 minutes	full power
3	8-12 minutes	full power
4	12-16 minutes	full power
5	16-20 minutes	full power
6	20-25 minutes	full power

Potatoes may still feel firm when done, but will soften upon standing. Overcooking will toughen and dehydrate them.

Vegetables are cooked to perfection in the microwave

Left to right: seafood, anchovy, and cheesy vegetable potatoes

Cheesy vegetable potatoes

full power
6 minutes

6 large baked potatoes*
250 mℓ white sauce*
salt and pepper to taste
100 g cheese, grated
125 mℓ cooked peas
125 mℓ cooked carrots, chopped
45 mℓ chopped green pepper
45 mℓ chopped onion
60 g butter

Cut potatoes in half and carefully scoop out flesh. Set aside shells and mash flesh. Season white sauce with salt and pepper and add half the cheese, the peas and carrots, and combine well. Add to potato flesh and mix well. Place green pepper and onion in a deep measuring jug and add butter. Microwave on full power for 3 minutes, stirring once. Add to potato mixture and mix well. Spoon mixture into empty potato shells and arrange in a casserole dish or on a plate. Top with remaining cheese and microwave on full power for about 3 minutes, or until hot.

Serves 6 – 12

Seafood potatoes

full power
10 minutes

6 large baked potatoes*
salt and pepper to taste
60 g butter
½ small onion, finely chopped
125 mℓ dry white wine
60 mℓ finely chopped mushrooms
250 g cooked crab (or crab sticks) or cooked lobster, flaked
90 mℓ sour cream
60 g cheese, grated

Cut tops from baked potatoes and carefully scoop out flesh. Salt and pepper the shells and set aside. In a casserole dish, microwave butter on full power for 1 minute to melt. Add onion and microwave for 2 minutes. Then add wine and microwave on full power for 3 – 5 minutes, until liquid has been reduced by half. Stir in mushrooms and cooked crab or lobster. Add to potato flesh and mix well. Stir in sour cream and a third of the cheese. Spoon mixture into potato shells and arrange in a casserole dish or on a plate. Sprinkle with remaining cheese. Microwave for about 2 minutes until hot.

Serves 6

Anchovy potatoes

full power
3 minutes

4 large baked potatoes*
2 egg yolks
90 g Parmesan cheese, grated
6 anchovy fillets, mashed
60 g butter
30 g dry breadcrumbs

Cut tops from baked potatoes and carefully scoop out flesh. Set aside shells and mash flesh. Add beaten egg yolks, cheese and mashed anchovies. Microwave butter on full power for 1 minute to melt, then stir into potato mixture. Pile potato mixture into shells and arrange in a casserole dish or on a plate. Sprinkle with breadcrumbs. Microwave on full power for about 2 minutes until piping hot.

Serves 4

Potatoes Lyonnaise

full power
34 minutes

45 mℓ butter or margarine
500 g onions, thinly sliced
2 cloves garlic, finely chopped
600 g potatoes, peeled and thinly sliced
200 mℓ chicken stock
5 mℓ salt
pepper to taste
5 mℓ chopped tarragon or dill (optional)
chopped parsley to garnish

In a 2 litre casserole dish, microwave butter on full power for 45 seconds to melt. Add onion and garlic and stir to coat. Microwave, covered, for 12 – 15 minutes, until onion is very tender, stirring once. Add potatoes, stock, seasoning and herbs, mixing gently. Cover and microwave on full power for 10 minutes. Stir well, then microwave for a further 6 – 8 minutes until potatoes are tender. Sprinkle with chopped parsley.

Serves 6

Potatoes Parmesan

full power
19 minutes

90 g butter
500 g potatoes, peeled and cut into 2 cm cubes
½ small clove garlic, finely chopped
60 g Parmesan cheese, freshly grated
8 savoury biscuits (Tuc), crumbed
dash paprika
salt and pepper to taste
30 mℓ chopped parsley
a little extra grated Parmesan cheese

Microwave butter in a large casserole dish. Add potatoes and garlic, stirring to coat, and microwave, covered, on full power for 15 minutes. Combine Parmesan cheese, biscuit crumbs, paprika, salt, pepper and parsley and stir three quarters of the mixture into the potatoes. Microwave for 2 – 3 minutes until potatoes are tender. Sprinkle the remaining crumb and cheese mixture over, top with a little extra cheese and microwave for 1 minute.

Serves 4 – 6

Potatoes au gratin

full power
42 minutes

60 g butter
750 g onions, peeled and thinly sliced
750 g potatoes, peeled and thinly sliced
5 mℓ freshly grated nutmeg
salt and black pepper to taste
30 mℓ chopped parsley
200 g Swiss cheese, grated
375 mℓ milk

Microwave butter in a large casserole dish on full power for 1 minute. Add onion, stirring to coat evenly with butter. Cover dish and microwave for about 20 minutes, until onions are tender. Combine potatoes with nutmeg, salt, pepper and parsley, tossing to coat evenly. Place half the potatoes in a large casserole dish. Add half the onion, then half the grated cheese. Repeat layers. Microwave milk on full power for 1 minute, then pour over cheese. Microwave, covered, on full power for 18 – 20 minutes, until potatoes are tender.

Serves 6 – 8

Cheesy potatoes

full power
3 minutes

4 large baked potatoes*
80 g butter
90 g Gruyère cheese, grated
salt and pepper to taste
1 egg yolk
45 mℓ sour cream

Cut tops from baked potatoes and carefully scoop out flesh. Microwave butter on full power for 1 minute to melt. Add to potato flesh, mashing well. Stir in three quarters of the cheese, the salt, pepper, beaten egg yolk and sour cream. Pile potato mixture into potato shells and top with remaining cheese. Place in a casserole dish or on a plate and microwave on full power for about 2 minutes until piping hot.

Serves 4

Mashed potatoes

full power
high
20 minutes

4 medium potatoes
45 mℓ water
salt and pepper
45 mℓ margarine
approximately 45 mℓ milk
1 mℓ baking powder

Peel and quarter potatoes. Place in a 1 litre bowl. Add water and a little salt and pepper. Cover and microwave on full power for 16 – 18 minutes, or until potatoes are soft. Drain off water, then stand for 2 – 3 minutes. Add margarine and milk to potatoes, then beat until smooth. Add baking powder and taste for seasoning. Beat once again until fluffy. Reheat for 2 minutes on high.

Serves 4

Spinach creams

full power
medium
22 minutes

1 large bunch spinach
1 egg
salt and black pepper
pinch nutmeg

For the cream sauce
150 mℓ milk
1 slice onion
piece of carrot
pinch mace
15 mℓ butter
30 mℓ cake flour

Wash spinach very well and remove coarse stems. Pat leaves dry, then place in a large bowl and cover with plastic wrap. Cut two slits in the plastic to prevent 'ballooning' during cooking. Microwave on full power for 6 minutes. Drain well. Grease or spray six custard cups. Line bases and sides of cups with spinach leaves. Place remaining spinach in a food processor bowl or blender and purée. Add egg, salt, black pepper and a pinch of nutmeg.

To make the sauce, place milk, vegetables and mace in a large jug. Microwave for 2 minutes. Allow to stand for 5 minutes before straining the milk. Microwave butter in the jug for 2 minutes. Add flour and stir well. Pour in flavoured milk. Microwave for 2 minutes, stirring after 1 minute.

Add the sauce to the spinach purée. Process to combine. Divide purée among cups. Cover purée with any long pieces of spinach which remain over the edges of the cups. Cover each cup with plastic wrap and make a small slit in each cover. Microwave on medium for 10 minutes. Allow to stand for 3 minutes before turning spinach creams onto a flat serving platter. Serve hot.

Serves 6

Baked layered potato

full power
high
18 minutes

4 large potatoes, peeled and sliced
2 – 3 leeks, sliced
100 mℓ milk
75 mℓ cream
salt and black pepper
3 mℓ dry mustard
60 g Emmenthaler cheese, grated
15 mℓ dry breadcrumbs
paprika

Arrange the potatoes and leeks in layers in a greased shallow casserole dish. Combine the milk and cream. Pour over the potatoes. Sprinkle with the seasonings. Cover and microwave on full power for 15 minutes. Combine the cheese and breadcrumbs, and sprinkle on top of potatoes. Cover and microwave on high for 3 minutes. Dust with paprika and serve immediately.

Serves 4 – 6

Baby potatoes with parsley butter

full power
16 minutes

500 g small potatoes, unpeeled
60 mℓ water
30 mℓ butter
45 mℓ finely chopped parsley
½ small clove garlic, finely chopped (optional)
salt and pepper to taste

Wash potatoes and place in a 2 litre casserole dish. Add water and microwave on full power for 12 – 14 minutes, or until tender. Drain well and keep warm. Microwave butter, parsley and garlic in a glass measuring jug for 2 minutes. Pour over potatoes and season with salt and pepper.

Serves 4 – 6

Note: These potatoes can be cooked ahead of time, then reheated with butter on medium for 3 – 4 minutes.

Stuffed butternut

Stuffed butternut

full power
24 minutes

2 medium butternuts
15 mℓ oil
1 onion, chopped
2 sticks celery, chopped
60 g ham, chopped
salt and black pepper
60 g Cheddar cheese, grated
cayenne pepper
pinch oregano
15 mℓ dry breadcrumbs

Cut butternuts in half and remove seeds and membranes.
Place cut side down in a shallow dish. Cover and
microwave on full power for about 15 minutes. Turn over
halfway through cooking time. Microwave oil for 1 minute.
Add onion and celery, and microwave for 3 minutes.
Combine onion mixture and ham. Scoop butternut pulp out
of the skins. Combine pulp and onion mixture. Season to
taste. Use this mixture to fill shells, piling the filling high.
Combine remaining ingredients and sprinkle on top of
filling. Microwave, covered, for 4 – 5 minutes, until filling
is piping hot and the cheese bubbling.

Serves 4 – 6

Stuffed baby marrows

full power
15 minutes

6 medium baby marrows
30 mℓ margarine
1 small onion, chopped
2 rashers bacon, chopped
1 tomato, peeled and chopped
2 mℓ dried thyme
salt and black pepper
45 mℓ fresh breadcrumbs
1 mℓ paprika
15 mℓ chopped chives

Cut a wedge lengthways along the top of each baby marrow
to take the filling. Level off base, so that the marrow does
not roll over. Roughly chop the wedges of marrow. In a
small casserole dish, microwave margarine on full power
for 2 minutes. Add onion and bacon, and toss in margarine.
Microwave for 3 minutes. Add chopped baby marrow,
tomato, thyme, salt and pepper. Microwave, uncovered,
for 3 – 4 minutes. Fill baby marrow shells with this mixture.
Combine breadcrumbs, paprika and chives. Sprinkle a little
on top of each marrow. Arrange marrows on a plate in a
radial design. Cover and microwave for about 6 minutes.
Cooking time will depend on size of the marrows. Serve hot.

Serves 6

Stuffed tomatoes

full power
14 minutes

6 tomatoes
15 mℓ oil
1 small onion, chopped
2 sticks celery, chopped
100 mℓ frozen peas
200 mℓ fresh white breadcrumbs
2 mℓ mixed herbs
10 mℓ Maggi liquid seasoning
1 mℓ dry mustard
pinch turmeric
salt and black pepper
80 g Cheddar cheese, grated
parsley to garnish

Cut tops off tomatoes and remove pulp. Place tomato shells
in a circle on a plate. In a large casserole dish, microwave
oil on full power for 1 minute. Add onion. Microwave
for 2 minutes. Now add celery, peas and tomato pulp.
Microwave, uncovered, for 6 minutes. Add breadcrumbs,
herbs and seasonings. Stir to mix. Lastly stir in half the
cheese. Fill shells with this mixture. Sprinkle remaining
cheese on top. Cover and microwave for 4 – 5 minutes.
Serve hot, garnished with a little parsley.

Serves 6

Cabbage casserole

full power
11 minutes

30 mℓ water
salt and a dash pepper to taste
1 small cabbage, shredded
30 mℓ butter
30 mℓ cake flour
3 mℓ salt
dash pepper
250 mℓ milk
pinch caraway seeds
90 g mature Cheddar cheese, grated
pinch dry mustard
125 mℓ wholewheat breadcrumbs

In a 2 litre casserole dish, combine water and seasoning.
Add cabbage, cover and microwave on full power for
7 – 9 minutes for each 500 g. Rotate dish halfway through
cooking time if necessary. Stand for 5 minutes.
   Microwave butter in a 500 mℓ glass measuring jug on full
power for 30 seconds. Stir in flour and seasoning and mix
well. Gradually stir in milk. Microwave for 1 minute, stir,
then microwave for 1½ – 2 minutes longer, stirring every
30 seconds until the mixture boils. Add caraway seeds,
cheese and mustard, and mix thoroughly. Microwave for
1 minute, then mix well. Drain liquid from cabbage and
stir in sauce. Top with breadcrumbs and microwave for
1 minute.

Serves 4 – 6

Mixed vegetable sauté

full power
8 minutes

45 mℓ butter
3 carrots, julienned
5 baby marrows, julienned
200 g mushrooms, sliced
1 turnip, julienned
salt and black pepper
30 mℓ lemon juice
15 mℓ chopped parsley
10 mℓ chopped chives

Place butter in a shallow casserole dish. Microwave on full
power for 1 minute. Add carrots and toss in butter. Cover
and microwave for 3 minutes. Add baby marrows,
mushrooms and turnip. Season and toss lightly. Cover and
microwave for 3 – 4 minutes. Vegetables should still be
crisp. Add lemon juice, parsley and chives. Stir carefully to
combine. Serve piping hot.

Serves 4 – 6

Green beans almondine

full power
12 minutes

30 mℓ butter
50 g flaked almonds
300 g frozen sliced green beans
60 mℓ water
salt and pepper to taste

Microwave butter in a glass measuring jug on full power for
1 minute. Add almonds, mixing well, and microwave for
about 4 minutes until lightly browned, stirring after each
minute. Set aside. Place green beans in a large casserole
dish. Add water, cover and microwave on full power for
6 minutes. Drain beans, then return to casserole dish. Add
nuts and butter, salt and pepper, tossing to coat evenly.
Microwave on full power for 1 minute. Serve hot.

Serves 4

Casseroled onions

full power
high
12 minutes

10 – 12 small onions	60 mℓ tomato sauce
30 mℓ water	salt and black pepper
60 mℓ honey	15 mℓ margarine

Place onions and water in a shallow casserole dish. Cover
and microwave on full power for 3 minutes. Drain.
Combine honey and tomato sauce, and season. Pour over
onions. Dot with small pieces of margarine. Cover and
microwave on high for 7 – 9 minutes. Serve hot.

Serves 6

Corn on the cob

Corn on the cob

full power

Remove husks and beards if necessary, and place sweet corn in a glass casserole dish. Cover and microwave on full power for the following times:

1 ear	2-3 minutes
2 ears	4-6 minutes
3 ears	6-7 minutes
4 ears	7-8 minutes
6 ears	8-9 minutes

Rotate ears halfway through the cooking time, and stand for 5 minutes before serving. Serve with melted butter, salt and pepper.

Cauliflower cheese

full power
9 minutes

1 medium cauliflower, trimmed
125 mℓ mayonnaise
10 mℓ prepared mustard
salt and pepper to taste
90 g mature Cheddar cheese, grated
dash paprika

Wash cauliflower and place in a 2 litre casserole dish. Cover and microwave on full power for 5 – 6 minutes per 500 g. Let stand, covered, for 5 minutes while making the sauce. Combine mayonnaise, mustard, and seasonings in a glass measuring jug and microwave for 1 minute. Stir to blend, then spoon sauce evenly over cauliflower. Sprinkle with grated cheese and microwave for 1½ – 2 minutes, until cheese melts. Sprinkle with paprika.

Serves 4 – 6

Ratatouille with cheese

full power
21 minutes

750 g brinjal
60 mℓ oil
2 – 3 cloves garlic, chopped
1 onion, thinly sliced
250 g baby marrow, thinly sliced
1 green pepper, seeded and sliced
2 sticks celery, thinly sliced
1 x 410 g can whole tomatoes, chopped
125 mℓ tomato purée
30 mℓ tomato paste
8 mℓ sugar
45 mℓ cake flour
8 – 10 mℓ salt
3 mℓ pepper, or to taste
5 mℓ dried mixed herbs
2 mℓ dried oregano
pinch dried thyme
200 g Cheddar cheese, grated
fresh parsley to garnish

Pierce brinjals well with a fork and place on a microwave rack. Microwave on full power for 7 minutes, then set aside to cool. Place oil, garlic and onion in a large, deep casserole dish. Cover and microwave on full power for 5 minutes. Add baby marrow, green pepper and celery, mixing well. Peel brinjals and cut into 2 cm cubes. Add to vegetables. Cover and microwave on full power for 5 minutes.

Combine tomatoes and juice, tomato purée, tomato paste, sugar, flour, seasonings and herbs. Mix well, then spoon half the mixture over the vegetables. Add half the cheese. Top with remaining tomato mixture, then with remaining cheese. Cover and microwave on full power for 3 – 4 minutes, until mixture is hot and bubbly. Sprinkle with parsley just before serving.

Serves 6

Baked green pepper

Baked green peppers

full power
high
16 minutes

4 green peppers
15 mℓ oil
2 rashers bacon, chopped
1 onion, chopped
250 g chicken livers, cleaned and chopped
salt and black pepper
60 g mushrooms, chopped
1 egg
200 mℓ cooked rice
15 mℓ chopped parsley
pinch thyme
60 mℓ grated Cheddar cheese

Cut a slice off the top of each green pepper. Remove core and seeds. Cover and microwave peppers on full power for 4 minutes, turning them over halfway through the cooking time. In a shallow dish, microwave the oil for 1 minute. Add bacon and onion and microwave for 3 minutes. Add chicken livers. Microwave for a further 3 minutes. Season well. Add mushrooms, egg, rice, parsley, thyme and three quarters of the cheese. Use this mixture to stuff green peppers. Top with remaining cheese. Stand peppers in a shallow serving dish and cover. Microwave for 5 minutes on high. Serve immediately.

Serves 4

Brinjal in cream sauce

full power
medium
15 minutes

3 medium brinjals
salt
45 mℓ butter
1 clove garlic, crushed
75 mℓ chicken stock
10 mℓ cake flour
100 mℓ cream
1 mℓ dried marjoram
15 mℓ chopped parsley

Wash and dice unpeeled brinjals. Sprinkle with a little salt. Allow to stand for 30 minutes, then pat dry with paper towel. Place butter in a shallow casserole dish. Microwave on full power for 1 minute. Add brinjal and garlic, and toss well in butter. Add chicken stock, cover and microwave on full power for 8 – 10 minutes, until tender. Stir in flour, cream and marjoram. Cover and microwave on medium for 4 minutes. Dust with parsley. Serve hot.

Serves 4

Stir-fried cabbage

full power
16 minutes

30 mℓ oil
1 onion, chopped
2 cloves garlic, crushed
½ medium-sized cabbage, shredded
30 mℓ soy sauce
black pepper
2 mℓ caraway seeds
10 mℓ chopped parsley

In a shallow casserole dish, microwave oil on full power for 2 minutes. Add onion and garlic, and toss in oil. Return to microwave for 3 minutes. Stir in cabbage. Cover and microwave for 8 – 10 minutes, stirring every 2 minutes. Stir in soy sauce, black pepper and caraway seeds. Microwave for 1 minute. Dust with parsley.

Serves 4

Carrots Vichy

full power
11 minutes

6 carrots, julienned
30 mℓ orange juice
2 medium-sized cucumbers, julienned
30 mℓ butter
salt and black pepper
15 mℓ chopped parsley

Place carrots in a shallow casserole dish and add orange juice. Cover and microwave on full power for 7 minutes. Add cucumber, butter and seasonings. Cover and microwave for 4 minutes. Stir once during cooking time. Dust with parsley and serve.

Serves 6

Garlic mushrooms

full power
8 minutes

12 – 14 large black mushrooms, wiped
60 g butter
1 – 2 cloves garlic, crushed
5 mℓ fresh marjoram or 2 mℓ dried marjoram
15 mℓ chopped parsley
salt and black pepper
5 mℓ lemon juice

Place mushrooms in a greased shallow casserole dish. Overlap mushrooms if necessary, as they shrink a great deal when cooked. Place butter in a small bowl. Microwave on full power for 2 minutes. Add remaining ingredients. Brush each mushroom with butter mixture. Pour leftover butter into the casserole dish. Cover with plastic wrap and cut two slits in plastic to prevent 'ballooning' during cooking. Microwave for 5 – 6 minutes. Do not overcook, as the mushrooms continue to cook for some time after they have been removed from the oven.

Serves 6

Paté-stuffed mushrooms

full power
6 minutes

10 – 12 large mushrooms
125 mℓ creamy chicken liver paté*
125 mℓ dry breadcrumbs
30 mℓ chopped parsley
90 mℓ grated mozzarella cheese

Wipe mushrooms clean, remove stems and arrange on two microwave dishes. Divide paté among the mushroom caps. Combine breadcrumbs, parsley and mozzarella cheese and sprinkle on top of paté. Microwave each dish on full power for 3 minutes until stuffing is heated through. Serve hot.

Makes 10 – 12 mushrooms

Mushrooms with spinach and cheese

full power
6 minutes

10 – 12 large mushrooms
250 g frozen chopped spinach, thawed
1 egg
30 mℓ thick white onion soup powder
60 mℓ smooth cottage cheese
dash nutmeg
salt and pepper to taste
30 mℓ dry breadcrumbs
60 mℓ grated Gouda cheese

Wipe mushrooms clean, remove stems and arrange on two microwave dishes. Drain spinach and mix with remaining ingredients, reserving 30 mℓ of the Gouda cheese. Place spoonfuls of the mixture on each mushroom and sprinkle remaining cheese on top. Microwave each dish on full power for 2½ – 3 minutes. Smaller mushrooms will be done more quickly.

Makes 10 – 12 mushrooms

Left to right: mushrooms with spinach and cheese, pâté-stuffed mushrooms and savoury mushrooms (p. 38)

Desserts

The variety of desserts which can be cooked in the microwave is never-ending. Recipes using gelatine are easily made, as are ice-cream toppings and hot desserts which can be cooked in advance and reheated before serving. Although traditional double-crust pies are unsuccessful because the fillings bubble over and the tops do not brown, crumbles are simply delicious in every form. Baked puddings should be removed from the microwave while still slightly moist, as cooking will continue during standing time. Fresh fruit cooked in a cooking bag or casserole dish with a little sugar (it is seldom necessary to add water) retains its full flavour and has a bright colour. Check and stir or rearrange fruits often to prevent overcooking. Those cooked with their skins on, such as baked apples, should first be pricked to prevent them from bursting during the cooking process. Puréed fruits make a good sauce to pour over ice-cream, or to stir into yoghurt.

FRESH FRUIT COOKING CHART

FRUIT	QUANTITY	COOKING TIME (On full power)	PREPARATION
Apricots	450 g	7-9 minutes	Cut in half and stone. Sprinkle with sugar to taste
Cape gooseberries	450 g	4-5 minutes	Sprinkle with sugar to taste
Cooking apples, puréed	450 g	8-10 minutes	Peel, core and slice. Add sugar to taste
Cooking apples, baked whole	4	7-8 minutes	Core and stuff, if desired
Peaches	4 medium	4-6 minutes	Peel, halve and stone. Cook halves or slices. Add sugar to taste
Pears	4 medium	7-9 minutes	Peel, halve and core. Sprinkle with a little lemon juice or cook in a syrup made of 60 g sugar, 80 mℓ water, piece cinnamon stick
Plums and cherries	450 g	4-5 minutes	Cut plums in half. Remove stones. Remove cherry stalks. Add a strip of lemon rind and sugar to taste
Quinces	450 g	6-8 minutes	Peel, core and slice thickly. Cook in a sugar syrup
Rhubarb	450 g	8-10 minutes	Wash and cut into 3 cm lengths. Add 100 g sugar and a strip of lemon rind
Soft Fruits			
Loganberries	450 g	4-5 minutes	Add sugar to taste
Mulberries	450 g	4-5 minutes	Remove stems and add sugar to taste
Strawberries	450 g	4-5 minutes	Hull and add sugar to taste

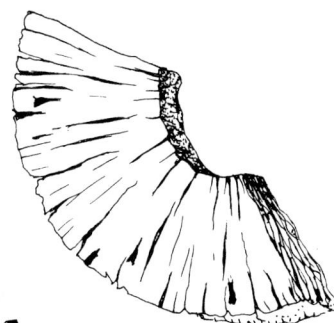

To dissolve gelatine

Dissolving gelatine in any liquid is simply done in the microwave as less utensils are used and the amount of time taken is also reduced. Depending on the volume of liquid, the length of time the gelatine mixture is microwaved may vary slightly. Measure the liquid in a microwave-proof measuring jug, sprinkle gelatine onto liquid and stir to combine. Allow the mixture to stand for a few minutes, until it has thickened. Microwave, uncovered, on medium for about 1 minute, stir and use. Dissolved gelatine may also be kept warm on low or defrost for a few minutes before being used.

Basic custard

full power
7 minutes

500 mℓ milk
30 mℓ custard powder
30 mℓ sugar

Pour milk into a large jug, saving a little to mix with the custard powder. Microwave milk, uncovered, on full power for 4 minutes. Combine remaining milk, custard powder and sugar. Pour a little of the hot milk onto custard mixture. Stir well. Pour custard mixture into the jug. Mix well. Microwave for a further 3 minutes, stirring at the end of each minute during the cooking time. The custard is ready to use.

To prevent a skin from forming, cover custard with a piece of greaseproof paper. Push paper onto custard so that there is no air trapped on the surface. When custard is required, lift paper off and remove excess custard from paper with the back of a knife. The thickness of the custard may be varied by using more or less custard powder.

Makes 500 mℓ

Crème brûlée

full power
defrost
11 minutes

500 mℓ cream
30 mℓ sugar
6 egg yolks
10 mℓ vanilla essence
100 mℓ white sugar
60 mℓ brown sugar
slices of kiwi fruit to garnish

Pour the cream into a jug and add 30 mℓ sugar. Microwave on full power for 3 minutes. Stir well to make sure the sugar has dissolved. Beat egg yolks until fluffy and light in colour. Add vanilla and cream. Beat to combine. Pour into six individual serving dishes. Cover and microwave on defrost for 7 – 8 minutes. Delicate food such as custard continues to cook for some time after being microwaved. To test that it is ready, shake the custard carefully. The inside should quiver like jelly. Cool, then chill well.

Combine the white and brown sugars. Divide between the six dishes and sprinkle evenly on top of each custard. Place custards on a baking sheet and grill conventionally for a few minutes, turning each custard as the top starts to caramelize. When deep golden brown, remove from the oven and chill once more. Serve with a few slices of kiwi fruit, or any other tart fruit.

Serves 6

Caramel coffee dessert

Caramel coffee dessert

defrost
16 minutes

4 eggs
1 x 379 g can condensed milk
700 mℓ cold strong coffee
30 mℓ brandy

Beat eggs very lightly. Add remaining ingredients and beat to combine. Pour into a glass ring mould. Cover with plastic wrap, and pierce to prevent 'ballooning' during cooking. Microwave for 16 minutes on defrost. Cool and refrigerate for a few hours before turning out and serving.

Serves 6

Fruit salad supreme

A heavenly fruit salad that is best served well chilled

high
4 minutes

2 eggs
100 g sugar
30 mℓ cake flour
juice of 1 lemon
1 x 410 g can pineapple pieces, drained and juice reserved
250 mℓ cream
90 mℓ smooth cottage cheese
1 x 310 g can mandarin oranges, drained
250 mℓ miniature marshmallows (or large marshmallows, chopped)
50 g desiccated coconut, toasted*
60 mℓ maraschino cherries, quartered
250 mℓ seedless green grapes, halved
50 g flaked almonds, toasted*

In a large glass measuring jug, combine eggs, sugar, flour, lemon juice and 190 mℓ of the reserved juice from the pineapple. Microwave on high for 3 – 4 minutes, stirring well after each minute. The mixture should be thickened. Stir until smooth and let cool to room temperature. Whip cream lightly and fold into egg mixture, along with cottage cheese. Fold in remaining ingredients except almonds, cover and chill overnight. Just before serving, fold in almonds.

Serves 10 – 12

Banana and granadilla slice

full power
medium
3 minutes

For the crust	For the filling
100 g blanched almonds, toasted* and chopped	30 mℓ water
75 g coconut, toasted*	15 mℓ gelatine
45 mℓ sugar	400 mℓ natural yoghurt
60 g margarine	45 mℓ honey
	2 granadillas
	2 egg whites
	2 bananas, sliced

To make the crust, combine almonds, coconut and sugar. Rub in margarine. Line a 26 x 12 cm loaf pan with greaseproof or parchment paper. Grease well, so that the crust can be pressed in firmly. Line the pan with approximately half the crust, reserving the rest for the topping. Microwave on full power for 2 minutes. Cool.

To make the filling, combine water and gelatine in a jug, and allow to stand for a couple of minutes. Microwave on medium for 1 minute. Stir well before using. (Dissolved gelatine may be kept warm using the defrost cycle.) Combine yoghurt and honey, and add granadilla pulp. Beat egg whites until stiff. Stir gelatine into yoghurt mixture, then fold in egg whites. Arrange banana slices on the base of the crust. Pour yoghurt mixture over this. Sprinkle with remaining crust mixture. Chill for 4 hours. Turn out and cut into squares or slices. This dessert may also be made in two 21 x 11 cm loaf pans.

Serves 8

Apricot cream

full power
medium
8 minutes

8 apricots
60 mℓ water
sugar to taste
250 mℓ milk
2 eggs, separated
75 mℓ cold water
25 mℓ gelatine
100 mℓ cream
a little whipped cream and sliced apricot to garnish

Wash apricots, cut in half and remove stones. Place in a shallow casserole dish and add 60 mℓ water and a little sugar. Cover and microwave on full power for 4 minutes. Purée apricots and sweeten to taste. Pour milk into a jug and microwave, uncovered, for 3 minutes. Beat egg yolks very well. Pour onto hot milk and beat again. Combine custard and apricot purée. Allow to cool.

Pour 75 mℓ water into a jug and add gelatine. Stand for a few minutes. Microwave, uncovered, on medium for 1 minute. Meanwhile, beat the cream until thick. Stir gelatine into apricot custard. Chill over ice until mixture begins to thicken. Whisk egg whites until soft peaks form. Carefully fold cream, then egg whites into custard mixture. Pour into a rinsed mould and then refrigerate for at least 3 hours.

To turn out mould, dip into hot water for 3 seconds. Carefully draw a small area of the pudding away from the side of the mould – this will introduce an air bubble. Turn over onto a plate and wait for a few seconds before removing mould. Decorate with stars of whipped cream and a few slices of apricot.

Serves 6

VARIATIONS
Plum cream: Substitute 8 plums for the apricots, then continue as for apricot cream.

Granadilla cream: Substitute 150 mℓ granadilla pulp (about 10 fruits) for the apricots and the water. Microwave granadilla pulp and sugar to taste for 4 minutes on full power, then continue as for apricot cream.

Chocolate mousse

Although this rich mousse makes a large quantity, half the mixture can be frozen if desired

medium
6 minutes

150 g dark chocolate	45 mℓ light rum
60 g milk chocolate	10 mℓ vanilla essence
45 mℓ strong coffee	15 mℓ gelatine
6 eggs	60 mℓ water
3 egg yolks	375 mℓ cream
200 g sugar	whipped cream to garnish

Place chocolate and coffee in a deep measuring jug and microwave on medium for 5 minutes or until chocolate is melted, stirring frequently. Allow to cool.

Apricot cream

Beat eggs and yolks until very light and fluffy, about 10 minutes. Add sugar and beat until mixture is shiny, about 5 minutes. Add melted chocolate, rum and vanilla. Mix until thoroughly blended.

Sprinkle gelatine over water in a glass measuring jug. Let stand for 3 minutes, then microwave on medium for about 45 seconds to melt gelatine. With mixer running, slowly beat gelatine into chocolate mixture. Beat cream to soft peaks and fold into chocolate mixture. Pour into a large serving bowl (or two medium-sized bowls) and chill for at least 4 hours. Serve garnished with whipped cream.

To freeze, chill, then cover well and freeze for up to 3 weeks. Thaw in refrigerator.

Serves 16

Note: To change the flavour of the mousse, add orange liqueur, brandy or coffee liqueur instead of rum.

Chocolate fondue

A quick, easy dessert that is delightful to serve and fun to eat

full power
4 minutes

360 g dark chocolate, broken up
125 mℓ cream
30 mℓ dark rum
banana slices, pineapple chunks, strawberries or
    squares of madeira cake to serve

Place chocolate, cream and rum in a deep serving dish and microwave on full power for 3½ – 4½ minutes to melt chocolate. Stir well until mixture is smooth, and serve immediately. To serve, give each person a skewer or fondue fork and a dish of fruit or cake pieces. Let each person dip pieces into the chocolate.

Serves 6

Pears Alicia

Pears Alicia

full power
19 minutes

250 mℓ water	small piece cinnamon stick
75 g sugar	6 firm pears, peeled
125 mℓ haneport wine	20 mℓ cornflour
45 mℓ curaçao	30 mℓ brandy
2 strips orange rind	angelica and orange rind
15 mℓ apple jelly	strips to decorate

Pour water into a casserole dish. Add sugar and cover. Microwave on full power for 4 minutes. Add haneport, curaçao, orange rind, apple jelly and cinnamon, then stir to combine. Add pears and cover. Microwave for 7 – 10 minutes. The time will vary, depending on the type and ripeness of pears used. Remove pears and cinnamon.

Blend together cornflour and brandy. Add a little of the hot liquid to the cornflour, then pour the cornflour mixture into the sauce. Stir well. Microwave, covered, for 5 minutes, stirring twice during cooking time. The liquid should be of a pouring consistency, as it thickens when cold. Add pears and coat well with sauce. Cover and cool, then chill. Recoat pears with sauce from time to time. Decorate each pear with a 'leaf' of angelica and a strip of orange rind. Serve well chilled with plenty of whipped cream.

Serves 6

Champagne cream

full power
6 minutes

180 g castor sugar
125 mℓ water
2 oranges
2 lemons
500 mℓ chilled champagne or sparkling wine
500 mℓ cream
60 mℓ brandy
6 finger biscuits, broken into pieces
a little brandy

Place sugar and water in a deep bowl and microwave on full power for 2 minutes. Stir until sugar dissolves, then microwave for 4 minutes. Grate rind from one orange. Remove peel in thin strips from one lemon and set aside. Squeeze juice from oranges and lemons and strain. Add to sugar syrup along with orange rind. Let cool. Pour in champagne and turn mixture into freezer trays. Cover and freeze until frozen around edges.

Turn mixture into a large bowl and beat very well. Beat cream to stiff peaks, then fold into champagne mixture, mixing until well combined. Stir in 60 mℓ brandy, cover and freeze for about 4 hours, until frozen. About 30 minutes before serving, place biscuit pieces in six serving glasses and sprinkle with a little brandy. Leave to soak. To serve champagne cream, scoop into glasses and garnish with thin strips of lemon peel. Serve immediately.

Serves 6

Chocolate cream pie

full power
medium
6 minutes

For the crust
100 g pecan nuts, chopped
12 – 14 marie biscuits, crumbed
45 mℓ sugar
60 g butter
45 mℓ cream

For the filling
15 mℓ gelatine
60 mℓ cold water
150 g dark chocolate, broken up
125 mℓ boiling water
2 eggs
45 mℓ sugar
dash salt
5 mℓ vanilla essence
50 g pecan nuts, chopped
250 mℓ cream, whipped
whipped cream and grated chocolate to garnish

To make the crust, combine the nuts, biscuit crumbs and sugar. Microwave butter on full power for 1 minute to melt. Add to crumb mixture, mixing well. Add cream and combine well. Press mixture lightly into the bottom and sides of a 23 cm glass flan dish and microwave for 2 minutes. Let cool.

For the filling, sprinkle gelatine over cold water in a glass measuring jug and stand for 5 minutes. Microwave on medium for 1 minute to dissolve the gelatine. Place the chocolate in a glass bowl and microwave on full power for 1½ – 2 minutes. Stir in the 125 mℓ boiling water and gelatine and mix very well. Beat eggs, sugar, salt and vanilla essence until light and fluffy. Add nuts and chocolate mixture. Mix well, then gently fold in the whipped cream. Spoon mixture into the crust and chill until set. Decorate with whipped cream and chocolate. Cut into wedges to serve.

Serves 8 – 10

In a conventional oven: Bake the crust at 180 °C for about 8 – 10 minutes.

Chocolate cheese triangle and banana and granadilla slice (p. 106)

Chocolate cheese triangle

medium
high
4 minutes

25 mℓ water	*For the coating*
10 mℓ gelatine	45 mℓ sugar
80 g butter	45 mℓ water
80 g sugar	50 g dark chocolate, chopped
125 g cream cheese	30 mℓ cocoa
1 egg	45 mℓ butter
15 mℓ lemon juice	a few slivered almonds
2 mℓ cinnamon	
75 g almonds, toasted* and chopped	
30 mℓ brandy	
30 mℓ milk	
18 tennis biscuits	

Combine water and gelatine. Stand for 1 minute, then microwave on medium for 1 minute. Stir well before using. Gelatine may be kept warm on low for a few minutes if necessary. Beat butter and sugar until light and fluffy. Add cream cheese and beat again. Add egg, lemon juice, cinnamon and nuts. Beat once more. Stir in gelatine.

Combine brandy and milk. Dip biscuits into milk mixture one at a time. Arrange on a piece of aluminium foil in a square made up of nine biscuits. Spread a thin layer of cheese mixture over biscuits. Repeat with remaining biscuits. Heap cheese mixture along centre row of biscuits, working cheese into a triangular form. Draw the outer edges of the foil up, so that the biscuits meet and form the apex of a triangle. Seal firmly and refrigerate. Care must be taken at this point that the biscuits meet perfectly, as the cheese mixture sets firmly and the biscuits cannot be moved at a later stage.

To make the coating, place sugar, water, chocolate and cocoa in a bowl and stir to combine. Microwave on high for 3 minutes, stirring at least twice during cooking time. Stir very well. Add butter and stir until melted. Allow coating to cool until it is thick enough to leave a trail. Unwrap cheese triangle. Stand on a cooling rack. Pour coating over the cake, taking care to coat the whole cake evenly. Arrange nuts along top immediately. Refrigerate until coating has set. Serve this rich dessert in small slices.

Serves 8 – 10

Banana crumble

medium
7 minutes

4 bananas, sliced	*For the topping*
15 mℓ lemon juice	90 g cake flour
grated rind of ½ lemon	45 mℓ margarine
400 mℓ basic custard*	15 mℓ castor sugar
	1 mℓ cinnamon
	25 mℓ finely chopped nuts
	30 mℓ brown sugar

Place bananas in a greased 22 cm pie dish. Sprinkle with lemon juice. Add rind to custard and pour over bananas. To make the topping, sift flour, then rub in margarine. Add castor sugar and cinnamon. Sprinkle over custard. Combine nuts and brown sugar and sprinkle on top. Microwave on medium for 7 minutes. Serve hot or cold.

Serves 6 – 8

Boston cream cake

full power
medium
18 minutes

For the hot milk sponge	300 mℓ milk
2 eggs	2 egg yolks, beaten
200 g sugar	15 mℓ butter
120 g cake flour	15 mℓ apricot liqueur or 15 mℓ brandy
5 mℓ baking powder	5 mℓ vanilla essence
125 mℓ milk	
30 mℓ butter	*For the chocolate glaze and white icing*
45 mℓ apricot jam	30 g dark chocolate
	15 mℓ butter
For the custard filling	175 g icing sugar
70 g sugar	5 mℓ vanilla essence
30 mℓ cake flour	hot water
20 mℓ cornflour	10 mℓ milk
dash salt	

For the sponge, beat eggs at high speed for 4 minutes, then gradually add sugar, beating for 4 – 5 minutes or until sugar is nearly dissolved. Combine flour and baking powder and add to egg mixture, stirring until just blended. Place milk in a jug, add butter and microwave on full power for 20 – 30 seconds, just to melt butter. Add milk to cake mixture, stirring until smooth. Turn into a greased and lined 20 cm round baking dish and microwave on medium for 7 – 8 minutes, rotating dish every 2 minutes if necessary. Then microwave on full power for 1½ minutes or until done. Cool on a wire rack for about 10 minutes, then turn out and cool completely.

To make the custard, combine sugar, flour, cornflour and salt in a 1 litre bowl. Gradually stir in milk, mixing well. Microwave on full power for 4 minutes, stirring every minute. Microwave for 1 minute more. Gradually stir a small amount of milk mixture into beaten egg yolks, then return to bowl, mixing well. Microwave on full power for 45 seconds, stirring every 15 seconds. Add butter, liqueur and vanilla, and stir just until butter melts. Cover surface with waxed paper and cool without stirring. Chill well. Use to fill cake.

For the glaze, place chocolate and butter in a jug and microwave on full power for 1½ – 2 minutes or until the chocolate has melted. Stir in 100 g of the icing sugar and the vanilla, then 10 mℓ hot water. Add a further 15 – 30 mℓ hot water a little at a time and blend well, until mixture is of pouring consistency. For the white icing, combine remaining 75 g icing sugar and 10 mℓ milk to make a drizzling consistency.

To assemble, slice cake horizontally into two layers and spread bottom layer with apricot jam. Place on a serving plate. Top with custard filling, spreading to within 1 cm of the edges. Place remaining cake half on top. Pour over chocolate glaze and spread evenly so that it runs over edges. Drizzle white icing in a spiral pattern on top of chocolate icing, then quickly draw a sharp knife from the centre to the edge of the cake several times. Let icing set, then chill the cake. Serve cut into wedges.

Serves 10 – 12

In a conventional oven: Bake sponge cake at 190 °C for 25 – 30 minutes.

Hot fruit salad

high
4 minutes

juice of 2 lemons
juice of 3 oranges
1 x 410 g can pineapple pieces, drained and juice reserved
300 g sugar
500 mℓ water
45 mℓ cake flour
a little lemon juice
6 bananas, sliced
4 oranges, segmented
125 mℓ red pitted cherries
450 g green seedless grapes

Combine lemon, orange and pineapple juices with sugar, water and flour in a deep casserole dish. Microwave on high for 3 – 4 minutes, stirring after each minute. Stir until smooth. Sprinkle lemon juice over sliced bananas and reserve. Add pineapple pieces, orange segments, cherries and grapes to the sauce mixture. Stir in bananas. Serve warm, topped with whipped cream.

Serves 10

Boston cream cake

Creamy cheesecake

full power
medium
high
23 minutes

For the crust
60 g butter
250 mℓ marie biscuit crumbs
45 mℓ brown sugar

For the filling
250 g smooth cottage cheese
2 eggs
100 g sugar
dash salt
5 mℓ vanilla essence
15 mℓ lemon juice
125 mℓ sour cream

In a 23 cm glass pie dish, microwave butter on full power for 1 minute. Stir in biscuit crumbs and sugar. Press mixture into bottom and sides of the dish and microwave on full power for 1½ minutes.
  For the filling, beat together cottage cheese, eggs, sugar, salt, vanilla and lemon juice. Stir in sour cream and microwave on medium for 10 – 12 minutes, stirring well every 2 minutes. Pour into baked crust and microwave on medium for 3 minutes. Carefully stir through the filling, rotating dish if necessary, and microwave on medium for 2 minutes. Stir through filling again, then microwave on high for about 3 minutes more, or until centre is just set. Chill. Serve sprinkled with cinnamon or with a fruit sauce.

Serves 6 – 8

Baked chocolate pudding

full power
10 minutes

240 g cake flour
200 g sugar
75 mℓ cocoa
5 mℓ bicarbonate of soda
5 mℓ baking powder
250 mℓ mayonnaise (not salad cream)
250 mℓ water
5 mℓ vanilla essence
cream or custard for serving

Stir together dry ingredients in a large mixing bowl. Combine mayonnaise, water and vanilla essence and add to dry ingredients. Beat for 2 minutes, scraping bowl at least once. Pour mixture into a greased, deep 26 cm baking dish. Microwave on full power for 8 – 10 minutes, rotating dish if necessary. Let stand for 10 minutes before serving. Spoon into individual pudding dishes and top with cream or custard.

Serves 12

In a conventional oven: Bake at 180 °C for 35 – 40 minutes. Turn out and cool.

Sherry cream soufflé

Sherry cream soufflé

medium
1 minute

30 mℓ gelatine
125 mℓ water
375 mℓ medium sherry
6 eggs, separated
175 g sugar
15 mℓ lemon juice
250 mℓ cream
whipped cream, chopped nuts and crystallized flowers to decorate

Sprinkle gelatine over water in a glass measuring jug and stand for 5 minutes. Microwave for 1 minute on medium to dissolve gelatine. Add sherry, mixing well, then let mixture cool until it is the consistency of unbeaten egg white.
  Beat egg whites until frothy, then gradually beat in 120 g of the sugar. Add lemon juice and beat until stiff. Beat egg yolks until frothy. Add remaining sugar and beat until thick. Add slightly thickened sherry mixture to egg yolk mixture and beat well. Whip 250 mℓ cream and fold into egg yolk mixture. Fold in a quarter of the egg white, then fold in remaining egg white. Spoon mixture into a 23 cm soufflé dish with a deep waxed paper collar attached. Chill for 3 – 4 hours. To serve, pipe whipped cream stars around the top of the soufflé, remove collar and pat chopped nuts around the sides. Place a crystallized flower in the centre. Keep refrigerated until required.

Serves 10 – 12

combine. Stir in nuts, followed by date mixture. Pour into pie shell. Microwave on medium for 14 minutes. The centre should still be tacky. Allow to cool before serving. Serve slices with plenty of whipped cream.

Serves 8

In a conventional oven: Bake on the middle shelf at 160 °C for 45 minutes.

Pecan meringue pie

high
medium
7 minutes

3 egg whites
pinch cream of tartar
200 g castor sugar
5 mℓ vanilla essence
20 'Salty crack' biscuits, crumbed
100 g pecan nuts, coarsely chopped
cream for serving

Beat egg whites with cream of tartar until soft peaks form. Gradually beat in castor sugar until peaks become stiff. Fold in vanilla essence, biscuit crumbs and pecans. Spoon into a well-greased 20 cm glass pie dish and microwave on high for 3 minutes, then reduce power to medium and microwave for 3½ – 4 minutes more. Cool on a wire rack for a few minutes before serving. Cut into wedges while still warm, and serve with cream.

Serves 8 – 10

In a conventional oven: Bake at 180 °C for 25 minutes.

Mocha pie

high
defrost
4 minutes

1 x 25 cm crumb crust*
50 mℓ cream, whipped and chocolate leaves* to decorate

For the filling
150 mℓ milk
20 marshmallows
30 mℓ instant coffee powder
2 egg yolks
250 mℓ cream

To make the filling, pour milk into a jug or bowl and add marshmallows. Microwave on high for 2 minutes, then on defrost for 2 minutes. Stir in coffee. Stir from time to time to make sure that the marshmallows have melted completely. Beat egg yolks until fluffy and light. Pour in marshmallow mixture and beat well. Allow to cool, but do not chill. Beat cream until thick. Fold in marshmallow mixture. Pour into prepared crust and chill until firm. Decorate with swirls of cream and chocolate leaves.

Serves 6 – 8

Macadamia nut pie

Macadamia nut pie

full power
medium
20 minutes

1 x 22 cm sweet shortcrust pastry pie shell*
250 mℓ water
15 mℓ margarine
180 g dates, chopped
3 eggs
90 g white sugar
90 g soft brown sugar
4 mℓ vanilla essence
30 mℓ cream
1 mℓ cinnamon
1 mℓ ginger
pinch nutmeg
30 mℓ cake flour
80 g macadamia nuts, chopped
whipped cream for serving

Place a piece of paper towel on the base of the pie shell. Add a few dried beans to weight it down. Microwave on full power for 2 minutes. Remove beans and paper towel. Microwave pie shell for 1 minute more. Cool slightly.
   To make the filling, place water and margarine in a bowl. Microwave for 3 minutes. Add dates and allow to cool. Beat the eggs well. Add both sugars, vanilla and cream, and beat very well. Sift in the dry ingredients and beat to

Apple crumble

full power
9 minutes

1 x 385 g can pie apples
70 g brown sugar
50 mℓ raisins
5 mℓ grated lemon rind
15 mℓ lemon juice
15 mℓ water
60 g cake flour
60 g butter
45 mℓ brown sugar
30 mℓ chopped nuts
15 mℓ brown sugar

Place pie apples in the bottom of a 20 cm baking dish and sprinkle with brown sugar. Scatter raisins and lemon rind on top and sprinkle with a mixture of lemon juice and water. Rub together flour, butter and 45 mℓ brown sugar until crumbly. Sprinkle evenly over fruit. Top with nuts and 15 mℓ brown sugar. Microwave on full power for 8 – 9 minutes, rotating dish a quarter turn every 3 minutes, if necessary. Stand for 5 minutes before serving with cream or ice-cream.

Serves 6

Date dessert

This dessert can be successfully reheated the day after it has been made

medium
high
12 minutes

90 g cake flour
3 mℓ bicarbonate of soda
salt
100 g soft brown sugar
60 g margarine, softened
2 eggs
3 mℓ vanilla essence
125 mℓ sour cream
125 g dates, chopped
60 mℓ chopped pecan nuts

For the cream topping
125 mℓ sour cream
45 mℓ fresh cream
45 mℓ brown sugar

Sift flour, bicarbonate of soda and salt into a bowl. Add brown sugar, margarine, eggs, vanilla essence and sour cream. Mix well, then stir in dates and pecans. Pour into a greased, deep, 25 cm pie plate. Place pie plate on top of an inverted saucer. Microwave on medium for 6 minutes, then on high for approximately 5 minutes. Remove from oven and allow to cool for 10 minutes before pouring cream topping over. To make the topping, combine all ingredients in a bowl, then microwave on medium for 30 seconds. Serve dessert warm. To reheat, cover and microwave on medium for 2 – 3 minutes, depending on the size of the piece being reheated.

Serves 6 – 8

In a conventional oven: Bake at 180 °C for 25 – 30 minutes.

Basic crêpe mixture

full power
30 seconds

120 g cake flour
1 mℓ salt
2 eggs
150 mℓ milk
150 mℓ water
30 mℓ butter

To make batter, place all ingredients except butter, in a blender or processor. Blend for 30 seconds, scrape down sides of goblet, and process for a further 30 seconds. Place butter in microwave on full power for 30 seconds. Add to batter. Blend for a few seconds more to combine. Stand batter for 30 minutes. The batter should be the consistency of milk for paper-thin crêpes. Dilute the batter with a little more water if necessary. For thicker crêpes or pancakes, add less liquid to original mixture. Heat a crêpe pan until a slight haze forms. Wipe the pan with a little oil. Spoon sufficient of the mixture into the pan to coat the base thinly. Cook for a few seconds. Carefully loosen edges with a spatula, then turn crêpe over and cook for a few seconds more. Lift out of pan and place on a sheet of greaseproof paper.

Makes about 20 crêpes

Note: Crêpes and pancakes freeze very well. Make a large number, then stack ten, one on top of the other, on a piece of greaseproof paper. Add another layer of paper. Repeat until all the crêpes are packed, place in a plastic bag and freeze. To thaw, lift off a stack of ten crêpes, place on a plate and cover with plastic wrap. Microwave on defrost for 4 minutes. The crêpes will peel off perfectly. Use as required.

Crêpes Marguerite

high
8 minutes

10 – 12 crêpes*

For the filling
1 x 410 g can apricots or plums
75 g butter
100 g icing sugar

For the topping
75 mℓ apricot or plum liqueur
extra apricot or plum halves
maraschino cherries

Drain apricots, reserving syrup, and chop. Cream butter and sugar. Add apricots and 30 mℓ of the syrup. Blend well. Place about 30 mℓ of the mixture on each crêpe and roll up. Place in a greased heatproof dish. Stir liqueur into any remaining filling and pour over crêpes. Decorate with extra fruit and cherries. Cover and microwave for about 8 minutes on high. Serve hot.

Serves 5 – 6

Apricot sorbet

full power
6 minutes

125 g dried apricots
600 mℓ water
100 g sugar
60 mℓ lemon juice
45 mℓ apricot liqueur
2 egg whites
30 mℓ icing sugar

Soak apricots for 1 hour in water. Place in a casserole dish and add sugar. Cover with plastic wrap. Cut two slits in plastic to prevent 'ballooning' during cooking. Microwave on full power for 6 minutes. Cool slightly, then add lemon juice and liqueur. Using a blender, purée apricots. Place in an ice tray and freeze until firm. Beat egg whites until stiff, then slowly beat in icing sugar. Cut sorbet into blocks and, using a food processor, process in two batches until soft. Add half the egg white at a time and process to combine. Return to freezer. Freeze until firm. Serve in glasses, decorated with wafers.

Serves 6

VARIATION
Apricot ice-cream: Add 125 mℓ cream to sorbet when processing the frozen apricot mixture.

Caramel ice-cream and apricot sorbet

Caramel ice-cream

full power
high
8 minutes

1 x 379 g can condensed milk
4 eggs, separated
5 mℓ vanilla essence
500 mℓ cream
whipped cream and a few hazelnuts to decorate

Line the base of a 32 x 10 cm loaf pan with foil. Pour condensed milk into a very deep bowl (if the bowl is too small, the boiling condensed milk will run over the sides). Microwave, uncovered, for 4 minutes on full power and 4 minutes on high. Allow to cool. Beat egg yolks, vanilla and caramelized condensed milk very well. Whip cream until thick, then fold into caramel mixture. Beat whites until stiff, but not dry. Fold into caramel mixture. Pour mixture into loaf pan and freeze overnight. Run a spatula around edges of pan. Turn ice-cream out onto a plate. Decorate immediately with stars of whipped cream and a few hazelnuts. Return ice-cream to freezer until ready to serve.

Serves 12

Hot fruit salad sauce

Jellied kir

Makes a light dessert or a refreshing jelly to serve between courses of a hot meal

medium
full power
1½ minutes

30 mℓ gelatine
125 mℓ cold water
125 mℓ hot water
70 g sugar
500 mℓ dry white wine
30 mℓ crème de cassis liqueur
lemon slices to garnish

Sprinkle gelatine over cold water in a glass measuring jug. Let stand for 5 minutes, then microwave on medium for 1 minute to dissolve gelatine. Add hot water and sugar, and stir well. Microwave on full power for 30 seconds. Stir until sugar dissolves. Add wine and crème de cassis and mix well. Pour into a 1 litre mould, or six individual moulds, and chill until set. Unmould onto serving plates, garnish with lemon slices and serve.

Serves 6

Hot fruit salad sauce

full power
18 minutes

1 x 410 g can apricot halves
1 x 410 g can peach slices
1 x 410 g can pineapple chunks
1 x 410 g can stoned black cherries
small piece cinnamon stick
100 mℓ van der Hum
60 mℓ cornflour

Pour the undrained fruit into a large casserole dish. Add cinnamon. Cover and microwave on full power for 12 minutes. Remove cinnamon. Combine van der Hum and cornflour. Stir a little of the hot liquid into the cold mixture, then pour the cornflour mixture into the fruit. Stir well. Microwave, covered, on full power for 6 minutes. Stir the fruit mixture every 2 minutes. Serve hot over ice-cream.

Serves 10 – 12

Apple sauce

full power
8 minutes

500 g cooking apples, peeled, cored and sliced
45 mℓ water
30 mℓ sugar, or to taste
dash salt

Place apples and water in a bowl and cover with a lid or plastic wrap. Turn back corner of plastic wrap or slit to prevent 'ballooning' during cooking. Microwave on full power for 8 minutes. Rotate dish a quarter turn every 2 minutes if necessary. Remove from oven and mash cooked apples. Stir in sugar and salt. Serve warm or cold.

Serves 4 – 6

Note: For added flavour, add 1 or 2 cloves to the apples while cooking, or add a dash of cinnamon with the sugar.

Butterscotch topping

full power
8 minutes

30 mℓ golden syrup   45 mℓ butter
200 g brown sugar   15 mℓ lemon juice
250 mℓ milk and water mixed 15 mℓ custard powder

Place syrup, brown sugar, milk and water, and butter in a large bowl. Microwave, uncovered, on full power for 4 minutes. Stir at least once during cooking time. Combine lemon juice and custard powder, adding a little extra water if necessary, to form a smooth paste. Add a little hot mixture to custard, then pour custard mixture into hot liquid. Stir well. Microwave for 3 – 4 minutes, stirring every minute during cooking time. Serve hot over ice-cream.

Makes 300 mℓ

Caramel sauce

defrost
low
12 minutes

2 x 53 g Bar Ones, cut up
150 mℓ cream
30 mℓ hazelnuts, chopped

Using a jug, combine Bar Ones and cream. Cover and microwave on defrost for 8 minutes. Stir every 2 minutes, then microwave, covered, on low for 4 minutes. Stir in nuts and serve hot over ice-cream.

Serves 6 – 8

Chocolate fudge sauce

Vary the flavour by using different liqueurs – orange, coffee or cherry, even brandy or rum

full power
3 minutes

30 mℓ honey   100 g milk chocolate
125 mℓ cream   5 mℓ vanilla essence
100 g dark chocolate   15 – 30 mℓ liqueur

Place honey, cream and chocolate in a 1 litre casserole dish or measuring jug and microwave on full power for 2½ – 3½ minutes. Stir until completely smooth. Add vanilla and liqueur and mix well. Serve warm.

Makes about 375 mℓ

Hot chocolate sauce

full power
medium
6 minutes

60 mℓ water   60 mℓ golden syrup
30 mℓ butter   60 mℓ sugar
60 mℓ cocoa powder   5 mℓ vanilla essence

Combine all ingredients in a large bowl. Microwave on full power for 3 minutes, stirring every minute during cooking time. Then microwave on medium for 3 minutes. Serve hot with ice-cream.

Makes 120 mℓ

Orange sauce

full power
12 minutes

60 g butter
60 g sugar
1 x 200 g can frozen orange juice
100 mℓ water
30 mℓ cornflour
orange rind
30 mℓ van der Hum

Place butter in a bowl and microwave on full power for 2 minutes. Stir in sugar. Microwave, uncovered, for 2 minutes. Add orange juice and stir to combine. At this point lumps may form but they will disappear when the sauce is heated. Microwave, uncovered, for 3 minutes. Combine water and cornflour. Stir a little of the hot liquid into cornflour mixture, then pour all this liquid into hot orange juice. Stir well. Microwave, uncovered, for 5 minutes. Stir every minute during cooking time. Now add orange rind and van der Hum. Serve hot over ice-cream.

Makes 300 mℓ

Maple nut sauce

full power
4 minutes

15 mℓ cornflour   dash salt
200 g brown sugar   60 g butter
125 mℓ cream   5 mℓ vanilla essence
45 mℓ maple syrup   50 g pecan nuts, chopped

Combine cornflour and brown sugar in a 2 litre casserole dish. Stir in cream, syrup and salt. Add butter. Cover and microwave on full power for 3 – 4 minutes, stirring after 2 minutes. The mixture should be thickened and sugar dissolved. Stir in vanilla and nuts. Serve warm or cool.

Makes about 375 mℓ

Maple nut sauce served over ice-cream

Baking

Many cakes and breads can be baked in the microwave in less time than it takes to prepare them, so something delicious can always be served ovenfresh in next to no time.

The recipes in this chapter have been selected because they are particularly suitable for the microwave.

Follow the instructions carefully and your baking will be an instant success.

Quick breads

Many quick breads react well to microwave baking. Coffee cakes, fruit breads, muffins and yoghurt breads rise well and have a good appearance. Although scones can be baked in the microwave, they do not brown. However, the scone dough in recipes such as Caramel cherry ring or Golden nut ring, page 123, gives a finished product which looks appetizing and tastes delicious.

Cakes

Cakes bake quickly and rise to greater volume in the microwave, giving an airy, fluffy texture. They do not brown as they would conventionally, but with a sprinkling of icing sugar or a coating of icing, it is difficult to tell the difference (see page 22). Microwaving does not affect the flavour of cakes, so they taste just as great as if baked conventionally. Dark cakes, such as chocolate, ginger and carrot cakes, have a good appearance. Angel and chiffon cakes should not be baked in the microwave.

Biscuits and bars

Large batches of biscuits or cookies take longer to microwave than to bake conventionally, as only a few can be baked at a time. The texture and colour also differ because many biscuits need hot dry air to form the characteristic crisp crust. However, bars and squares, such as date bars and chocolate chip squares, microwave with excellent results. Their texture and appearance compare favourably with conventional baking, and they can be ready to serve in about 10 minutes.

Pastry and pies

Shortcrust pastry becomes tender and flaky when baked in the microwave oven but does not brown, so it will not have the golden appearance you are used to. Brushing with a little egg yolk, vanilla essence mixed with water, or adding a few drops of yellow food colouring to the dough will improve the colour. Most microwaved pies use a prebaked shell. If the pastry is not partially or fully baked before adding the filling, it absorbs moisture and becomes soggy.

Crumb crusts are perfect with many fillings. The butter for the crust can be microwaved in the pie dish, then crumbs and other ingredients added and mixed. Microwave the crumb crusts for a short time, and cool before using.

Pastries that need hot dry air to give the characteristic finish, such as puff pastry and choux pastry, are not suitable for microwave cooking.

Yeast breads

Dough for yeast breads can be proved in the microwave in half the normal time by using short bursts of microwave energy with resting periods of about 10 minutes. Follow the directions for mixing and proving yeast breads as accurately as possible. Once the dough has risen, it can be shaped and baked conventionally, as microwaved bread neither browns nor forms a crisp golden crust. However, the batter yeast bread recipes for microwave baking can be topped with cheese, seeds or crushed wheat to give colour and extra flavour to the crust.

To prove yeast doughs in the microwave oven

Mix and knead the dough according to recipe directions. Place in a large, greased bowl and cover. Microwave on full power for 15 seconds, then rest for 10 minutes. Repeat the process 2 or 3 times until the dough has doubled in bulk. It can then be punched down and shaped as desired. If you use a suitable container you may prove the dough a second time in the microwave before baking conventionally.

DEFROSTING OF BREADS AND CAKES

FOOD	QUANTITY	APPROXIMATE TIME (On defrost)	METHOD
Bread, whole or sliced	1 kg	6-8 minutes	Unwrap. Place on paper towel. Turn over during defrosting. Stand 5 minutes.
Bread	26 x 12 cm	4-6 minutes	Unwrap. Place on paper towel. Turn over during defrosting. Stand 5 minutes.
Bread	1 slice	10-15 seconds	Unwrap. Place on paper towel. Stand 1-2 minutes. Time accurately.
Bread rolls	2 4	20-25 seconds 30-40 seconds	Unwrap. Place on paper towel. Stand 1-2 minutes. Time accurately.
Cupcakes or muffins	4	1-1½ minutes	Unwrap. Place on paper towel. Stand 5 minutes.
Sponge cake	22 cm	2-3 minutes	Unwrap. Place on paper towel. Turn over after 1 minute. Stand 5 minutes.
Doughnuts or sweet buns	4	1½-2 minutes	Unwrap. Place on paper towel. Turn over after 1 minute. Stand 5 minutes.
Loaf cakes or ring cakes	26 x 12 cm or 22-25 cm diameter	5-7 minutes	Unwrap. Place on paper towel. Turn over after 3 minutes. Stand 10 minutes.
Bars	20-22 cm square	4-6 minutes	Unwrap. Place on paper towel. Stand 5-10 minutes.
Crumpets	4	25-30 seconds	Unwrap. Place on paper towel. Stand 3-4 minutes. Time accurately.
Pancakes or crêpes	10	3-4 minutes	Unwrap. Place on plate. Cover with plastic wrap.
Pies or tarts	20-23 cm	4-6 minutes	Unwrap. Stand 10 minutes.
Pies, cooked (small individual, to thaw only)	1 4	25-30 seconds 2-3 minutes	Unwrap. Place upside down on paper towel. Stand 2 minutes.

When baking

- It is easy to overbake in the microwave oven, and baking times will vary with oven models, so most recipes give a range of times. Check the cake or loaf after the minimum time and cook for longer if necessary. Overcooking by even 1½ or 2 minutes will result in a cake with hard and dry outer edges.
- For even baking, turn pans frequently if the cake or loaf seems to be baking unevenly.
- Baked foods rise to a greater volume in the microwave than in a conventional oven, so be sure the container is large and deep enough to accommodate the mixture.
- Prepare pans and dishes for baking by spraying or greasing them generously. Line with waxed paper or paper towel for layer cakes. Sprinkle greased pans with finely chopped nuts or fine biscuit crumbs for ring cakes or breads, so that they will turn out of the pan easily.
- Sprinkling a greased baking pan with flour may result in a doughy coating on the outside of the food.
- A ring-shaped cake pan allows the centre of the cake to cook at the same rate as the outer edges. Although glass and microwave ring pans are available, it is easy to prepare one by placing an ordinary glass in the centre of a round glass baking dish.

- Fill cake pans a third to half full. If there is any batter left over, use it to make cupcakes.
- The tops of many baked items will still be slightly moist when cooked. Resist the temptation to turn cakes or loaves out of the pan immediately, as the top will dry during standing time.
- After microwaving, place the pan on a flat, heat-resistant surface so that the bottom will finish baking during standing time.
- In many microwave recipes the amount of liquid can be reduced, but with cakes the liquid is needed to make them moist, so use the amount of liquid stated.
- Let a cake mixture stand for 3 or 4 minutes before microwaving in order to start the reaction between the baking powder and the liquid.
- Try placing the cake pan on an inverted saucer in the microwave. The microwaves can penetrate the bottom of the pan more easily and cooking will be more even.
- To test when cakes, coffee cakes, quick breads or bars are done, insert a tooth pick in the centre and it should come out clean.
- When baking cakes or bars in a square dish, remember to shield the corners with foil to prevent overcooking or drying.

Fruit cake

full power
medium
27 minutes

150 g sultanas	230 g cake flour
150 g raisins	5 mℓ baking powder
150 g currants	3 mℓ cinnamon
60 g mixed peel	2 mℓ ground ginger
150 g butter	1 mℓ nutmeg
200 g soft brown sugar	pinch of ground cloves
200 mℓ water	10 mℓ cocoa
5 mℓ bicarbonate of soda	125 mℓ sherry
100 g glacé cherries, chopped	75 g pecan nuts or almonds, chopped
125 g dates, chopped	a few blanched almonds (optional)
5 mℓ instant coffee powder	100 mℓ brandy
2 eggs, beaten	

Place sultanas, raisins, currants, peel, butter, sugar and water in a large bowl. Cover with plastic wrap and cut two holes in plastic to prevent 'ballooning' during cooking. Microwave on full power for 7 minutes. Stir at least twice during cooking time. Add bicarbonate of soda, cherries, dates and instant coffee. Allow to cool completely.

Stir in eggs. Sift all dry ingredients and add, alternately with sherry, to the fruit mixture until all ingredients have been combined. Stir in pecans. Pour into a lined 18 cm cake pan. If the cake is not going to be iced, arrange a few almonds attractively on top of the cake before baking. Cover top of cake with greaseproof paper. Microwave on medium for 18 – 20 minutes. Allow cake to cool before turning out of pan. When cool, slowly pour brandy over cake. Wrap in aluminium foil and store until required.

Makes 1 cake

In a conventional oven: Bake at 140 °C for 2 hours.

Sponge cake

full power
4 minutes

3 eggs
100 g sugar
3 ml vanilla essence
100 g cake flour
dash salt
3 ml baking powder

Beat eggs, sugar and vanilla essence together until very light and fluffy. Sift together flour, salt and baking powder, and fold into egg mixture. Pour into a 26 cm greased and lined round glass baking dish and microwave on full power for 4 – 4½ minutes. Let stand in the dish for 5 minutes, then turn out and cool. Alternatively, pour mixture into two 16 cm greased and lined baking dishes and microwave on full power, one at a time, for 2½ – 3 minutes.

Makes 1 large or 2 smaller sponges

In a conventional oven: Bake at 190 °C for 15 – 18 minutes for the large cake, 10 – 12 minutes for the smaller ones.

Banana cake

medium
full power
14 minutes

125 g butter, softened
275 g sugar
2 eggs
250 ml mashed bananas
2 ml almond essence
270 g cake flour
2 ml baking powder
3 ml bicarbonate of soda
pinch salt
60 ml yoghurt
banana fudge icing* to decorate

Grease a 25 cm ring pan. Cream butter and sugar until light and fluffy. Beat in eggs, one at a time. Add banana and almond essence. Sift dry ingredients together. Add about a third of the dry ingredients to banana mixture. Beat to combine. Add a third of the yoghurt and beat. Continue until all ingredients have been combined. Pour mixture into ring pan. Microwave on medium for 12 minutes. Increase to full power and microwave for a further 1 – 2 minutes. Allow cake to stand in pan for about 15 minutes before turning out onto a rack. Cool completely before icing with banana fudge icing.

Makes 1 ring cake

In a conventional oven: Add 2 ml extra baking powder. Bake in two layer pans at 180 °C for 30 minutes, or in a bundt pan for 35 – 40 minutes.

Van der Hum sponge

full power
medium
24 minutes

1 packet vanilla cake mix
1 packet vanilla instant pudding
4 eggs
60 ml oil
60 ml van der Hum
180 ml orange juice
60 ml water
strips of orange rind to decorate

For the icing
130 g icing sugar, sifted
15 ml orange juice
15 ml water
15 ml van der Hum
15 ml golden syrup

Grease or spray a 25 cm ring pan. Place all ingredients for cake into a mixing bowl. Beat for 3 – 4 minutes using an electric mixer. Pour mixture into pan. Microwave cake on full power for 4 minutes. Reduce power to medium and microwave for about 20 minutes, or until a cake tester can be inserted into the cake and when removed remains clean. Allow cake to stand for about 15 minutes before turning out onto a cooling rack.
   To make the icing, combine all the ingredients in a bowl. Beat until smooth. Drizzle over cooled cake and decorate with strips of orange rind.

Makes 1 ring cake

In a conventional oven: Bake at 180 °C for 40 – 45 minutes. Turn out and glaze with icing.

Jam cake

medium
full power
14 minutes

180 g cake flour
3 ml bicarbonate of soda
salt
2 ml cinnamon
2 ml mixed spice
160 g sugar
160 g margarine, softened
125 ml gooseberry jam
4 eggs
100 ml milk
5 ml grated lemon rind
50 g hazelnuts, chopped
lemon glaze* to decorate

Sift dry ingredients into a mixing bowl. Add remaining ingredients, except icing. Beat very well until light and smooth. Pour into a well-greased 25 cm ring pan and microwave on medium for 12 minutes. Increase to full power and microwave for 2 minutes. Allow cake to become almost cool before turning out. Drizzle with lemon icing.

Makes 1 ring cake

In a conventional oven: Bake at 180 °C for 40 – 45 minutes.

Upside-down cakes bake perfectly in the microwave

Upside-down cake

full power
12 minutes

150 g cake flour	*For the topping*
150 g sugar	60 g butter
10 mℓ baking powder	70 g brown sugar
3 mℓ salt	1 x 410 g can pineapple slices
1 egg	6 maraschino cherries, halved
60 g butter, softened	
pineapple liquid and milk to make 125 mℓ	
5 mℓ vanilla essence	

To make the topping, place butter in a 20 cm round glass baking dish and microwave on full power for 1 minute. Tilt dish to coat bottom evenly. Sprinkle brown sugar evenly over the bottom. Arrange pineapple slices and cherries in the dish.

Place all ingredients for the cake in a bowl and beat on low speed until mixture is smooth, about 3 minutes. Spread mixture evenly over pineapple. Place dish on inverted saucer and microwave on full power for 9 – 11 minutes, or until a toothpick inserted near the centre comes out clean. Invert cake onto serving plate and let dish stand over cake for a few minutes. Serve warm or cool.

Makes 1 cake

In a conventional oven: Bake at 180 °C for 25 minutes, or until skewer inserted in centre comes out clean.

VARIATION

Peach upside-down cake. Use 1 x 410 g can peach slices instead of pineapple and add a few drops almond essence to the cake mixture.

Pineapple cake

full power
8 minutes

240 g self-raising flour
120 g brown sugar
120 g soft butter or margarine
2 eggs
1 x 230 g can pineapple slices, drained and juice reserved
120 g raisins or sultanas
honey to glaze

In a large mixing bowl, combine flour, sugar, butter and eggs. Add 90 mℓ reserved pineapple juice, mixing thoroughly. Beat for 2 minutes until mixture is smooth and glossy. Chop four slices pineapple and add, with raisins, to the mixture. Spread evenly in a greased 25 cm microwave ring pan. Place pan on an inverted saucer and microwave on full power for 7 – 8 minutes. Remove cake from oven and brush top with warmed honey. Stand on a rack until cool, then remove cake from pan. Store wrapped in foil in a covered container.

Makes 1 ring cake

In a conventional oven: Add 10 mℓ baking powder to the dry ingredients. Follow mixing method, then spread mixture evenly in a greased and floured loaf pan or cake pan. Bake at 160 °C for 1½ – 1¾ hours. Brush cake with warmed honey and leave to cool in pan.

Butter cake

full power
16 minutes

330 g cake flour	200 g butter, softened
380 g sugar	250 mℓ milk
10 mℓ baking powder	8 mℓ vanilla essence
3 mℓ salt	1 egg

Combine flour, sugar, baking powder and salt in a large mixing bowl. Add butter, milk, vanilla and egg and beat on low speed for 30 seconds. Scrape down bowl and beat on low for 2 minutes. Line two 20 cm round glass baking dishes with single layers of paper towel cut to fit the bottom. Turn cake mixture into dishes and spread evenly. Microwave one cake at a time on an inverted saucer on full power for 7 – 8 minutes, rotating dish half a turn after 4 minutes if necessary. Remove from oven and stand on a wooden board for 15 minutes before turning out. Sandwich together and ice as desired.

Makes two 20 cm layers

In a conventional oven: Bake at 180 °C for 25 minutes, or until a skewer inserted in the centre comes out clean. Turn out and cool on a wire rack.

Strawberry coffee cake

Streusel coffee cake

full power
8 minutes

150 g sugar
60 g butter or margarine
3 mℓ vanilla essence
1 egg
125 mℓ milk
180 g cake flour
10 mℓ baking powder
2 mℓ salt

For the streusel topping
100 g brown sugar
30 mℓ cake flour
10 mℓ cinnamon
30 mℓ butter
50 g nuts (hazel or pecan), chopped

Beat sugar, butter, vanilla essence and egg until light and fluffy. Stir in milk. Sift dry ingredients together and add to mixture. Stir until smooth. Make streusel mixture by combining all ingredients thoroughly. Spread half the batter in a greased 23 cm baking dish and sprinkle with half the streusel mixture. Cover with the remaining batter and top with the remaining streusel mixture. Microwave on full power for 7 – 8 minutes, rotating dish a quarter turn every 3 minutes if necessary. Remove from oven and stand for 10 minutes before serving. Serve warm.

Serves 9 – 12

In a conventional oven: Bake at 180 °C for 25 minutes.

VARIATIONS
Apple coffee cake: Chop the contents of a 385 g can of pie apples and spread half over the first layer of cake mixture. Sprinkle with half the streusel mixture, then repeat the cake, apple and streusel layers.

Jam coffee cake: In a measuring jug, microwave 100 mℓ fruit jam or marmalade on full power for 45 – 60 seconds to soften. Drizzle half the warmed jam over the first layer of cake mixture, sprinkle with half the streusel mixture, then repeat the cake, jam and streusel layers.

Southern peach coffee cake: Drain a 425 g can of peach slices well, then soak the peach slices in 30 mℓ brandy. Drain. Arrange the peach slices on the first layer of cake mixture, sprinkle with half the streusel mixture, then repeat the cake, peach and streusel layers.

Strawberry coffee cake: Slice 200 g fresh strawberries and sprinkle with 30 mℓ castor sugar and 30 mℓ kirsch liqueur. Stand for 10 minutes, then drain. Arrange the strawberry slices on the first layer of cake mixture, sprinkle with streusel mixture, then repeat the cake, strawberry and streusel layers.

Carrot cake

full power
11 minutes

180 g cake flour	750 mℓ grated carrot ✱ 3 cups
10 mℓ cinnamon	300 g sugar
8 mℓ bicarbonate of soda	250 mℓ oil
5 mℓ nutmeg	100 g walnuts, chopped
3 mℓ salt	3 eggs, beaten

For the icing
250 g smooth cottage cheese or cream cheese
120 g butter, at room temperature
50 g walnuts, chopped
5 mℓ vanilla essence
about 400 g icing sugar, sifted

Sift together flour, cinnamon, bicarbonate of soda, nutmeg and salt. Set aside. Combine grated carrot, sugar, oil, walnuts and eggs, mixing well. Add dry ingredients and mix well. Turn mixture into a deep, greased 25 cm microwave ring pan. Place pan on an inverted saucer and microwave on full power for 10 – 11 minutes. The cake should shrink away slightly from edges of pan. Turn pan during baking if the cake looks as if it is cooking unevenly. Cool slightly before inverting onto a serving plate.

To make the icing, beat cheese until smooth. Add butter and beat well. Add nuts and vanilla and mix thoroughly. Gradually add icing sugar, beating well to the desired consistency. Spread over cake.   *Makes 1 ring cake*

In a conventional oven: Bake at 180 °C for 35 – 40 minutes.

Lemon and yoghurt loaf

full power
medium
13 minutes

150 mℓ plain yoghurt
100 mℓ oil
150 g sugar
250 g self-raising flour
2 eggs
pinch salt
5 mℓ grated lemon rind
30 mℓ lemon juice
lemon glaze*

Beat yoghurt, oil and sugar together until well combined. Sift in flour. Beat to combine. Add remaining ingredients, mixing well. Pour into a greased or sprayed 26 x 12 cm microwave loaf pan and microwave on full power for 3 minutes. Reduce power to medium. Microwave for a further 8 – 10 minutes. Allow cake to cool in dish on a rack. Turn out after 20 minutes. When cold, drizzle lemon glaze over top. Allow glaze to set before serving cake.

Makes 1 loaf

In a conventional oven: Add 4 mℓ baking powder to ingredients and bake at 160 °C for 45 – 55 minutes.

Basic scone mix

500 g cake flour
30 mℓ baking powder
10 mℓ salt
30 mℓ sugar
180 g butter

Sift together flour, baking powder, salt and sugar. Rub in butter until mixture resembles fine crumbs. Keep refrigerated in a tightly covered container and use as directed in recipes such as Golden nut ring or Caramel cherry ring, or in other recipes calling for basic scone dough. To make up scone dough, add enough milk mixed with egg to make a soft but not sticky dough, and use as desired.

Makes 700 g

Caramel cherry ring

full power
high
10 minutes

60 g butter
100 g brown sugar
2 mℓ cinnamon
45 mℓ golden syrup
50 g pecan nuts, halved
45 mℓ maraschino cherries, quartered
250 g basic scone mix*
1 egg
190 mℓ milk

Place butter in a microwave ring pan and microwave on full power for about 45 seconds to melt. Tilt pan so that butter coats evenly. Sprinkle with brown sugar and cinnamon. Microwave for 1 minute, then stir well and spread evenly in pan. Drizzle with golden syrup. Arrange halved pecans evenly around pan and sprinkle with cherries. Place scone mix in a mixing bowl. Combine egg and milk, and add enough liquid to dry ingredients to form a soft, but not sticky, dough. Form dough into ten balls. Place balls of dough on top of cherries in ring pan. Let rest for 5 minutes. Place pan on an inverted saucer and microwave on high for 6 – 8 minutes, rotating pan during cooking if necessary. Let rolls stand in pan for about 3 minutes, then invert onto a serving plate and let pan stand over rolls a few minutes. Serve warm.   *Makes 1 ring of 10 pieces*

In a conventional oven: Bake at 200 °C for 20 – 25 minutes until well risen and golden brown. Invert onto serving plate and serve warm.

Golden nut ring

full power
medium
9 minutes

20 mℓ butter
50 g walnuts, chopped
45 mℓ brown sugar
15 mℓ sugar
5 mℓ cinnamon
60 mℓ golden syrup
250 g basic scone mix*
1 egg
190 mℓ milk

Place butter in a microwave ring pan and microwave on full power for 20 – 30 seconds. Tilt pan so that butter coats evenly. Mix together nuts, brown sugar, sugar and cinnamon. Place golden syrup in a small glass measuring jug and microwave on full power for 15 seconds to warm.
　　Place scone mix in a mixing bowl. Combine egg and milk and add enough liquid to dry ingredients to make a soft, but not sticky, dough. Knead lightly, then roll out on a lightly floured board and cut into ten 5 cm rounds. Brush each round with warmed syrup, then dip in nut mixture, coating well. Place rounds in ring pan with edges overlapping. Microwave on medium for 6 – 8 minutes, rotating pan half a turn after 3 minutes. Let cool in pan for 5 minutes. Invert onto a serving plate and sprinkle with any remaining nut mixture. Serve warm.

Makes 1 ring of 10 pieces

In a conventional oven: Bake at 200 °C for 20 minutes. Turn out onto a wire rack and let cool slightly before serving.

Sour cream apple bake

full power
12 minutes

1 egg, beaten
30 mℓ cake flour
125 mℓ golden syrup
125 mℓ sour cream
3 mℓ caramel flavouring
3 large apples, peeled,
　cored and sliced

For the topping
230 g butter
200 g brown sugar
1 egg
180 g cake flour
5 mℓ bicarbonate of soda
3 mℓ salt
250 mℓ sour cream
3 mℓ caramel flavouring

Combine egg, flour, syrup, sour cream and caramel flavouring, beating well. Mix in apple slices and turn into a deep 23 cm baking dish.
　　For the topping, cream butter and sugar well. Add egg and beat until light and fluffy. Sift dry ingredients and add to the creamed mixture along with sour cream and caramel flavouring. Mix until smooth, then pour over apple mixture. Microwave on full power for 10 – 12 minutes. Serve from the dish, with cream or custard.

Serves 10 – 12

In a conventional oven: Bake at 180 °C for 45 minutes.

Wholewheat batter bread and cinnamon sticky buns

Cinnamon sticky buns

full power
8 minutes

250 g basic scone mix*
1 egg
180 mℓ milk

For the filling and topping
120 g butter
50 g pecan nuts, chopped
100 g brown sugar
8 mℓ cinnamon
60 g raisins

Place scone mix in a mixing bowl. Mix egg with milk and add enough of this liquid to dry ingredients to make a soft dough. Knead gently several times, then roll out into a large rectangle on a lightly floured surface.

For the filling and topping, microwave butter on full power for about 2 minutes to melt. Brush dough generously with melted butter, then pour remaining butter into a deep, 23 cm glass baking dish. Mix together pecans, brown sugar, cinnamon and raisins. Sprinkle two thirds of the filling mixture over the dough and sprinkle remainder in the

baking dish. Roll up dough, swiss roll fashion, and cut into 3 cm thick slices. Arrange slices close together in the prepared baking dish. Microwave on full power for 5 – 6 minutes. Stand in the dish for 3 – 4 minutes, then turn out onto a plate and serve warm.

Makes about 12 buns

In a conventional oven: Bake at 190 °C for 20 – 25 minutes, until lightly golden brown and well risen. Turn out at once.

Basic batter bread

This recipe can be adapted to make a variety of tasty yeast breads

full power
10 minutes

15 mℓ active dry yeast
300 mℓ warm water
30 mℓ honey
30 mℓ butter
5 mℓ salt
360 g cake flour

Dissolve yeast in warm water in a large glass bowl. Stir in the honey, mixing well. Microwave the butter on full power for 10 seconds to soften, then add to the yeast mixture along with salt and 240 g of the flour. Beat on high speed for 1 minute, scrape down bowl and beat for 1 minute more. Stir in remaining flour, mixing well. Cover bowl and microwave for 15 seconds on full power, then rest in microwave oven for 10 – 12 minutes. Repeat heating and resting at least twice more, or until dough has doubled in bulk.

Stir down with a wooden spoon and turn into a well-greased 20 cm round casserole dish with straight sides. Cover with greased waxed paper and microwave on full power for 15 seconds, then rest in the microwave oven for 10 – 12 minutes. Repeat heating and resting at least twice more, or until dough has risen to level with the top of the casserole dish. Remove cover and microwave on full power for 8 – 9 minutes. Let bread stand in dish for 3 – 4 minutes, then turn out and cool. Store tightly covered.

Makes 1 loaf

In a conventional oven: Microwave as directed to prove dough, then bake at 190 °C for 30 – 35 minutes. Turn out on a wire rack to cool.

VARIATIONS

Bacon and pepper bread: Stir in 3 mℓ freshly ground black pepper and 200 g bacon, cooked and diced, when stirring down dough. Increase microwave time when baking by 30 seconds to 1 minute.

Cheddar cheese bread: Reduce butter to 15 mℓ and add 100 g grated Cheddar cheese and a pinch of dry mustard to the remaining flour. Increase microwave time when baking by 30 seconds to 1 minute.

Raisin batter bread: Add 10 mℓ cinnamon with remaining flour. Add 100 g raisins after stirring the batter down.

Wholewheat batter bread

An easy-to-make health loaf with a number of variations

full power
11 minutes

15 mℓ active dry yeast
300 mℓ warm water
30 mℓ honey
30 mℓ butter or margarine
5 mℓ salt
180 g cake flour
190 g wholewheat flour

In a large mixing bowl, dissolve yeast in warm water. Stir in honey. Microwave butter on full power for 15 – 20 seconds, and add to the yeast mixture along with salt, cake flour and 60 g of the wholewheat flour. Beat for 1 minute, scrape down bowl and beat for 1 minute more. Stir in remaining flour, mixing well. Cover and microwave on full power for 15 seconds, then rest for 10 – 12 minutes. Microwave again on full power for 15 seconds and rest. Repeat at least once more, or until the dough has doubled in bulk.

Stir down dough, then turn into a well-greased 20 cm round casserole dish with straight sides. Cover with greased

waxed paper and microwave for 15 seconds on full power, then rest in microwave for 10 – 12 minutes. Repeat heating and resting at least twice more, or until dough has risen to level with top of casserole dish. Remove cover and microwave on full power for 8 – 9 minutes. Let bread stand in casserole for 3 – 4 minutes, then turn out and cool. Store tightly covered.

Makes 1 loaf

In a conventional oven: Microwave as directed above to prove dough, then bake at 190 °C for 30 – 35 minutes. Turn out onto a wire rack and cool.

VARIATIONS

Bran and wheat bread: Reduce wholewheat flour to 60 g and increase cake flour to 240 g. Add 1 egg with the salt, butter and all the cake flour. Then add 60 mℓ wheat germ and 60 mℓ natural bran with the remaining wholewheat flour.

Sunflower yoghurt bread: Reduce warm water to 190 mℓ, and add 125 mℓ plain yoghurt and 60 mℓ sunflower seeds with remaining flour.

Wholewheat onion bread: Finely chop ½ onion and add with the remaining flour.

Brown yoghurt bread

full power
6 minutes

60 g cake flour	1 egg
60 g mealie meal	250 mℓ yoghurt
70 g wholewheat flour	80 mℓ molasses
5 mℓ bicarbonate of soda	15 mℓ oil
3 mℓ salt	30 mℓ wheat germ

Combine dry ingredients in a large mixing bowl. Mix together egg, yoghurt, molasses and oil and add to dry ingredients, mixing well to moisten. Grease a small microwave ring pan or a small loaf pan well and sprinkle with half the wheat germ. Spoon in bread mixture, smoothing evenly. Sprinkle remaining wheat germ on top. Microwave on full power, uncovered, for 4 minutes, then rotate pan a quarter turn. Microwave for 1½ – 2½ minutes longer, until a skewer inserted in the centre comes out clean. Let stand for 10 minutes in pan, then invert bread onto wire rack and cool.

Makes 1 loaf

In a conventional oven: Bake in a greased loaf pan at 180 °C for 45 minutes, until a skewer inserted in the centre comes out clean.

VARIATIONS

Savoury onion bread: Mix 45 mℓ dry onion soup mix with dry ingredients and increase oil by 5 mℓ.

Seed loaf: Add 30 mℓ sesame seeds and 45 mℓ sunflower seeds to dry ingredients. Increase oil by 5 mℓ. Omit wheat germ and sprinkle greased pan with 15 mℓ sesame seeds.

Clockwise: spicy apple muffins, apple nut bread, apple coffee cake (p. 122)

Basic microwave muffins

For best results, use a microwave muffin pan

high

240 g cake flour
100 g sugar
15 mℓ baking powder
3 mℓ salt
2 eggs, beaten
125 mℓ oil
125 mℓ milk

Sift together dry ingredients. Beat together eggs, oil and milk, and add to dry ingredients. Mix until just moistened. Fill paper muffin cups half full of batter and place in a microwave muffin pan. Microwave on high according to chart below. The muffins are done when a toothpick inserted in the centre comes out clean.

Makes 10 – 12 muffins

Number of muffins	Time (on high power)	Method
3	1½-2 minutes	Rotate the pan half a turn after half the cooking time. Batters with other ingredients (see variations) may take slightly longer than the time stated.
4	2-3 minutes	
5	2½-3½ minutes	
6	3-5 minutes	

In a conventional oven: Spoon mixture into greased muffin cups, filling two thirds full. Bake at 190 °C for 20 minutes, until well risen and golden brown.

VARIATIONS

Spicy apple muffins: Add 3 mℓ cinnamon to dry ingredients and add 1 peeled and chopped apple with liquid. Top with cinnamon sugar topping.

Herby cheese muffins: Add 3 mℓ mixed herbs, 5 mℓ chopped parsley and pinch dry mustard to dry ingredients. Stir in 50 g grated cheese with liquid. Top with extra grated cheese.

Lemon coconut muffins: Add 5 mℓ grated lemon rind and 60 mℓ toasted coconut* to dry ingredients. Add 15 mℓ lemon juice to liquid and top with more toasted coconut.

Orange nut muffins: Add 5 mℓ grated orange rind and 50 g chopped pecan nuts to dry ingredients. Replace 25 mℓ of the milk with orange juice in the liquid. Top with streusel topping.

MUFFIN TOPPINGS

Streusel topping: Combine 100 g brown sugar, 30 mℓ cake flour, 10 mℓ cinnamon, 30 mℓ butter and 50 g chopped nuts.

Nut crunch topping: Combine 80 mℓ cake flour, 30 mℓ brown sugar, 30 mℓ butter, 45 mℓ chopped nuts, 30 mℓ cornflake crumbs.

Cinnamon sugar topping: Combine 45 mℓ brown sugar with 3 – 5 mℓ cinnamon.

Banana molasses bread

high
14 minutes

3 ripe bananas
1 egg
70 g sugar
70 g brown sugar
30 mℓ molasses
30 mℓ butter, melted
15 mℓ oil
240 g cake flour
5 mℓ bicarbonate of soda
3 mℓ salt
100 g walnuts, chopped

Mash bananas until no lumps remain. Add egg and beat well. Beat in sugars, molasses, melted butter and oil. Sift together dry ingredients and stir into banana mixture. Fold in three quarters of the nuts. Grease a microwave ring pan well and dust with remaining chopped nuts. Spoon in banana mixture and microwave on high for 11 – 14 minutes, until a toothpick inserted in the centre comes out clean. Rotate pan a quarter turn every 4 minutes of cooking time. Let stand in pan for 5 minutes, then turn out and cool.

Makes 1 ring loaf

In a conventional oven: Bake in ring mould or loaf pan at 160 °C for about 1 hour, until a skewer inserted in the centre comes out clean.

Gingerbread ring

high
15 minutes

280 g cake flour
10 mℓ freshly grated ginger
8 mℓ bicarbonate of soda
5 mℓ cinnamon
3 mℓ salt
dash ground cloves
120 g butter, at room temperature
100 g brown sugar
100 g sugar
2 eggs
250 mℓ buttermilk
250 mℓ molasses
15 mℓ grated orange rind
15 mℓ grated lemon rind
a little extra cinnamon

Mix together flour, ginger, bicarbonate of soda, cinnamon, salt and cloves. Cream butter and sugars and add to flour mixture. Beat in eggs, buttermilk, molasses and rinds, mixing thoroughly. Grease a large microwave ring pan and sprinkle with a little cinnamon, shaking out excess. Turn gingerbread mixture into pan and microwave on high for 13 – 15 minutes, turning the pan if the mixture seems to be baking unevenly. Stand in the pan for about 20 minutes before turning out to cool.

Makes 1 large ring

In a conventional oven: Bake at 160 °C for 1 – 1¼ hours, or until a skewer comes out clean.

Apple nut bread

high
12 minutes

120 g butter
200 g sugar
2 eggs, beaten
30 mℓ sour milk or buttermilk
1 small apple, peeled and grated
50 g sultanas
50 g nuts (hazel or pecan), chopped
240 g cake flour
5 mℓ bicarbonate of soda
dash salt

Beat butter and sugar until creamy. Add eggs and beat until fluffy. Add sour milk, apple, sultanas and half the nuts, mixing well. Stir in sifted dry ingredients. Grease fluted microwave ring pan and dust with remaining chopped nuts. Spread batter in pan and microwave on high for 10 – 12 minutes, rotating ring pan a quarter turn every 4 minutes. A toothpick inserted in the centre should come out clean when the loaf is done. Let loaf stand in pan for 5 minutes, then turn out onto cooling rack. Serve warm or cool.

Makes 1 ring loaf

In a conventional oven: Bake in a ring mould or greased loaf pan at 180 °C for 45 – 55 minutes. Turn out to cool.

Date bars

full power
high
18 minutes

For the filling
250 g dates, chopped
300 mℓ water
25 mℓ lemon juice

For the crumble topping
90 g cake flour
2 mℓ bicarbonate of soda
60 g oats
1 mℓ cinnamon
120 g soft brown sugar
50 mℓ chopped pecan nuts
125 g margarine

Place dates, water and lemon juice in a bowl. Cover with plastic wrap and cut two slits in the plastic to prevent 'ballooning' during cooking. Microwave on full power for 5 minutes. Uncover and cool slightly.

To make crumble, sift flour and bicarbonate of soda. Stir in oats, cinnamon, sugar and pecans. Microwave margarine on high for 3 – 4 minutes, until completely melted. Pour into dry ingredients and mix well. Press half the crumble into a greased 22 cm square glass dish. Cover with date mixture and top with crumble. Press down well. Shield corners of dish with foil. Microwave on full power for 9 minutes. Cool, then cut into squares.

Makes 20 squares

In a conventional oven: Bake at 180 °C for 20 – 25 minutes.

Date bars (p. 127) and chocolate chip squares

Chocolate chip squares

full power
6 minutes

120 g butter, softened
150 g brown sugar
1 egg
15 mℓ milk
5 mℓ vanilla essence
150 g cake flour
3 mℓ baking powder
1 mℓ ground cinnamon
dash salt
1 x 100 g packet bakers' chocolate chips
50 g nuts, chopped (optional)

Cream butter and sugar until light and fluffy. Add egg and beat well. Stir in milk and vanilla. Combine flour, baking powder, cinnamon and salt and add to the butter mixture. Mix well, then stir in chocolate chips and nuts. Turn the mixture into a greased 20 cm baking dish and shield corners of dish with small pieces of foil. Microwave on full power for 5 – 6½ minutes, rotating dish a quarter turn every 2 minutes if necessary. Cool in the pan before cutting into squares.

Makes 16 large or 24 small squares

In a conventional oven: Bake at 180 °C for 25 – 30 minutes, until a skewer inserted in the centre comes out clean.

Muesli pie crust

full power
4 minutes

250 mℓ biscuit crumbs (about 14 biscuits)
125 mℓ muesli
5 mℓ ground cinnamon
30 mℓ ground almonds
100 g butter
45 mℓ cream

Mix biscuit crumbs, muesli, cinnamon and almonds together. Microwave butter on full power for 1½ – 2 minutes to melt. Add to dry ingredients, mixing well. Add cream and mix in. Press into bottom and sides of a 23 cm pie dish and microwave on full power for 2 minutes. Let cool before using.

Makes one 23 cm pie crust

In a conventional oven: Bake at 190 °C for 5 – 8 minutes.

Basic crumb crust

full power
2½ minutes

60 mℓ butter
250 mℓ marie or tennis biscuit crumbs (about 14 biscuits)
30 mℓ brown sugar

Microwave butter in a 23 cm pie dish on full power for 45 – 60 seconds. Add crumbs and brown sugar and mix well. Gently press the mixture into bottom and sides of the dish and microwave on full power for 1 – 1½ minutes. Cool before using.

Makes one 23 cm crust

VARIATIONS
Nutty crust: Proceed as for basic crust, adding 50 g chopped nuts and 30 mℓ cream to the crumbs.

Spicy crust: Use 250 mℓ ginger biscuit crumbs (about 14 biscuits). Add 3 mℓ cinnamon and 30 mℓ cream. Proceed as for basic recipe.

Butter crunch crust: Use 250 mℓ butter crunch biscuit crumbs (about 14 biscuits) and proceed as for basic recipe.

Chocolate crumb crust

full power
2½ minutes

10 – 12 chocolate cream biscuits, broken
60 mℓ butter
30 mℓ cream

Place biscuits in a food processor with a metal blade and process to fine crumbs. Microwave butter in a 23 cm pie dish on full power for 45 – 60 seconds. Add crumbs and cream, mixing well. Press into bottom and sides of the dish and microwave on full power for 1 – 1½ minutes. Cool before using.

Makes one 23 cm crust

Shortcrust pastry

full power
6 minutes

120 g cake flour	60 mℓ butter
3 mℓ salt	1 egg yolk
5 mℓ sugar	45 mℓ cold water

Combine flour, salt and sugar. Rub in butter until mixture resembles fine crumbs. Combine egg yolk and water and add enough to the dry ingredients to form a dough. Turn pastry onto a lightly floured surface and knead gently, then roll out and use as desired.

To microwave pastry shells, line pie dish with pastry. Cut a long foil strip about 3 cm wide and line the edge of the pastry shell. Place a double layer of paper towel in the base of the pastry shell, pressing gently into the edges. Microwave on full power for 3½ – 4 minutes, rotating dish after 2 minutes if necessary. Remove foil and paper towel and microwave for 1½ – 2 minutes more. Use cooked pastry shells for pies and tarts with cold or uncooked fillings.

Makes a 20 – 23 cm single crust

VARIATIONS
Herbed pastry: Leave out sugar and add 5 mℓ mixed herbs, or herb of your choice.

Cheese pastry: Omit sugar, add 1 mℓ dry mustard to the dry ingredients and stir in 50 mℓ grated cheese after rubbing in the butter.

Sweet pastry: Increase the sugar to 45 mℓ, add 1 mℓ vanilla essence, and proceed as for shortcrust pastry.

Lemon glaze

full power
3 minutes

250 g icing sugar, sifted	15 mℓ water
15 mℓ lemon juice	3 mℓ finely grated lemon rind

Place all ingredients in a bowl. Microwave on full power for 2 – 3 minutes. Stir well. Cool 5 minutes. Use as required.

Ices 1 cake

Coconut crunch topping

Spread on top of a butter cake or chocolate layer cake for a quick and delicious 'icing'

full power
2 minutes

200 g brown sugar	30 mℓ butter
15 mℓ cornflour	125 mℓ desiccated coconut
30 – 45 mℓ milk	50 g nuts, chopped

Combine brown sugar, cornflour, 30 mℓ milk and the butter. Microwave on full power for 1 minute. Stir thoroughly, then microwave for 1 minute more. Stir well, then add coconut and nuts. Mix well, adding a little more milk if mixture is very stiff. Spread on cake while the mixture is still warm.

Makes enough topping for two 20 cm layers

Butter cream icing

high
2 minutes

500 g icing sugar, sifted
30 mℓ milk
dash salt
5 mℓ vanilla essence
120 g butter

Combine sugar, milk, salt and vanilla in a bowl and mix to blend. The mixture will be very stiff. Cut butter into pieces and place on top. Microwave on high for 1 – 2 minutes, until mixture can be beaten smoothly. If icing is too hot, it may run off the cake. Cool the icing in the bowl, stirring occasionally before using.

Makes enough for icing two 20 cm layers

Banana fudge icing

medium
high
8 minutes

30 mℓ butter
175 g soft brown sugar
45 mℓ milk
140 g icing sugar, sifted
15 mℓ cream
1 banana, sliced
a little lemon juice

Place butter, brown sugar and milk in a bowl. Microwave on medium for 5 minutes. Stir well. Microwave on high for 3 minutes. Pour into a cold bowl and cool slightly. Beat icing sugar and cream into icing. The mixture should be of a 'drizzling' consistency. Use this icing to sandwich two cake layers together, then drizzle on top of cake, or drizzle all over a ring cake. Whilst still soft, decorate icing with banana slices dipped in a little lemon juice.

Ices 1 cake

Banana cake (p. 120) covered with banana fudge icing

Beverages

Microwaving speeds up and simplifies the making of beverages. Try these hot drinks for cold nights – you can make them quickly after a late show, or as an impromptu treat after dinner. Exotic chilled drinks are easily made in advance and there are recipes for homemade liqueurs too. When making single quantities, heat the liquid in a cup or heatproof glass, but take care not to use those with a metal trim. If heating more than 2 cups or glasses at a time, arrange them in a ring with a space between each one. Stir liquids before microwaving, and do not overfill cups as the liquid will spill over as it expands. Milk-based drinks should be watched carefully and as soon as they start to boil, the door should be opened. The microwave can also be used to reheat that forgotten cup of tea or coffee without it losing any flavour.

Strawberry party punch

Popular treat for a children's party

full power
2 minutes

1 x 90 g packet strawberry jelly
250 mℓ water
1 x 200 g can frozen lemon concentrate, thawed
1 ℓ pineapple juice
1 ℓ ginger ale, chilled
ice cubes
sliced strawberries to garnish

Place strawberry jelly powder in a large bowl and set aside. Microwave water on full power for 2 minutes, then stir into the jelly, mixing well to dissolve. Add lemon concentrate and stir well. Pour in pineapple juice and chill well. Just before serving, add the ginger ale and ice cubes. Garnish with sliced strawberries.

Serves about 20

Plantation frost

full power
3 minutes

500 mℓ water
15 mℓ instant coffee powder
45 mℓ sugar
3 bananas
125 mℓ cream

Place water and instant coffee powder in a large jug and microwave on full power for 2 – 3 minutes. Chill the coffee. Place chilled coffee, sugar and sliced bananas in a blender and blend until smooth. Stir in cream and serve in chilled glasses.

Serves 6

Danish coffee punch

full power
3 minutes

750 mℓ water
30 mℓ instant coffee powder
6 eggs
grated rind of 1 lemon
100 g sugar
125 mℓ brandy

Place 500 mℓ of the water and the coffee powder in a large jug and microwave on full power for 2 – 3 minutes. Add the remaining 250 mℓ water, then chill the coffee. With an electric mixer, beat the eggs with grated lemon rind until frothy. Gradually add the sugar, beating until mixture is thick. At low speed, stir in the cold coffee and the brandy. Serve in punch cups.

Serves 10 – 12

Hot apple wine

full power
medium
low
47 minutes

750 mℓ apple cider (or apple juice)
65 mℓ sugar
3 cinnamon sticks
6 whole cloves
rind of 1 small lemon, cut into strips
1 ℓ dry white wine
juice of 1 lemon
65 mℓ brandy

Combine apple cider, sugar, cinnamon, cloves and lemon rind in a 3 litre casserole dish. Microwave on full power for 4 minutes, stirring after 2 minutes and again at the end of the cooking time. Reduce power to medium and microwave, uncovered, for 10 minutes. Strain the mixture to remove spices. Return apple cider to the casserole, then add the wine and lemon juice. Microwave on full power for 3 minutes, then reduce power and microwave, covered, on low for about 30 minutes. Stir in brandy and serve warm.

Serves 12 – 16

Hot spicy tea

full power
2 minutes

1,5 ℓ boiling water
3 cloves
small piece cinnamon stick
15 mℓ tea leaves
juice of 1 orange
10 mℓ lemon juice
60 g sugar
orange and lemon slices to garnish

Pour the boiling water over the cloves, cinnamon and tea. Allow to infuse for 4 minutes. Strain. Meanwhile, place the fruit juices and sugar in a small jug and stir. Microwave on full power for 2 minutes, stirring after 1 minute. Strain into tea mixture. Serve hot with slices of orange and lemon as a garnish. (Illustrated left)

Makes 1,5 litres

VARIATION

For an alcoholic tea, soak 60 g raisins or sultanas in a little rum or brandy for a few hours. Add a few to each glass of steaming tea.

Hot spiced wine

full power
medium
25 minutes

250 mℓ orange juice
45 mℓ sugar
45 mℓ brown sugar
1 x 750 mℓ bottle red wine
1 cinnamon stick
4 whole cloves
3 whole allspice
1 small piece whole nutmeg
a little orange and lemon rind, cut into strips
orange slices to garnish

Combine orange juice and sugars in a large bowl, then microwave on full power for 5 minutes, stirring every few minutes. Add all the remaining ingredients. Microwave on medium for 20 minutes. Strain and serve hot. Garnish with orange slices.

Makes 1 litre

Mocha chocolate

full power
9 minutes

125 mℓ milk
250 mℓ water
50 g dark chocolate, chopped
60 g sugar

5 mℓ vanilla essence
250 mℓ freshly made coffee
125 mℓ cream
a little cinnamon to garnish

Combine the milk and water in a large jug. Microwave on full power for 4 minutes. Add chocolate to the hot milk mixture, then stir in the sugar and vanilla. Microwave on full power for 2 minutes. Now stir in the coffee and cream and microwave for 3 minutes. Pour into four small, heatproof glasses and sprinkle with a little cinnamon. Serve immediately.

Serves 4

Quick cappuccino

full power
7 minutes

750 mℓ freshly made coffee
125 mℓ cream
little cocoa to garnish

Pour the coffee into a large jug. Microwave on full power for 6 minutes. Stir in the cream. Microwave on full power for 1 minute. Pour half the coffee mixture into a blender and blend for 30 seconds or until very foamy. Pour into two cups. Repeat the process with the remaining coffee. Sprinkle a little cocoa on top of each.

Serves 4

Clockwise: mocha chocolate, hot spiced wine, quick cappuccino

South African coffee

full power
1 minute

150 mℓ van der Hum
45 mℓ brown sugar, or to taste
800 mℓ freshly made strong black coffee
150 mℓ whipped cream
cinnamon

Divide van der Hum and sugar between four Irish coffee glasses. Arrange glasses in a circle in the microwave oven. Microwave on full power for 1 minute. Place a long-handled metal spoon in each glass and pour in hot coffee until glasses are three quarters full. Stir to dissolve sugar. Carefully pour whipped cream over the back of a spoon so that it floats and does not sink into the coffee mixture. Sprinkle with cinnamon and serve immediately.

Serves 4

VARIATIONS
Leave out van der Hum and make the following coffees:

Mexican coffee: Add 150 mℓ Kahlua and sprinkle a little grated chocolate on top.

French coffee: Add 150 mℓ Mandarin Napoleon liqueur.

Jamaican coffee: Add 150 mℓ Coco Rico and top with a little grated chocolate.

Irish coffee: Add 150 mℓ Irish whiskey.

Mediterranean coffee

full power
low
56 minutes

1 ℓ water
45 mℓ instant coffee powder
60 mℓ chocolate syrup
70 g sugar
4 cinnamon sticks
5 mℓ whole cloves
3 mℓ anise flavouring
125 mℓ orange liqueur
rind of 1 orange, cut into strips
rind of 1 lemon, cut into strips
whipped cream to garnish

Place 500 mℓ of the water and the instant coffee in a deep jug. Microwave on full power for 3 minutes. Add chocolate syrup, sugar, cinnamon, cloves, anise and orange liqueur. Place remaining water in a deep 3 litre casserole dish and add coffee mixture. Microwave on full power for 8 minutes, stir well, then reduce power and microwave on low for 30 – 45 minutes, stirring occasionally. Add orange and lemon rind during last 15 minutes. Strain and serve in coffee cups, topped with whipped cream.

Serves 10 – 12

Hot brandied chocolate

full power
1½ minutes

15 mℓ drinking chocolate powder
5 mℓ instant coffee powder
15 mℓ brandy
180 mℓ milk
whipped cream to garnish

Place chocolate, coffee powder, brandy and milk in a large mug. Stir to mix, then microwave on full power for 1 – 1½ minutes. Serve topped with whipped cream.

Serves 1

Iced lemon coffee

full power
3 minutes

500 mℓ water
15 mℓ instant coffee powder
500 mℓ lemon sherbet or lemon-flavoured ice-cream
30 mℓ grenadine syrup

Place water and instant coffee powder in a large jug. Microwave on full power for 2 – 3 minutes, then chill the coffee. Place coffee, sherbet or ice-cream and grenadine syrup in a blender and blend until smooth. Serve in tall glasses.

Serves 4

Hot spiced rum

full power
6 minutes

15 mℓ brown sugar
4 strips lemon rind
1 mℓ cinnamon
500 mℓ water
10 mℓ butter
120 mℓ rum

Divide the sugar, lemon rind, cinnamon, water and butter between four heatproof glasses. Microwave on full power for 6 minutes. Remove the lemon rind and stir well. Stir in the rum and serve piping hot. If desired, add a twist of fresh lemon to each glass.

Serves 4

Homemade coffee liqueur

full power
5 minutes

250 mℓ water
300 g sugar
60 mℓ pure instant coffee
5 mℓ vanilla essence
280 mℓ vodka

Combine water, sugar and coffee in a bowl. Microwave, uncovered, on full power for 5 minutes. Stir at least twice during cooking time. Add vanilla and cool. Stir in vodka. Pour into a bottle and cover. Label and store in a cool, dark place. Shake bottle from time to time. Allow liqueur to mature for about 6 months before using.

Makes 700 mℓ

Coffee liqueur

Youngberry liqueur

full power
3 minutes

250 g fresh youngberries
190 g sugar
750 mℓ gin

Wash youngberries and drain. Place sugar and 125 mℓ of the gin in a measuring jug and microwave on full power for 2 minutes. Stir and microwave for 1 minute. Pour sugar mixture over berries in a bowl, stir gently, then cool to room temperature. When cool, place mixture in a large jar with a tight-fitting lid. Add remaining gin. Close tightly and keep in a cool place. Turn jar every few days. The liqueur is ready to drink after about 3 weeks, but it is better if left for about 2 months before using.

Makes about 750 mℓ

Youngberry liqueur

134

Hot spiced sherry

medium
low
1¼ hours

1 x 300 g can frozen orange juice, thawed
1 x 750 mℓ bottle dry or medium sherry
600 mℓ water
12 cloves
60 g sugar
2 cinnamon sticks
3 mℓ mixed spice
30 mℓ butter

Mix orange juice with sherry. Add water and remaining ingredients except butter. Place mixture in a 3 litre deep casserole dish and microwave, covered, on medium for 10 minutes. Reduce power to low and microwave, still covered, for about 1 hour, letting flavours blend. Add butter and stir to dissolve. Serve warm.

Serves 12 – 16

Rio chocolate

full power
7 minutes

60 g dark chocolate, chopped
750 mℓ milk
250 mℓ water
15 mℓ instant coffee powder
1 mℓ ground nutmeg
2 mℓ cinnamon
60 mℓ sugar
75 mℓ brandy
whipped cream, grated chocolate and cinnamon sticks to garnish

Combine the chocolate, milk, water, instant coffee, spices and sugar in a large jug or bowl. Microwave, uncovered, on full power for 6 – 7 minutes, stirring every 2 minutes. Add the brandy. Whisk very well, until foamy. Pour into cups or heatproof glasses. Top generously with whipped cream and sprinkle with grated chocolate. Stand a piece of cinnamon stick in the cream and use to stir.

Makes just over 1 litre

Cocoa

full power
7 minutes

60 mℓ cocoa powder   10 mℓ grated orange rind
45 mℓ sugar   a few drops almond essence (optional)
750 mℓ milk   4 marshmallows

Combine the cocoa and sugar in a 1 litre glass measuring jug. Add a little of the milk and mix to a smooth paste. Stir in remaining milk and add orange rind and almond essence, if used. Microwave on full power for 6 – 7 minutes. Pour cocoa into four mugs and top each with a marshmallow.

Serves 4

Sweets & nuts

For those with a sweet tooth, the microwave works wonders, producing delectable dainties with no mess and no fuss. This section is packed with recipes for a wide selection of sweet treats, homemade chocolates and crunchy nuts that are ideal for children's parties or to give that final touch to a special dinner. Hints on how to work successfully with melted chocolate have also been included.

Working with chocolate

Chocolate responds very well to being microwaved. However, as it is particularly sensitive to heat, care must be taken.

- When making chocolate leaves, or moulded or dipped chocolates, a grey film sometimes appears on the surface of the chocolate one or two days after the chocolates have been made. This is due to overheating, so it is best to microwave chocolate on defrost.
- When working with chocolate, the consistency often becomes too thick. Simply place chocolate in the microwave for a few seconds to soften.
- Chocolate is sometimes poured into piping bags and used to decorate chocolates or cakes. If the chocolate hardens, place the piping bag in the microwave for a few seconds – this saves a great deal of time and chocolate.
- Always chop or break up chocolate before microwaving.

Chocolate leaves

defrost
2 minutes

50 g dark chocolate, preferably cooking chocolate
fresh rose leaves or ivy leaves

Chop chocolate and place in a container. Microwave, uncovered, on defrost for 1 – 2 minutes. Wash and dry leaves well. If using rose leaves, spread chocolate on the underside of the leaf. Do not spread too thinly. Place on a piece of foil. Refrigerate for a few minutes. Carefully peel leaf away from chocolate. Store until needed in a sealed container. Refrigerate if weather is very hot. If using ivy leaves, spread chocolate on top of the leaf.

Makes about 30 leaves

White chocolate and almond fudge

full power
6 minutes

100 g slab milky bar
100 g butter
500 g icing sugar, sifted
60 mℓ milk
10 mℓ vanilla essence
1 mℓ almond essence
60 mℓ flaked almonds

Break up chocolate and place in a large bowl with butter. Microwave on full power for 1 minute. Add icing sugar, milk and essences and mix to combine. Microwave, uncovered, on full power for 5 minutes. Remove from oven and stir well. Stir in nuts. Pour into a greased 30 x 22 cm pan and refrigerate for 30 minutes. Cut into squares, then refrigerate for a further 30 minutes. Pack into an airtight container.

Makes about 40 squares

VARIATION
Chocolate fudge: Leave out milky bar and flaked almonds, and add 125 mℓ cocoa. Microwave all ingredients together on full power for 5 minutes.

Chocolate cherry fudge

Chocolate cherry fudge

full power
2½ minutes

360 g milk chocolate, broken into pieces
60 mℓ evaporated milk
dash salt
3 mℓ vanilla essence
10 maraschino cherries, chopped
100 g walnuts, chopped

Lightly grease a 20 cm square baking dish and set aside. Place chocolate, evaporated milk and salt in a 1 litre bowl and microwave on full power for 2 – 2½ minutes to melt chocolate. Stir in vanilla essence, mixing until smooth. Mix in cherries and nuts and pour into prepared pan. Cool until firm, then cut into squares.

Makes about 500 g

Chocolate glaze

This glaze has a beautiful, glossy appearance and is ideal for pouring over chocolate eclairs or Devonshire cream cake. Frozen bananas may also be dipped into this glaze. Freeze again for a few minutes before serving.

defrost
8 minutes

250 g chocolate, broken up
45 mℓ oil

Place chocolate in a bowl and microwave, uncovered, on

defrost for 6 – 8 minutes. Stir chocolate every 2 minutes. Add oil and mix well. The chocolate should be completely smooth before it is ready to use. Pour chocolate over a layer cake or loaf cake and allow to set.

Makes 200 mℓ

Piped chocolate creams

defrost
10 minutes

250 g chocolate, preferably cooking chocolate
100 mℓ cream
100 g butter
100 mℓ icing sugar, sifted
liqueur to taste, or flavouring oil (available from speciality shops)

Break chocolate into small pieces and place in a bowl. Add cream. Microwave on defrost for 6 – 8 minutes, stirring every 2 minutes during cooking time. Chocolate should be completely combined with cream when cooking time is completed. Cool, but do not chill. Place butter in a bowl and microwave on defrost for 2 minutes to soften slightly. Beat in icing sugar and flavouring. Carefully beat in the chocolate cream. It is important not to melt the butter as the cream is added. Beat well. Pipe into small paper cases. Allow to become firm at room temperature. If the weather is particularly hot, refrigerate for a short while. Stand chocolate at room temperature for a few minutes before serving.

Makes about 40

Rum truffles

defrost
6 minutes

100 g dark chocolate, chopped
30 mℓ butter
30 mℓ icing sugar
100 mℓ fresh cake crumbs
2 egg yolks
10 mℓ rum
chocolate vermicelli

Place chocolate in a shallow dish. Microwave, uncovered, on defrost for 3 minutes. Add butter, icing sugar and cake crumbs. Mix well. Microwave on defrost for 3 minutes. Add egg yolks and rum, and mix well. Refrigerate for 1 hour, or until firm enough to roll into small balls. Shape and roll in chocolate vermicelli. Place in paper cups.

Makes about 30

Raisin cups

defrost
3 minutes

60 g raisins, chopped
30 mℓ brandy, rum or liqueur
125 g chocolate, broken up
preserved ginger, thinly sliced

Chocolate selection

Soak raisins in brandy for a few hours. Place chocolate in a shallow dish and microwave, uncovered, on defrost for about 3 minutes. Brush the inside of paper cases with chocolate and allow to set in the refrigerator. Brush once again with chocolate. Allow to set. Spoon a little of the raisin mixture into the cases. Do not overfill, as the chocolates will leak when the top is added. Cover with melted chocolate and decorate with slivers of ginger whilst chocolate is still soft. Allow to set for at least 30 minutes in the refrigerator. Peel off paper cases and place the chocolates in fresh cases. If chocolate hardens whilst using, place in the microwave and heat on defrost for 1 minute or until the chocolate reaches desired consistency.

Makes about 30

Marshmallow treat

full power
15 seconds

2 chocolate-coated digestive biscuits
½ large marshmallow

Place 1 biscuit, chocolate side up, on a small plate and place the half marshmallow on top. Microwave on full power for 15 seconds, or until marshmallow puffs up. Immediately place 2nd biscuit, chocolate side down, on the marshmallow. This makes a delicious sweet treat. To microwave more than one treat at a time, increase time by a few seconds, but watch carefully and stop as soon as the marshmallow puffs up.

Makes 1

Nut clusters

defrost
3 minutes

100 g chocolate, broken up
100 g hazel or pecan nuts, chopped
5 mℓ grated orange rind
a few drops orange oil (available from speciality shops)

Place broken pieces of chocolate in a shallow dish. Microwave on defrost for about 3 minutes. Add the nuts, rind and oil. Mix well and allow to cool slightly. Using two teaspoons, drop small quantities of the mixture in cluster shapes on waxed paper. Allow to set before removing from the paper. Place in small paper cases.

Makes about 30

Coconut and chocolate bars

full power
6 minutes

70 g butter
250 mℓ marie biscuit crumbs (about 14 biscuits)
100 g chocolate, grated
60 g desiccated coconut
100 g nuts (walnuts or pecans), chopped
160 mℓ sweetened condensed milk

Microwave butter on full power for 1 minute in a 20 cm square glass baking dish. Stir in crumbs and press evenly to cover bottom of dish. Microwave for 1 – 1½ minutes. Sprinkle with grated chocolate, then coconut and chopped nuts. Pour condensed milk evenly over surface. Microwave on full power for 3 – 4 minutes until mixture is bubbly all over the surface. Cool, then cut into bars.

Makes 60

Coconut and chocolate bars

Microwave meringues

full power
1½ minutes

1 egg white
3 mℓ flavouring, such as vanilla, rum or almond essence
pinch salt
250 g icing sugar

Combine all ingredients and beat well until mixture forms a ball. Roll mixture into small balls about the size of walnuts and place in paper baking cups or in wafer cake cups. Arrange seven at a time on a plate, leaving a space between each as they puff up. Microwave on full power for 1½ minutes. Remove from oven and cool.

Makes about 30

VARIATION
For colourful meringues, add a few drops of food colouring with the flavouring, and continue as for microwave meringues. These meringues are very popular at children's parties.

Crunchy toffee

full power
6 minutes

100 g nuts, chopped
200 g brown sugar
70 g butter
45 mℓ water
90 g dark or milk chocolate, grated

Sprinkle nuts over the bottom of a well-greased 20 cm square dish. Combine sugar, butter and water in a deep bowl and microwave on full power for 5 – 6 minutes, stirring every 2 minutes. Mix well, then immediately spread over nuts. Sprinkle grated chocolate over hot toffee, cover dish and stand for 5 minutes until chocolate has melted. Carefully spread chocolate over the top. Chill until set, then turn out and break into pieces.

Makes about 500 g

Sugar caramel

full power
12 minutes

200 g sugar
160 mℓ water

Mix sugar and water together in a medium-sized bowl. Microwave on full power for 2 minutes. Stir. Microwave for a further 8 – 10 minutes, depending on how dark the caramel is required. Do not allow caramel to become too brown, as cooking continues for some time. Use as a base for cream caramel, dipping fruit and nut friandise, as part of a dessert, or for making spun sugar.

Makes about 300 mℓ

Friandise

300 mℓ sugar caramel*
fruits such as naartjie segments, grapes, strawberries and cherries
a few dates
a selection of nuts

Remove pith from naartjie segments. Leave stems on grapes, strawberries and cherries. Wash and dry thoroughly.

Make caramel, removing from microwave when light golden in colour. Have two oiled forks ready and a well-oiled baking sheet. Dip fruit sections, one at a time, into caramel, remove and allow excess caramel to drip off. Place on baking sheet. Continue in this way until all the fruit has been used up. Should the caramel become too thick to work with, microwave for 1 minute on high. Continue as before. When caramelized fruits are hard, lift off baking sheet, trim off any excess caramel and serve in tiny paper cups.

Makes 50 friandises

Popcorn balls

high
5 minutes

3 – 3,5 ℓ popped popcorn
200 g sugar
1 x 90 g packet raspberry jelly powder
250 mℓ golden syrup

Place popcorn in a large bowl and set aside. Combine sugar and jelly powder in a deep bowl. Add syrup and stir until ingredients are well mixed. Microwave on high until all the ingredients have dissolved and mixture boils, about 3½ – 4 minutes, stirring after every minute. Microwave for 1 minute more. Pour syrup over the popcorn and mix well. Wait until the mixture is cool enough to handle, then shape into balls with buttered hands. Do not press corn tightly together.

Makes about 12 balls

Nut and date balls

defrost
8 minutes

100 g pecan nuts, chopped
75 g dates, coarsely chopped
125 mℓ crunchy peanut butter
45 mℓ icing sugar
15 mℓ lemon juice
3 mℓ grated lemon rind
15 mℓ butter, at room temperature
3 mℓ vanilla essence
dash ground cinnamon
280 g dark chocolate or cooking chocolate
100 g milk chocolate

Combine all ingredients except chocolate and mix well. Chill for 1 hour, then shape mixture into small balls and place on a baking sheet lined with waxed paper. Chill for 2 hours. Break chocolate into small pieces and place in a deep glass bowl. Microwave on defrost for 7 – 8 minutes, stirring after every minute. Let chocolate cool slightly, then dip balls one at a time. Return to baking sheet, or to a wire rack to cool.

Makes about 30

Fruit and nut friandises

Preserves

The microwave oven is ideal for making jams, chutneys, marmalades and preserves. Not only does your kitchen remain cool and steam-free but there are no messy saucepans to scour, and very little chance of burning utensils and fingers. The preserves themselves retain the bright, clear colours and rich flavours of the fruit. Even small quantities of jams and chutneys can be made without the ingredients scorching or sticking to the saucepan. Preparation is so quick you can make a batch of marmalade before breakfast! The greatest difference between jams made the traditional way and those made in the microwave is that the preserve will cook on its own, with only an occasional stir, and will not burn. As microwaves are particularly attracted to sugar molecules, there is the possibility of the preserve boiling over. With this in mind, choose very large or deep bowls. Remember the bowls become very hot, so always use oven gloves when handling them. For the best results when making preserves, use very fresh, slightly under-ripe fruits. Those high in pectin, such as citrus fruit and apples, preserve well.

When preserving fruits

- Select good quality, barely ripe fruit. Soft or bruised fruit will result in an inferior product. Wash, wipe and peel the selected fruit according to the type.
- Wash jars well. Sterilize according to instructions below.
- Using a brush dipped in water, remove any sugar crystals which may have adhered to the sides of the bowl.
- To test whether jam or marmalade is ready:
  - Stand a sugar thermometer in the preserve but do not leave the thermometer in the microwave when it is switched on, unless it is specifically designed for microwave use. For a good set when making jam, the temperature should reach 105 °C.
  - Spoon a little jam onto a saucer and when it is cool push the surface gently with your finger. If the jam wrinkles, it is set.
  - When you think the jam is ready, stir well with a wooden spoon. Lift a spoonful of jam out of the bowl, cool slightly then allow the jam to drop off the spoon. It should drop off in 'flakes'.
- Allow the jam to cool only slightly before pouring it into hot, sterile jars. Fill them right to the top and when the jam is cool, top up the jars once more and cover with brandy papers or waxed papers. To make brandy papers, cut circles of greaseproof or parchment paper the size of the top of the jars. Dip into brandy and place on cooled jam. To make waxed papers, dip the circles of paper into melted candle wax. Allow to set before placing on top of the jam.
- To prevent air bubbles from forming, do not allow the jam to cool for too long before pouring it into jars. If the jam is poured into jars whilst still too hot, the fruit may rise in the jars.

To sterilize jars for preserving

Pour a little water into the jars. Place no more than three jars in the microwave oven. Microwave on full power for up to 5 minutes, depending on the size of the jars and on the thickness of the glass. Pour out the water and stand the jars upside down to drain. Plastic lids, each containing a little water, may be sterilized in the microwave but do not sterilize metal lids this way.

Apricot jam

full power
35 minutes

1 kg half-ripe apricots
1 kg sugar
juice of 1 lemon

Wash the fruit well. Cut in half and remove stones. Combine the apricots and sugar in a large bowl. Allow to stand overnight. Add lemon juice and stir well. Cover with plastic wrap and cut two slits in the plastic to prevent it from 'ballooning' during cooking. Microwave on full power for 10 minutes, stirring every 2 minutes. Uncover and microwave for 25 minutes, stirring every 5 minutes. The jam should now be at setting point. Remove from the microwave. Allow jam to cool for at least half an hour to prevent the fruit from rising in the jar when it has cooled. Pour the warm jam into warm, dry bottles. When cool, top up with a little more jam. Cover the top of the jam with a disc of brandy paper or waxed paper. Cover, label and store.

Fills 3 x 400 mℓ bottles

Kumquat preserve

full power
44 minutes

750 – 800 g kumquats	400 g sugar
800 mℓ boiling water	160 mℓ water
20 mℓ bicarbonate of soda	30 mℓ lemon juice

Wash the kumquats and place in a large bowl. Pour the boiling water over fruit and add the bicarbonate of soda. Cover with plastic wrap and make two slits in the plastic to prevent 'ballooning' during cooking. Microwave on full power for 5 minutes. Allow to cool. Drain off water and rinse well in cold water. Using a small, sharp, pointed knife, make incisions right through the sides of fruit. Place fruit once again in a large bowl, cover with boiling water, and plastic wrap. Microwave on full power for 10 minutes. Allow to cool slightly, then squeeze out the pips.

Place sugar and water in a large bowl. Microwave, uncovered, on full power for 10 minutes, stirring every few minutes. Strain the syrup through a sieve lined with cotton wool. Return to bowl, then microwave for 3 – 4 minutes until syrup is boiling once more. Add kumquats and lemon juice. Microwave, uncovered, on full power for 15 minutes. The syrup should have thickened, and the fruit should be translucent. Pour into sterilized bottles. Cover loosely and allow to cool. Once cool, top up with syrup. Cover tightly, label and store.

Fills 2 x 400 mℓ bottles

Granadilla curd

Granadilla gives this old favourite a truly South African flavour

full power
high
medium
7 minutes

125 g butter
3 eggs
125 g castor sugar
8 granadillas
5 mℓ grated lemon rind
juice from 3 lemons
5 mℓ cornflour

Microwave butter on full power for 2 minutes. Meanwhile, beat together eggs and castor sugar until light and fluffy. Add granadilla pulp, lemon rind and most of the lemon juice. Mix remaining lemon juice and cornflour to a smooth paste and stir into egg mixture, along with the melted butter. Microwave, uncovered, on full power for 2 minutes. Stir well. Microwave on high for 2 minutes more, stirring at the end of each minute. Change setting to medium and microwave for 1 minute. Stir very well. The mixture should be thick enough to coat the back of a wooden spoon. Cool slightly. Pour into two medium-sized jars and top with brandy papers or waxed papers. Cover when cold. Label and store in the refrigerator.

Fills 2 x 400 mℓ jars

Fig preserve served with streusel muffins (p. 126)

Fig preserve

full power
57 minutes

500 g small green figs	For the syrup
1 ℓ water	600 g sugar
5 mℓ slaked lime	750 mℓ boiling water
750 mℓ boiling water	10 mℓ lemon juice

Wash the figs well and remove stems. Cut a small cross in the rounded end. Place figs in a bowl. Combine the water and slaked lime. Pour over figs and stand for 12 hours. Rinse figs very well, then stand in fresh cold water for about 15 minutes. Drain and add 750 mℓ boiling water to figs. Cover with plastic and make two holes in the plastic to prevent 'ballooning' during cooking. Microwave on full power for 7 minutes. Drain well.

To make the syrup, combine sugar, water and lemon juice in a large bowl. Cover and microwave for 10 minutes, stirring twice during the cooking time. Add fruit to boiling syrup. Then microwave, uncovered, for 30 minutes, stirring from time to time during cooking. Drain the figs from the syrup. Pack into warm, dry bottles. Microwave the syrup, uncovered, for 10 minutes. Pour over figs, and cover loosely with lid. When cool, tighten lid and store.

Fills 2 x 400 mℓ bottles

Bottled yellow peaches

full power
40 minutes

750 mℓ water
300 g sugar
1 small piece cinnamon stick
1 small piece lemon rind
1 kg yellow cling peaches

Combine water and sugar in a large bowl. Microwave on full power for 10 minutes, then stir well to dissolve the sugar. Add cinnamon and lemon rind, and microwave for another 10 minutes. Peel the peaches, cut into halves or quarters and remove the stones. Add peaches to the syrup. Microwave for 8 – 10 minutes, stirring once or twice during cooking time. Remove cinnamon and lemon rind. Pack peaches into warm, dry, sterilized bottles. Microwave the syrup for a further 10 minutes. Fill jars with syrup, cover tightly and store.

Fills 2 x 800 mℓ jars

Ginger marmalade

full power
40 minutes

3 oranges
1 ℓ water
500 g green apples
1,5 kg sugar
1 piece fresh ginger, grated
25 mℓ chopped preserved ginger
2 mℓ ground ginger

Wash the oranges well. Squeeze the juice. Remove the membranes and pips, then mince or chop the peel finely. In a large bowl, combine orange juice, minced peel and water. Tie the membranes and pips in a piece of muslin and add to bowl. Cover bowl with plastic wrap and make two slits in the plastic to prevent 'ballooning' during cooking. Microwave on full power for 20 minutes. Remove the muslin bag. Peel, core and dice apples finely. Add all the remaining ingredients to the bowl. Microwave, uncovered, on full power for 15 – 20 minutes, stirring every 5 minutes. Check for setting point, allowing extra time if necessary. Pour into warm, sterilized jars. Cover loosely. When cold, top up bottles and cover tightly. Label and store.

Fills 3 x 400 mℓ bottles

Golden jelly marmalade

full power
1¾ hours

1 kg oranges
2 lemons
2 ℓ water
1,25 kg sugar

Using a zester, remove the zest from the oranges and lemons or peel thinly and cut rind into fine shreds. Cover zest with boiling water, stand for 10 minutes, then drain. Peel the oranges and the lemons. Chop the pulp, place in a

Four fruit marmalade

large bowl and add 1 litre water. Cover with plastic wrap and cut two slits in the plastic to prevent 'ballooning' during cooking. Microwave on full power for 20 minutes. Strain pulp through a jelly cloth and reserve liquid. Meanwhile, cover the zest with 500 mℓ water and microwave on full power for 10 minutes. Drain and add this liquid to the pulp. Return pulp to bowl, add 500 mℓ water and re-cover. Microwave on full power for 15 minutes. Strain pulp again through jelly cloth. Reserve liquid and discard pulp.

In a large bowl, combine reserved liquid, zest and sugar. Microwave, uncovered, for 50 – 55 minutes on full power, stirring every 5 minutes. Skim from time to time, if necessary. To prevent the marmalade from rising in the jar, allow to cool slightly before pouring into warm, sterilized jars. Cool completely, top up with a little more marmalade, then cover tightly. Label and store.

Fills approximately 3 x 400 mℓ bottles

Four fruit marmalade

full power
55 minutes

2 oranges	850 mℓ boiling water
2 grapefruit	2 kg sugar
2 lemons	15 mℓ molasses or dark treacle
2 naartjies	60 mℓ whisky

Wash and dry fruit. Squeeze juice and set aside. Remove pips and pith, and tie in a piece of muslin. Slice peel according to taste – thin, medium or coarse. Place juice, sliced peel and muslin bag in a large mixing bowl. Add half the boiling water, stand for 1 hour, then add remaining boiling water. Cover with plastic wrap and make two slits in the plastic to prevent 'ballooning' during cooking.

Microwave on full power for about 25 minutes (depending on the thickness of the peel). Uncover, remove muslin bag and stir in sugar and molasses. Microwave, uncovered, for 25 – 30 minutes until setting point is reached, stirring every 5 minutes. If any scum forms on top, scoop it off. Allow marmalade to cool. Stir in the whisky, then pour into sterilized bottles. Cover, label and store.

Fills 3 x 400 mℓ bottles

Cherries in brandy

full power
7 minutes

500 g cherries, stems removed
1 cinnamon stick
230 g sugar
125 mℓ water
15 mℓ lemon juice
150 mℓ brandy

Wash and dry cherries. Pack into a warm, sterilized glass jar together with a cinnamon stick. Combine sugar, water and lemon juice in a bowl. Microwave on full power for 3 minutes, stirring every minute during cooking time. Now microwave without stirring for 4 minutes. Allow to cool slightly, and add brandy. Pour over cherries, seal, label and store in a dark place. Keep for at least one month before using. Serve the cherries on top of ice-cream. The liquid can also be strained, and drunk as a liqueur.

To make a cherry sauce, mix a little cornflour with the cold cherry liquid and microwave on full power for 1 – 2 minutes, stirring every 30 seconds. Add a few chopped cherries to the thickened sauce. Serve hot over ice-cream.

Fills 1 x 800 mℓ jar

Cherries preserved in brandy

Banana chutney

full power
20 minutes

10 ripe bananas, sliced
400 mℓ white vinegar
75 g seedless raisins
1 onion, finely chopped
150 g brown sugar
1 green pepper, seeded and chopped
3 mℓ salt
3 mℓ ground ginger
1 mℓ cayenne pepper
2 cloves garlic, crushed
10 mℓ dry mustard

Combine all ingredients in a large bowl. Cover with plastic wrap and cut two slits in the plastic to prevent 'ballooning' during cooking. Microwave on full power for 20 minutes. Stir twice during cooking time. Pour into clean, dry jars and cool before sealing. Store in a cool, dry place.

Fills approximately 2 x 400 mℓ jars

Spicy cucumber pickle

This is excellent served with cheese, salads, or as a snack

full power
11 minutes

3 medium cucumbers
375 mℓ water
200 mℓ vinegar
15 mℓ salt
10 mℓ peppercorns
2 bay leaves
2 cloves garlic, chopped

Wash the cucumbers. Using a fork, score the cucumbers down the length. Slice thickly. Combine the remaining ingredients in a large bowl. Cover and microwave on full power for 7 minutes. Add cucumber slices and microwave, covered, on full power for 4 minutes. Pour into a large bottle whilst still hot. Cool, cover and refrigerate. This pickle will keep in the refrigerator for some weeks.

Fills approximately 1 x 800 mℓ bottle

Cucumber pickle

This pickle is delicious served sliced or chopped in salads, on sandwiches or with cheese

full power
16 minutes

2 very large cucumbers
30 mℓ salt
300 mℓ white vinegar
5 mℓ dill
5 mℓ mustard seed
80 g sugar
1 large onion, sliced

Peel cucumbers. Slice thickly down length of cucumber and discard fleshy centre portion. Place cucumber strips in a flat, non-metallic basin and sprinkle with salt. Stand for 8 hours. Drain off liquid and pat dry with paper towel.

Place vinegar, dill, mustard seed and sugar in a large bowl. Cover with plastic wrap and make two slits in the plastic to prevent 'ballooning' during cooking. Microwave on full power for 7 minutes. Divide cucumber strips into three batches. Microwave each batch, uncovered, for 3 minutes on full power. Add a little onion to each batch once it is cooked, then place cucumbers in a clean, dry jar. Cover with pickling liquid. Cover jar and refrigerate. Keep for a few days before using. This pickle lasts for up to 6 months.

Fills 1 x 800 mℓ jar

Pickled onions

full power
10 minutes

1 kg pickling onions
30 g salt
300 mℓ white vinegar
60 mℓ sugar
10 mℓ mustard seed
10 mℓ pickling spice
2 – 3 blades mace
2 red chillies

Carefully remove tops and roots from onions. Place in a large bowl and cover with boiling water. Stand for 30 seconds, drain and cover with cold water. Peel onions under cold water. Place onions in a bowl, layering them with salt. Stand overnight. Using a colander, rinse well.

Combine all remaining ingredients in a large bowl. Microwave on full power for 5 minutes. Add onions, then microwave again on full power for 5 minutes. Pack onions into clean, dry jars. Pour over the hot, strained vinegar. Cover loosely while still hot. Tighten lid when cool and stand for at least 3 weeks before serving. To make pickled onions with an extra bite, add 1 or 2 additional chillies to bottled onions.

Fills 3 x 400 mℓ bottles

Mixed vegetable pickle

full power
8 minutes

Use a selection of the following vegetables:

½ small cauliflower	*For the pickling liquid*
1 small cucumber	300 mℓ white vinegar
2 – 3 carrots	1 bay leaf
a few small onions	1 small piece fresh ginger
green beans	1 green chilli
baby marrows	1 small piece mace
salt	6 whole allspice

First prepare vegetables. Cut cauliflower into small florets. Slice unpeeled cucumber thickly and cut into quarters. Peel carrots, then slice thickly. Peel and quarter onions. Slice beans into short lengths. Cut unpeeled baby marrows thickly. Layer vegetables in a bowl with salt. Cover and stand overnight. Drain, then rinse well in a colander and allow to dry.

Combine all remaining ingredients in a large bowl. Cover

with plastic wrap and make two slits in the plastic to prevent 'ballooning' during cooking. Microwave on full power for 4 minutes. Add vegetables, cover and microwave on full power for another 4 minutes. Using a slotted spoon, pack vegetables into clean, dry jars. Strain pickling liquid and cool. Cover vegetables with the liquid. Cover jars, label and store.

Fills about 2 x 400 mℓ jars

Piccalilli

full power
21 minutes

1 cucumber
250 g small onions, peeled
1 piece vegetable marrow, 10 – 15 cm long, peeled
1 cauliflower
4 baby marrows
100 g green beans
20 mℓ salt

For the sauce
600 mℓ white vinegar
15 mℓ pickling spice
200 g brown sugar
60 mℓ cake flour
10 mℓ turmeric
10 mℓ dry mustard
7 mℓ ground ginger

Cut the vegetables into small, even-sized pieces. Place in a bowl, sprinkle with salt and stand for 12 hours. Rinse and drain. To make the sauce, pour the vinegar into a large jug and add the pickling spice. Microwave on full power for 5 minutes. Strain. Meanwhile, combine all the remaining ingredients in a large bowl. Pour on the hot vinegar and stir well. Microwave on full power for 8 minutes, stirring every 2 minutes. Add vegetables. Microwave on full power for a further 8 minutes, stirring from time to time. Cool, pack into clean dry bottles, cover and store. This pickle may be eaten immediately.

Fills 4 x 400 mℓ bottles

Chilli vinegar

full power
1½ minutes

60 g fresh green or red chillies
1 ℓ cider vinegar

Place chillies in a glass bowl and just cover with water. Microwave, covered, on full power for 1 – 1½ minutes. Drain and rinse in cold water. Place chillies in a sterilized bottle or jar and add vinegar. Seal and stand in a cool dark place for about 10 days before using.

Makes 1 litre

Flavoured oils and vinegars

Lemon vinegar

medium
2 minutes

1 ℓ red or white wine vinegar
1 long spiral lemon peel
3 – 4 sprigs fresh mint
2 cloves garlic, split

Place vinegar in a glass jug and microwave on medium for about 2 minutes, or until warm. Place the remaining ingredients in a jar or bottle and pour vinegar over. Seal and stand in a sunny place for several days before using. Use for fish or chicken, or in a dressing for fish salads.

Makes 1 litre

VARIATION
Herb vinegar: Use 1 sprig rosemary, 2 sprigs fresh dill, 1 sprig thyme and 1 bay leaf instead of lemon peel, mint and garlic. Proceed as for Lemon vinegar.

Pickle vinegar

medium
4 minutes

2 ℓ white vinegar
40 g black mustard seed
15 mℓ fresh ginger root, peeled and chopped
10 mℓ whole allspice
10 mℓ cloves
15 mℓ black peppercorns
8 mℓ celery seeds
180 g brown sugar
10 mℓ grated horseradish
1 clove garlic, peeled
½ lemon, sliced

Place vinegar in a large casserole dish and microwave on medium for 4 – 4½ minutes, or until warm, but not boiling. Divide remaining ingredients evenly between two sterilized jars or bottles. Pour warm vinegar over, seal and place in a sunny spot for several days. After the sun has extracted oils from the spices, strain the vinegar and use for pickling fruits or vegetables.

Makes 2 litres

Spiced French vinegar

Combined with oil, this vinegar makes an exciting French dressing

high
4 minutes

1 ℓ cider vinegar
75 g sugar
10 mℓ whole cloves
5 mℓ whole allspice
3 blades mace
10 mℓ celery seeds
10 mℓ mustard seed
10 mℓ whole black peppercorns
10 mℓ turmeric
10 mℓ sliced ginger root
1 clove garlic, peeled

Combine all ingredients, except garlic, in a large glass bowl. Microwave on high for 3 – 4 minutes, until the mixture is hot. Place mixture in a sterilized bottle or jar, add garlic and seal. Let stand in a cool place for 3 weeks before using.

Makes 1 litre

Spiced oil

medium
1½ minutes

10 coriander seeds, lightly crushed
2 cloves garlic, cut in half
2 pieces cinnamon stick
5 whole allspice
5 whole cloves
1 – 2 hot chillies
1 small piece fresh ginger root
750 mℓ oil

Place all ingredients, except oil, in a glass bowl and microwave on medium for 1 – 1½ minutes, stirring every 30 seconds. Place warm ingredients in a sterilized bottle or jar and add oil to almost fill. Seal and store in a cool place for about 10 days before using. Use oil to fry or marinate vegetables, or combine with vinegar for salad dressings.

Makes 750 mℓ

VARIATIONS
Double olive oil: Place 8 whole olives with their liquid in a glass jug and microwave on medium for 1 – 1½ minutes. Drain and place in a sterilized bottle and add olive oil to almost fill. Proceed as for Spiced oil.

Garlic oil: Place 15 – 20 unpeeled cloves garlic in a glass jug and just cover with water. Microwave on medium for 3 minutes to soften. Drain and thread garlic on a strong cord. Place garlic in a sterilized bottle, securing cord at the top and add oil to almost fill. Proceed as for Spiced oil.

Conversion tables

Metrication is part of our daily lives. Once you are accustomed to this simple way of measuring, cooking becomes easier and definitely more accurate. Remember, accuracy means success.

Small measurements:

METRIC	APPROXIMATE IMPERIAL
1 mℓ	¼ teaspoon
2 mℓ	½ teaspoon
5 mℓ	1 teaspoon
10 mℓ	1 dessertspoon
15 mℓ	1 tablespoon
45 mℓ	3 tablespoons

Mass:
This is an approximate conversion. 500 g is slightly heavier than 1 lb.

METRIC	APPROXIMATE IMPERIAL
30 g	1 oz
60 g	2 oz
100 g	3 oz
125 g	4 oz
250 g	8 oz
500 g	1 lb

Volumes:

METRIC	APPROXIMATE IMPERIAL
60 mℓ	¼ cup
80 mℓ	⅓ cup
125 mℓ	½ cup
190 mℓ	¾ cup
250 mℓ	1 cup
500 mℓ	2 cups
600 mℓ	1 pint
1,25 ℓ	1 quart

Approximate mass in grams per 250 ml:

INGREDIENTS	MASS
Butter or margarine	230 g
Cheese, grated	100 g
Cocoa powder	100 g
Coconut, desiccated	80 g
Cornflour	120 g
Dried fruit: raisins, etc	150 g
Flour: bread or cake flour	120 g
self-raising flour	140 g
wholemeal flour	130 g
Nuts, chopped	150 g
whole	100 g
Oats, uncooked	90 g
Rice, uncooked	200 g
Sugar: granulated	200 g
castor sugar	210 g
icing sugar	130 g

Menu planning

Once you have learned to cook simple foods in the microwave oven, you will want to use it to combine foods to cook a complete meal. Different foods cook in different ways and require different cooking times, so careful planning is needed to prepare foods in sequence.

As with any meal, microwave menus should be balanced for nutrition, colour, flavour, texture and appetite appeal. Plan meals so that not all the foods will need last-minute cooking or heating and take advantage of standing time and holding time to present foods at their best. Last-minute preparation should be reserved for foods that heat and cool quickly.

Appetizers can be prepared early in the day and refrigerated if necessary, and then reheated if they are to be served hot. Bread rolls should be warmed for a few seconds in the microwave just before serving.

Meats and main dishes usually require not only the longest cooking time of any part of the meal, but also the longest standing time, and other parts of the meal can be microwaved while the roast, chicken or casserole is standing. Cooking in advance foods that can easily be reheated simplifies the meal preparation and may improve the flavour of such foods as casseroles.

Vegetables and other foods that retain heat well can be cooked before those that require very short cooking, or ones that do not retain heat for a long period. For example, while the main dish is standing before serving, potatoes can be microwaved. They hold heat well so they can stand, wrapped in aluminium foil, while quick-cooking vegetables such as peas are microwaved.

Desserts can be made ahead of time and refrigerated until needed. Baked apples, crumbles and desserts to be served hot can be prepared in advance and microwaved while the main course is being eaten.

Planning tips

- Allow plenty of time to plan your first microwave meals. Try to serve at least one cold course or one dish that can be made ahead, leaving the microwave oven free for the main course and last-minute cooking.
- Soups, sauces, gravies and some vegetables can be cooked in advance, placed in serving dishes and microwaved to reheat when required.
- Fish, seafood, egg and cheese dishes cook very quickly, but do not retain heat well. It is difficult to reheat these dishes without overcooking, so they should be microwaved just before serving.
- It makes sense to cook foods that do not microwave well in a conventional oven, leaving the microwave oven free for other courses.
- Plan the menu so that while one course is being eaten, the next can be cooking or heating.
- Use aluminium foil to wrap cooked items, such as baked potatoes or chicken, to help retain heat. If large amounts of food need to be kept warm, use a warming oven or hot tray.
- Rice and pasta reheat quickly and well in the microwave oven, but they require the same cooking time as when boiled on the stove top. Cook those items conventionally, leaving the microwave free for other foods.
- Microwave as many foods as possible in the serving dish. This helps to retain heat during standing or holding time, and cuts down on the washing up.
- Any single serving placed on a plate can be reheated quickly for a latecomer with no change in texture or flavour.

Use the following sample menus as a guide to planning microwave meals.

Breakfast

Creamy yoghurt* served with fresh fruit
Farmer's breakfast*
Coffee, filter or instant*
Hot fresh toast and warm croissants
Four fruit marmalade*

- Make yoghurt the day before required.
- 20 minutes before serving, make the Farmer's breakfast.
- Place the Farmer's breakfast, toast and croissants in the microwave on low to keep warm whilst eating the first course.
- Whilst eating breakfast, keep filter coffee warm in the microwave, or boil water for instant coffee.

*Recipes included in this book.

Light lunch –
ideal when not much time is available

Chef's spinach salad*
Brown bread rolls
Ice-cream with
Hot fruit salad*

- Make the Chef's spinach salad in advance, either early in the day, or cook the leeks and chicken the day before.
- Combine all ingredients for the Hot fruit salad in advance, and 30 minutes before serving lunch, cook it in the microwave.
- 1 to 2 minutes before serving lunch, warm the brown bread rolls.
- Keep the Hot fruit salad warm in the microwave whilst eating the Chef's salad.

Summer lunch –
an interesting lunch and quick to serve, as everything is prepared in advance

Cream of carrot soup*
Club chicken casserole*
Fruity slaw* or Seasonal salad*
Chocolate mousse*
Coffee*

- Make Cream of carrot soup the day before required and serve chilled or piping hot – to reheat, microwave for 8 to 10 minutes after heating the Club chicken casserole, as covered casseroles retain heat for a long time.
- Make the Club chicken casserole the day before and 25 minutes before serving microwave, covered, on medium for 15 minutes. Keep warm in the microwave whilst eating soup.
- Make the Fruity slaw the day before, cover and refrigerate.
- Vegetables for the Seasonal salad may also be blanched in advance; merely combine a short while before serving.
- Make the Chocolate mousse the day before.
- Keep freshly filtered coffee warm in the microwave whilst eating the main course, or boil water for instant coffee.

Informal dinner

Caesar salad*
Pepper steak flambé*
Potatoes Lyonnaise*
Stuffed baby marrows*
Carrots Vichy*
Caramel ice-cream*
South African coffee*
Nut clusters*

- Make the Caesar salad 2 to 3 hours in advance and chill.
- Cook the Pepper steak flambé 12 to 15 minutes before serving.
- Microwave the Potatoes Lyonnaise 1¼ hours before serving.

- Prepare the Stuffed baby marrows 2 to 3 hours in advance, and microwave with the Carrots Vichy 30 minutes before serving. Cover and keep warm.
- Make the Caramel ice-cream the day before.
- Microwave the South African coffee for 1 minute after dinner.
- Make the Nut clusters in advance.

Celebration dinner

Potted shrimp*
Glazed stuffed roast pork*
Roast potatoes
Green beans almondine*
Garlic mushrooms*
Pears Alicia*
Quick cappuccino*
Rum truffles*

- Make the Potted shrimp the day before.
- Microwave the prepared Glazed stuffed roast pork 1¼ hours before serving. Cover and keep warm.
- Cook the Green beans almondine 12 to 15 minutes before serving.
- Microwave the Garlic mushrooms for 8 minutes whilst eating the first course.
- Prepare the Pears Alicia the day before.
- Make the Rum truffles in advance.
- Microwave the Quick cappuccino after dinner.

*Recipes included in this book.

Convenience foods

Using convenience foods is a quick way to serve snacks or meals, and they take only minutes to prepare in the microwave oven. The following chart gives a guide for defrosting, heating or cooking many frozen and canned foods. There are also instructions for baking cake and pudding mixes in the microwave, as well as packet or canned soups. More and more convenience or instant foods are finding their way onto supermarket shelves and into freezers, and they cannot all be included here. Recipes making use of many convenience foods are found throughout this book, but the hints that follow will help you convert most instant foods to quick and tasty meals.

When microwaving convenience foods

- Be sure foods are really heated through before serving. Steam or bubbling around the edges may not mean the food is completely heated. When the food is hot enough, the centre of the bottom of the dish will be warm to the touch.
- Most foods are covered when heating or reheating. Cover appetizers cooked with a sauce or main dishes with waxed paper or plastic wrap. Be sure to slash the plastic wrap. Sandwiches that are defrosted, then warmed, can be covered with paper towel or a napkin. Soups may be covered with waxed paper to prevent spattering.
- Do not cover baked foods when thawing or warming as they may become soggy.
- Remove casseroles, 'frozen dinners' or baked foods from foil trays before microwaving. Place those foods in a casserole dish or on a plate.
- Some foods, such as sausage rolls or double crust pastries, can be defrosted in the microwave, but give much better results if heated in a conventional oven.

Mixes

Hot sponge pudding mix

300 g packet

Follow packet instructions for mixing, then microwave on full power for 5½ – 6½ minutes. Serve warm.

Cooked pudding mixes

100 g packet

Use 500 mℓ milk and follow packet instructions for mixing. Place in a deep bowl and microwave for 2 – 2½ minutes, beating well every 45 seconds.

Cake mixes
Mix as directed on the packet, using 2 eggs. Grease a deep microwave ring pan and sprinkle with marie biscuit crumbs if desired. Pour batter into prepared pan and place on an inverted saucer in the microwave oven. Microwave on defrost for 6 minutes. Rotate the pan a quarter turn and microwave on full power for 5 – 6 minutes or until surface is almost dry, rotating dish a quarter turn every 3 minutes. Alternatively, microwave on full power for 4 minutes, rotate dish a quarter turn and microwave for

3 – 5 minutes or until surface is almost dry. When cooking is complete, stand the pan on a heatproof surface for 10 minutes, then turn cake out onto a wire rack to cool.

Cupcakes
Spoon prepared cake mix batter into paper cases in a microwave muffin pan or custard cups. Fill cases a third to half full. Arrange in a circle in the oven and microwave as follows:

Number	Time	Power
2	1 minute	full power
4	1¼ -1½ minutes	full power
6	2½ -3 minutes	full power

Soups

Packet Soups
Reconstitute according to packet instructions, reducing the liquid by about a fifth. For example, instead of 800 mℓ water use 650 mℓ.
- For thick soups such as cream of vegetable, microwave on full power for 6 – 7 minutes, stirring several times.
- For soups with liquid and solids, such as beef vegetable, microwave on high for 10 – 12 minutes, stirring occasionally.

Canned Soups
Add liquid according to directions and place soup in a deep bowl.
- For soups with water added, microwave on full power for 5 – 6 minutes.
- For soups with milk added, microwave on high for 8 – 10 minutes, stirring occasionally.

For extra flavour add a generous splash of sherry or white wine to vegetable soups, or brandy to meat soups. For a rich, creamy soup, stir in 60 – 90 mℓ cream or sour cream just before serving. For soups such as tomato or mushroom, add a generous helping of grated cheese after heating.

MICROWAVE CHART FOR CONVENIENCE FOODS

	QUANTITY	PREPARATION	DEFROST TIME	COOKING TIME	POWER LEVEL	METHOD
CANNED FOODS						
Soup	410 g	Place in bowl, add liquid as directed	–	5-6 minutes	full	Cover, stir frequently
Pasta in sauce	410 g	Place in dish	–	3-4 minutes	full	Cover, stir at least once
Baked beans	410 g	Place in dish	–	3-4 minutes	full	Cover, stir at least once
Peas or other small vegetables	410 g	Place in dish	–	3-4 minutes	full	Cover, stir gently once
Asparagus spears or other large vegetables	410 g	Place in dish	–	4-5 minutes	full	Cover, stir once
Meat in sauce	410 g	Place in dish	–	5-6 minutes	full	Cover, stir once
Sauces or gravy	410 g	Place in bowl	–	3-4 minutes	full	Cover, stir occasionally
Custard or pudding	approx 400 g	Place in bowl	–	3-4 minutes	full	Cover, stir once
Fruits, such as fruit cocktail or sliced peaches	410 g	Place in bowl	–	4-5 minutes	full	Cover, stir once
FROZEN FOODS						
Individual meat pies	3	Remove foil	1½-2 minutes	3-3½ minutes	full	Place on paper towel, carefully turn over halfway through heating
Sausage rolls or pastry snacks	6-8	Place on paper towel	2 minutes, stand 3 minutes	2-3 minutes	full	Pastry may become soggy so defrost in microwave and heat conventionally for best results
Quiche	20-23 cm	Remove from foil, place on plate	5 minutes, stand 5 minutes	6-8 minutes	full	Cover with waxed paper
Pizza	approx 230 g	Place on paper plate or towel	–	4-5 minutes	full	Cover with waxed paper to prevent spattering
Meat casserole	approx 500 g	Remove from foil, place in dish	4 minutes, stand 3 minutes, defrost 3 minutes more	10-12 minutes	full	Cover with waxed paper, stir if possible
'Boil in bag' fish	approx 160 g	Slit top of bag, place in bowl	4-6 minutes	2-3 minutes	full	Shake contents of bag before serving

For frozen baked goods, see chart page 118
For frozen vegetables, see page 95

Index